one-pot, slow-pot & CLAY-POT cooking

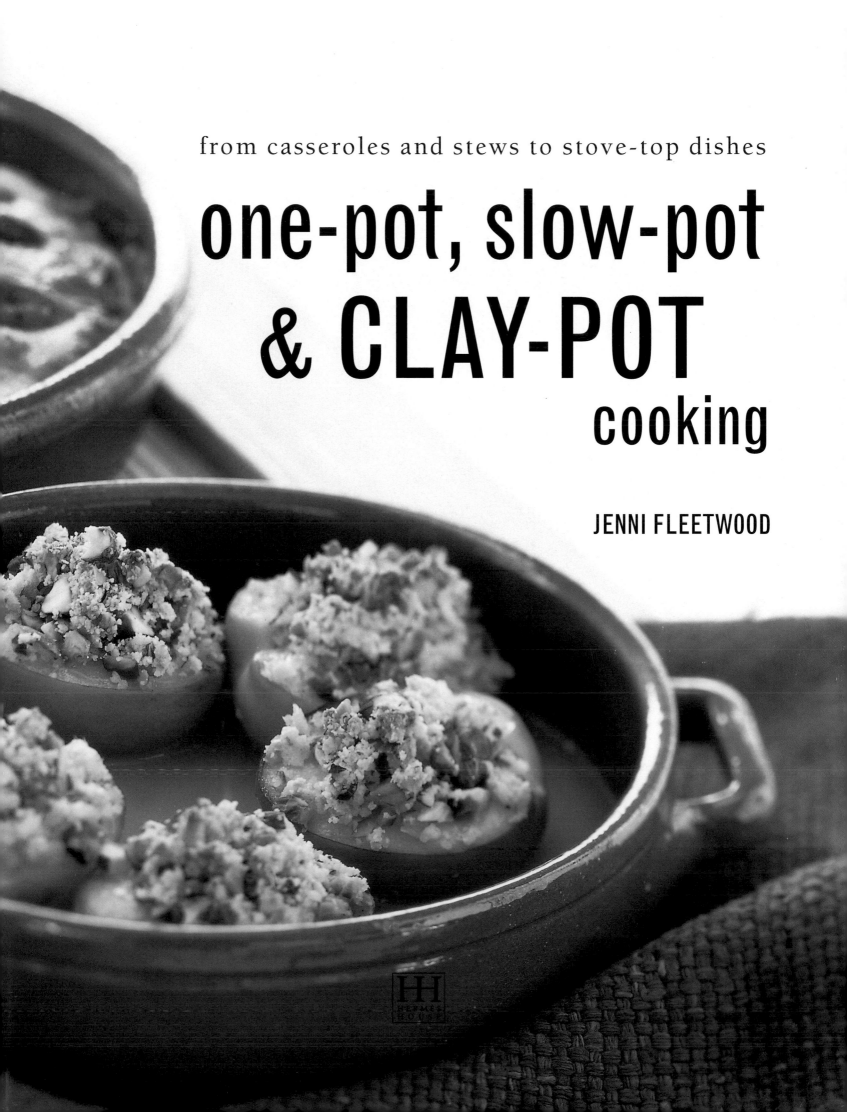

from casseroles and stews to stove-top dishes

one-pot, slow-pot
& CLAY-POT
cooking

JENNI FLEETWOOD

This edition published in 2002 by Hermes House

Hermes House is an imprint of
Anness Publishing Limited
Hermes House
88–89 Blackfriars Road
London SE1 8HA

Published in the USA by Hermes House
Anness Publishing Inc.
27 West 20th Street, New York, NY 10011

A CIP catalogue record for this book is available from the British Library.

Publisher: Joanna Lorenz
Managing Editor: Linda Fraser
Editorial Readers: Richard McGinlay and Joy Wotton
Indexer: Hilary Bird
Designer: Nigel Partridge
Photography: James Duncan, Ian Garlick, Michelle Garrett, Amanda Heywood, David Jordan,
Dave King, William Lingwood, Patrick McLeavey, Thomas Odulate, Craig Robertson, Sam Stowell
Recipes: Alex Barker, Michelle Berriedale-Johnson, Kit Chan, Jacqueline Clarke, Matthew Drennan,
Sarah Edmonds, Joanna Farrow, Brian Glover, Nicola Graimes, Christine Ingram, Lucy Knox,
Lesley Mackley, Sally Mansfield, Sallie Morris, Jennie Shapter, Anne Sheasby, Steven Wheeler,
Kate Whiteman, Jeni Wright

1 3 5 7 9 10 8 6 4 2

Front cover shows Braised Shoulder of Lamb with Pearl Barley
and Baby Vegetables, for recipe see page 99.
Previously published as *The One-pot and Clay-pot Cookbook*

NOTES
Bracketed terms are for American readers. For all recipes, quantities are given in both metric
and imperial measures and, where appropriate, measures are also given in standard cups and
spoons. Follow one set, but not a mixture because they are not interchangeable. Standard
spoon and cup measures are level. 1 tsp = 5ml, 1 tbsp = 15ml, 1 cup = 250ml/8fl oz
Australian standard tablespoons are 20ml. Australian readers should use 3 tsp in place of
1 tbsp for measuring small quantities of gelatine, cornflour, salt etc.
Medium (US large) eggs are used unless otherwise stated.

CONTENTS

INTRODUCTION

What do spicy stir-fries, nourishing soups, delectable stews, robust roasts, creamy risottos and citrus custards have in common? They're all one-pot dishes, easy to prepare, a pleasure to serve and the perfect choice for family and friends.

Elaborate dinner parties are a rarity these days. On the menu instead are simple dishes prepared with the minimum of fuss but with maximum flavour. Even celebrity chefs have turned their backs on fiddly food, preferring instead to take a second look at old favourites like Irish Stew, Spicy Venison Casserole, Cassoulet and Stoved Chicken. Coq au Vin has also made a come-back, and it is gaining new converts among a generation that has never tasted that delicious combination of chicken, red wine, bacon and shallots.

Cooking in a single pot is wonderfully liberating. All that is needed is a bit of leisurely preparation, and then the cook can relax, secure in the knowledge that there will be no last-minute sauces to make, no tricky toppings to produce. Serving a selection of side dishes would defeat the object of one-pot cooking (and is largely unnecessary when vegetables are included anyway), so you have the perfect excuse for offering only the simplest accompaniments, sparing yourself the anxiety that comes with trying to get everything ready at precisely the same time.

One-pot dishes tend to be fairly good-natured, and will seldom spoil if not eaten the moment they are ready. Some, like curries and casseroles, actually improve if made the day before,

Above: Paella, a classic one-pot seafood and rice dish from Spain, is traditionally cooked in a shallow, two-handled pan.

Left: A whole chicken cooked with forty cloves of garlic makes the perfect pot-roast, and it, like other one-pot dishes, needs little attention once it is in the oven.

Below: Clay pots come in a whole host of sizes and shapes. These tiny shallow cazuelas can be used to bake individual portions of both savoury and sweet tarts, roasted vegetables and custards.

the clay and throwing it away was wasteful and time-consuming, however. Clay pots were a huge improvement, and this material was used by many of the ancient civilizations. Today, clay pots based on ancient designs are still widely used all over the world. In North Africa, it is the conical tagine; in China, the sand pot; in Spain, the cazuela; and in France, the daubière and tian.

Chicken bricks, bean pots and clay pots come in all shapes and sizes. They need to be treated kindly, but are surprisingly durable. If you've never used one – or have forgotten just how good they make food taste – this book will give you plenty of inspiration, along with ideas for other delicious one-pot dishes of every kind.

Left: The tall, conical tagine from north Africa is one of the many ancient clay pot designs that are still widely used today.

so that all the flavours can bed down together and blend. Stir-fries, pasta and rice dishes need last-minute cooking, but if the preparation is done in advance, the effort is minimal.

This style of cooking is perfect for everyone, from students with a single hot plate to families feeding in relays. The meal can be cooked in the oven, on top of the stove or even in a free-standing appliance like a microwave oven, electric frying pan or slow-cooker. There's very little washing up, and if there are any leftovers, you may well be able to transform them into tasty pie fillings, simply by sandwiching them inside ready-rolled puff pastry or filo.

One-pot cooking can also be extremely healthy, especially if you use a clay pot, which ensures that vitamins and minerals are retained. This ancient form of cooking seals in all the food's natural juices by enclosing it in a porous clay container that has been soaked in water. As the container heats up, the water turns to steam, keeping the contents beautifully moist and tender. The only other liquid is that which comes from the food itself, so the full flavour of the food can be appreciated.

There's nothing new about cooking in clay. Thousands of years ago, hunters discovered that coating small birds and animals in clay before baking them in an open fire kept the meat juicy and prevented it from burning. Chipping off

Below: A fully glazed clay pot is the ideal container for this contemporary twist on a traditional Italian frittata. The glazing ensures that the flavours don't soak into the pot, which means that it can be used for both sweet and savoury dishes.

ONE-POT EQUIPMENT

If you are going to do a lot of cooking in just one pot, make it a good one. There's no point in planning a pot-roast for the whole family, only to find you haven't got a big enough pan, or that the one you have has a wobbly base. It is equally irritating to discover that your only decent casserole has a crack in it, or can only be used in the oven and not on top of the stove. Choose your cookware with care; it is worth investing in good quality equipment that will last.

Right:
Stainless-
steel pans
with a heavy
base are a good
choice for one-pot cooking.

Above: Frying pans with metal handles can be used under the grill (broiler) and in the oven.

Pots and Pans

When you are buying cooking equipment, it is very tempting to opt for a set of shiny pans, rather than individual items that might suit your purposes – and your personal circumstances – better.

Below left: A large pot with metal handles can be used on top of the stove and in the oven.

For one-pot cooking, you need a large pan with a heavy base, which will conduct the heat evenly and help to prevent the food from scorching should you inadvertently allow the amount of liquid to get too low. A good quality stainless-steel pan would be an excellent choice, but it is important to choose one with an aluminium or copper base, since stainless steel does not conduct heat well. For long, slow cooking, cast-iron pans coated in vitreous enamel, are ideal, as they can also be used in the oven. When buying a frying pan, choose one with a heavy base. When cooking a frittata or a dessert such as tarte Tatin, it is essential to use a frying pan with a handle that can withstand the heat of the grill (broiler) or oven; a point worth considering when you are buying a new frying pan.

Woks

One of the most useful items in the kitchen, the wok need not be reserved solely for stir-frying. It is the ideal pan for quick-cooked creamy dishes such as beef Stroganoff. The wok can also be used for making a risotto. Woks that

Left:
Woks have either one or two handles.

Right: When buying casseroles, it is a good idea to choose different shapes and sizes.

FREE-STANDING ELECTRIC COOKING POTS

It isn't vital to have a stove in order to cook a one-pot meal. Electric frying pans; slow-cookers (and combinations of the two); multi-purpose appliances, in which you can shallow fry, deep fry or even cook a casserole, all have the advantage that they have easy temperature control, use very little electricity and are easy to clean.

Casseroles

For one-pot cooking, choose a casserole that is big enough to serve six, even if you usually cook for four. This will give you plenty of room for stirring the contents without risking splashes and scalds. The ideal pot will be one that can be used on top of the stove as well as inside it, so that if you do need to do any pre-cooking, or if cooking juices need to be reduced by boiling, you will not need a second container. If you buy several casseroles, vary the shapes as well as the sizes. For cooking a whole chicken, for instance, an oval is more useful than a round dish. Look at the handles, too. It is important that they are easy to grasp, and that they do not become so hot that they are liable to burn you, even when you are using an oven glove. Appearance will obviously be a consideration, since you will be serving straight from the casserole, but consider practical aspects too.

have a flat base can be used on all types of cooker. They can have either one or two handles. Those with two handles are good for deep-frying and general cooking, while the wok with one handle is designed especially for stir-frying. The single handle makes the wok easy to pick up so that the ingredients can be stirred and tossed in the wok at the same time.

Baking Dishes

There are plenty of one-pot recipes that benefit from being cooked in large, shallow dishes, from oven-roasted vegetables to layered potato bakes. Buy several different shapes, bearing in mind the size of your oven. Having two rectangular dishes that will fit side by side can be a real boon if you want to cook one meal for serving immediately and another for the freezer.

Ramekins

You will also find it useful to have six or eight ovenproof ramekin dishes, for baking single portions, such as individual soufflés and oven-baked desserts.

Below: Choose two ovenproof baking dishes that will fit next to each other in your oven.

CLAY-POT EQUIPMENT

Visit any market in any town the world over, and you will find clay cooking pots for sale. Some will be rough, rustic items, only suitable for display, but others – like the Spanish cazuela or the North African tagine – will be intended not for the tourist trade, but for everyday cooking. Before buying, always seek local advice as to the durability and safety of the items, especially as regards any glazes that might be used. Buying a boxed item from a reputable store may not be as romantic, but it is probably more sensible. Clay cooking pots need special treatment, and it makes sense to follow the instructions that come with your particular utensil.

Left: The classic, high, domed Romertopf dish (top) and a large oval clay pot that is especially designed for cooking whole fish.

Romertopfs

Perhaps the most familiar unglazed clay pots are those produced by Romertopf. Their extensive range includes items suitable for cooking meat, fish, vegetables, fruit, even bread and cakes. The classic Romertopf is a rectangular pot with a deep, wide base and a domed lid. These come in several sizes. Other shapes include a long oval, suitable for accommodating a whole fish. This has a glazed base, to prevent liquid from penetrating the porous clay and leaving behind a lingering fishy smell.

Lids are designed to fit snugly, so that they cannot accidentally slip off, but there is a narrow gap between the lid and the base that allows any excess steam to escape from the clay pot.

Right: This deep, pan-shaped clay pot is designed for cooking bean dishes, but would also be good for baking potatoes, and for cooking soups and stews that have lots of liquid.

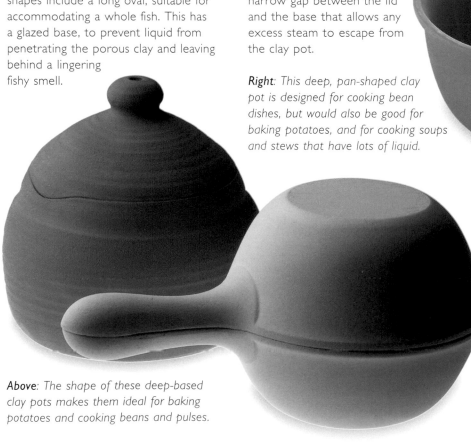

Above: The shape of these deep-based clay pots makes them ideal for baking potatoes and cooking beans and pulses.

Bean Pot/Potato Brick

There are several shapes of these deep, round pots. Some have a handle for easy lifting. Made entirely from clay, the pots have a domed lid. Although these pots are especially suitable for slowly cooking beans and pulses, they can also be used for soups and stews, and the shape is ideal for cooking both large and small potatoes. The potatoes are bathed in a layer of steam, which keeps them moist during cooking.

Whatever you are cooking, the pot and lid should first be soaked in water, then placed in a cold oven after the ingredients have been added.

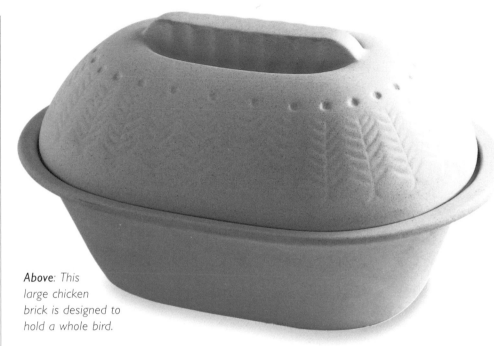

Above: This large chicken brick is designed to hold a whole bird.

COOKING BEANS

If you are cooking beans, check the recipe or the manufacturer's handbook. Before being added to the pot, such varieties as kidney, cannellini and soya beans need to be brought to the boil in a pan of water, then boiled vigorously for about 10 minutes to eliminate toxins from the beans. Drain the beans and leave them to cool before adding them to the bean pot. Any liquid added to the pot should be cold. This will prevent the pot from cracking or breaking.

Garlic Baker

This small terracotta dish with a domed lid is used for baking garlic. Like all clay pots, it must be placed in a cold oven and heated gradually. There is no need

to soak the pot in water first. The inside of the dish is glazed, so the garlic juices will not permeate it. The baker will accommodate four to six garlic bulbs. A small cross must be cut in the top of each garlic bulb, or the tops can be sliced off, to prevent them from bursting during cooking. The steam they release will be trapped under the domed lid of the garlic baker, and will keep the garlic cloves beautifully moist and tender. The garlic baker can also be used in a microwave oven.

Onion Baker

This clay pot looks like a larger version of the garlic baker. It consists of a shallow terracotta dish with a high, domed lid; it will accommodate four medium-sized onions, and can also be used for cooking onion wedges, shallots or baby onions. The lid can be soaked in water first, so that it releases steam during cooking. The steam helps to tenderize the onions. Towards the end of cooking, the lid should be removed so that the onions turn brown and become caramelized.

Chicken Brick

This is a large, unglazed fire clay cooking dish with a high lid. The largest ones are designed to hold a whole chicken, guinea fowl or duck, but can also be used to cook any large piece of meat or poultry. Smaller chicken bricks are ideal for small birds and portions. There is no need to add fat or liquid to the pot unless the recipe specifically requires this.

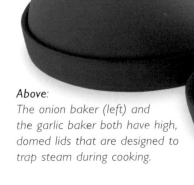

Above:
The onion baker (left) and the garlic baker both have high, domed lids that are designed to trap steam during cooking.

ADDING FLAVOURINGS

Roasting onions in a clay pot gives them a wonderful, sweet taste, but the flavour can be enhanced even further by adding sprigs of fresh herbs. Pungent fresh herbs such as rosemary, thyme and oregano work well; tuck small sprigs in among the vegetables for the best result.

Chinese Sand Pot

This covered earthenware pot, which is sometimes called a Chinese casserole, is usually glazed on the inside only and reinforced on the outside with wire. It comes from China, where it was originally used to cook stews over a slow charcoal fire. Several shapes and sizes are available. They are not expensive and can be bought in Asian and Chinese food and cooking equipment stores. The sand pot is ideal for slow-cooked dishes such as soups and stews that are baked in the oven. Do not use sand pots on top of the stove unless the manufacturer recommends this. Sand pots are fairly fragile, and are prone to crack easily. They do not need to be soaked before baking but like other clay pots are best placed in a cold oven.

Left: The Chinese sand pot was designed for cooking over a slow charcoal fire, but it is equally at home in a modern oven.

Tagine

This North African cooking pot consists of a large, shallow base and a tall, conical lid. The dish that is cooked in it is also known as a tagine.

Above: The traditional tagine (above left) has a shallow base and a tall, conical lid, while the contemporary version (right) has a deeper, larger base.

The food is placed in the base. As it cooks, steam rises and is trapped in the lid, keeping the food moist. Tagines are traditionally made from glazed brown earthenware, sometimes with a slightly rounded base. They come in a range of sizes, from small individual tagines to family-size ones that measure at least 20cm/8in across. There is also a modern version, with a heavy, cast-iron base and a glazed earthenware lid. Unlike the traditional tagine, which can only be used in the oven, or on a barbecue whose coals have been dowsed with sand, this design can also be used on top of the stove. This is very convenient, since it means that onions, vegetables and other ingredients such as meat and poultry can be browned in the base before the lid is fitted and the tagine is placed in the oven. Some glazed earthenware tagines can be used on top of the stove on a low heat, but it is best to use a heat diffuser; always check the manufacturer's instructions.

WHAT'S IN A NAME?

Clay, earthenware, terracotta, stoneware – we use the terms interchangeably, but are they all the same thing? Clay is essentially the raw material; it is a fine-grained mix of mineral origin that occurs in sedimentary rocks and soils. It is malleable when moist, but hardens when it is heated. When pots that are made from clay are baked, they become earthenware.

Terracotta is an Italian word that means "baked earth". It has come to refer to a type of hard, brownish-red earthenware that is traditionally left unglazed.

Stoneware is stronger than earthenware, having been fired at a higher temperature. It is usually perfectly safe to put stoneware in a hot oven, but always check the manufacturer's instructions.

Cazuelas

These shallow, lidless earthenware dishes originated in Spain. They are made in a variety of sizes. The smallest, suitable for Catalan-style sweet custards, measure 10–12.5cm/4–5in across, while the largest – used for cooking savoury dishes in the oven – measure 38cm/15in or even more. They vary in depth from about 2.5cm/1in to 7.5cm/3in. Cazuelas are either partially glazed on the outside, and fully glazed inside, or glazed inside and out. Neither type are soaked in water before use. After a while, the glaze on the cazuela may develop a slightly "crazed" appearance, but this is completely natural and will not affect the performance of the dish.

Individual cazuelas can be used for cooking single portions of all sorts of one-pot dishes, but they are ideal for making individual upside-down tarts. The lightly fried vegetables are spread out on the cazuelas, topped with rounds of puff pastry, then baked in the oven. The tarts are then inverted on serving plates.

Left: Spanish cazuelas come in a range of sizes and depths. The smallest are perfect for individual oven-baked custards, while the largest are good for slow-cooked stews and vegetable bakes, but will also accommodate whole fish and poultry as well as large joints of meat.

Tian

This traditional French baking dish originated in Provence. It is a shallow, usually oval, earthenware dish, and is used for baking vegetables, sometimes with rice and eggs. The dish that is cooked in it is also called a tian.

Right: Oval-shaped tians originated in Provence and are traditionally used for baking vegetables, but the shape is ideal for other oven-baked, one-pot dishes.

Right: A wide range of glazed earthenware bakeware is available – these dishes can often be used in the oven and under the grill.

Glazed Earthenware Bakeware

A wide selection of glazed ovenproof earthenware is available. These dishes can often be put straight into a hot oven, or used under a hot grill (broiler) for browning. They are also suitable for use in the freezer. Unlike clay pots and porous earthenware, they do not need to be soaked in water before use and will not absorb food flavours and become tainted.

ONE-POT COOKING TECHNIQUES

Cooking a dish in a single pot doesn't demand any particular expertise, but mastering a few simple techniques will make for greater efficiency, especially when preparing the ingredients. Many one-pot dishes need very little attention while they are actually cooking, but it is important to follow the instructions in individual recipes as regards stirring.

Stewing, Braising and Casseroling Meat

These are long, slow and moist methods of cooking either in the oven or on top of the stove. The meat is browned first to seal in the natural juices and improve the flavour and colour of the finished dish, then it is simmered slowly at a low temperature in liquid – wine, water, beer or stock.

1 Trim off any excess fat from the meat. For stewing and casseroling, cut the meat into 2.5cm/1in cubes. For braising use thickly cut steaks or cut the meat into thick slices.

2 Toss the meat a few pieces at a time in seasoned flour, then shake off any excess. The flour coating browns to give the casserole a good flavour and also thickens the liquid.

3 Heat 30ml/2 tbsp sunflower oil in a flameproof casserole. Add the meat in batches and cook over a high heat. When the meat is well browned on all sides, use a draining spoon to remove the meat before adding the next batch.

4 Add the sliced or chopped onions and other vegetables to the remaining fat and juices in the casserole and cook, stirring occasionally, for about 5 minutes.

5 Return the meat to the casserole, add herbs and pour in the cooking liquid. Stir to loosen the cooking residue from the base of the pan and then heat until simmering. Simmer gently on the hob or in the oven until the meat is tender. The casserole may be covered for the entire cooking time or uncovered towards the end to allow excess liquid to evaporate.

CUTS FOR STEWS, BRAISES AND CASSEROLES
These slow-cooked dishes are ideal for tough, inexpensive cuts of meat, such as cubes of stewing steak or slices of braising steak, less tender cuts of lamb such as shoulder, and diced or thickly sliced pork. Lamb leg steaks, although fairly tender, are also a good choice for braising.

Pot-roasting Meat

This long, slow method of cooking is ideal for slightly tough joints of meat such as topside of beef, lamb shoulder and shanks, and knuckle of pork.

1 Heat a little sunflower oil in a large flameproof casserole until very hot. Add the meat and cook over a high heat, turning frequently, until browned on all sides. Remove the meat from the pan.

2 Add the onions, leeks and any root vegetables to the pan, then cook, stirring, for a few minutes. Replace the meat on top of the vegetables and pour in a little liquid, such as stock, wine or beer. Cover and cook gently in the oven until the meat is tender.

Casseroling Chicken

Moist cooking methods not only bring out the flavour of poultry but also offer the opportunity for allowing herbs and spices and aromatics to infuse the light meat thoroughly. Whole birds and joints can be casseroled.

1 Brown the poultry pieces or bird all over first. Remove from the pan before softening chopped onion, carrot, celery and other flavouring ingredients in the fat remaining in the pan.

2 Replace the poultry before adding the chosen liquid – stock, wine or canned tomatoes. Season the casserole well, then bring it just to simmering point. Cover it closely and allow it to simmer very gently on top of the stove, or cook in the oven at 180°C/350°F/Gas 4.

COOKING TIMES FOR CASSEROLING CHICKEN
• For a whole bird allow 20 minutes per 450g/1lb, plus 20 minutes.
• Large portions 45–60 minutes.
• Boneless breasts about 30 minutes.
• Chunks or diced poultry 20–40 minutes, depending on their size.

Pan-frying Meat

This is the traditional cooking method for steaks such as sirloin and fillet, and it is also good for veal escalopes (US scallops) and veal chops, lamb chops, cutlets and noisettes, and pork chops, steaks and escalopes.

1 Cook steaks and chops in the minimum of fat, then add flavoured butter when serving, if you like. Dab a little sunflower oil on kitchen paper and use to grease the pan lightly. Heat the pan until it is very hot (almost smoking). Add the steak or chops and cook for 2–4 minutes on each side.

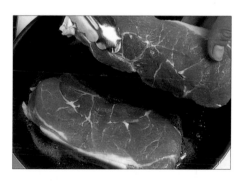

2 Pan-fry other lean cuts of meat in a mixture of butter and oil. Butter burns easily, so heat the oil in the pan first and add the butter just before the meat to avoid this. Make sure that the butter and oil are sizzling before adding the meat. Cook on both sides until browned. Beef and thin cuts of meat such as escalopes will be ready to serve. For some thicker cuts and meat such as pork that needs to be well-cooked, reduce the heat to low once the meat is browned and cook for 10–15 minutes, or until cooked through. Test by piercing the centre of the meat with the point of a sharp knife.

Pan-frying Poultry

This quick cooking method is ideal for chicken breast fillets and portions. Once the meat is cooked, the cooking juices can be made into a tasty sauce, simply stir in a little cream, add some chopped herbs and season to taste.

When frying poultry, remember that it must be cooked through. Escalopes and boneless breasts cook quickly, so are ideal for pan-frying over a high heat, but uneven thicker portions require careful cooking. With larger pieces, reduce the heat to low once the chicken is browned and cook it slowly for up to 30 minutes to ensure that the centre is cooked.

Stir-frying

This is a fast method of cooking tender meat. The meat should be cut into thin slices across the grain, and then cut into fine, long strips. Use a wok or a heavy frying pan.

Heat a little oil in a wok or frying pan until it is smoking hot. Add the meat in batches and stir-fry over a high heat. Remove the cooked meat before adding a fresh batch. When all the meat is cooked, add the other ingredients and stir-fry over a slightly lower heat.

CLAY-POT COOKING TECHNIQUES

Used with care, clay cooking pots last for years, but it is very important to follow the manufacturer's instructions closely. The advice that follows should be read in conjunction with your handbook.

Preparing a Clay Pot

All unglazed clay cooking pots must be soaked in cold water before every use. This is essential because it is the water retained in the clay that provides the moisture required during cooking. Ideally, the soaking time should be about 20 minutes. If it is the first time you have used the pot, leave it to soak for at least 30 minutes.

Place both the pot and its lid in a sink of cold water, inverting the lid on top of the base if necessary. The entire pot and the lid must be submerged. This thorough soaking is recommended before every use. If you are really short of time, you can just hold the pot under cold running water for about 1 minute, but this is not as satisfactory as soaking.

You can use your clay pot for lots of different recipes, but should avoid cooking fish or any highly flavoured dish in it the first time you use it. If you have more than one clay pot, consider keeping separate pots for savoury and sweet dishes.

Partially Glazed Clay Pots

Also available are clay pots that are glazed on the inside, but which have unglazed lids. With this type of pot, only the lid needs to be soaked, and this is done by holding it under running cold water for a few minutes. The ingredients are put into the pot, seasoned, and moistened with stock. The lid is fitted

and the pot is placed in a cold oven, which is then heated to 220°C/425°F/Gas 7. Steam released from the soaked lid helps to keep the food moist as it bakes. The lid can be removed towards the end of cooking to allow the food to brown, if necessary.

Cooking with a Clay Pot

Most clay pots should only be used in the oven. Unglazed pots are sensitive to sudden changes of temperature, which can cause the pot to crack or break if it is placed directly over the heat.

Some clay pots can be used on top of the stove on a very low heat, but it is recommended that a heat diffuser or flame-tamer is used. These are available from specialist cookware stores.

1 Some recipes suggest sautéing vegetables or meat in a frying pan to brown them before adding them to the clay pot. If you do this, let the browned foods cool slightly before putting them into the cold clay pot.

2 Once the browned foods have been added, it is okay to pour in warm or hand-hot cooking liquids. If what is in the pot is cold, any liquid added should be at room temperature.

USING A HEAT DIFFUSER

If your handbook states that your pot can safely be used on top of the stove you can obviously do so, but always use a heat diffuser between the heat source and the pot.

Some cazuelas can be used on top of the stove with a heat diffuser.

Cooking in an Oven

An unglazed clay pot must always be heated gradually.

Place the clay pot in a cold oven and then heat to the required temperature. It might crack if subjected to a sudden change of temperature.

You will notice that the recipes in this book advise you to place the clay pot, which will be cold, in a cold oven, then set the oven temperature to allow the oven and clay pot to heat slowly.

An electric oven heats up gradually, giving the clay pot time to acclimatize. If, however, you are using a traditional gas oven, the flames may be too fierce for the cold clay pot. You should start by setting the oven temperature to 190°C/375°F/Gas 5. After 5 minutes, increase the temperature to 200°C/400°F/Gas 6. Continue to increase the temperature of the oven gradually, each time raising it to the next setting on your cooker, until the required temperature is reached.

The exact cooking times for recipes containing liquids may vary from oven to oven, as the time taken for the liquid to come to the boil will differ.

Cooking with a Cast-iron Tagine on a Stovetop

In addition to the classic all-earthenware tagines, which can't be used on a stovetop, there is a modern version that has an earthenware lid and cast-iron base. The base can be used on the top of any type of stove, be it gas, electric or wood-burning, to brown ingredients such as onions, vegetables or meat before the other ingredients and liquid are added. The pot is then covered and the tagine or stew is simmered gently on top of the stove or in the oven.

Place the cast-iron tagine base on the stovetop, add a little oil and heat. Add the vegetables or other ingredients and cook over a medium-high heat, stirring occasionally, until browned

Browning in a Clay Pot

A certain amount of browning will occur during cooking, depending on the cooking temperature, cooking time and type of food. Some recipes suggest removing the lid for a short period of time towards the end of the cooking time to enhance the colour of baked items and roasts, and also to develop a crisper finish. The oven temperature for clay-pot cooking is fairly high, so the browning process will only take a few minutes; keep a close check on the food.

To remove the lid, lift the clay pot out of the oven using oven gloves and place it on a pot stand, wooden board or folded dishtowel. Take care when lifting the lid to avoid any escaping steam.

Adding Liquids to a Clay Pot

Never add boiling liquids – or even very hot liquids – to a cold clay pot or the sudden change in temperature may cause the claypot to crack.

If you need to add liquid to the clay pot during the cooking period, this liquid should be hot. This not only avoids a sudden temperature change, but also ensures that the food isn't cooled too much, which would slow the cooking.

Adding Flavourings

To get the best results, place herb sprigs and spices in among vegetables that are to be roasted or underneath joints of meat. This will ensure that the flavour penetrates as deeply as possible.

Adding Ingredients during Cooking

In some recipes, ingredients that don't need to be cooked for long, such as prawns or cooked ham, are added towards the end of the cooking time.

Remove the pot from the oven using oven gloves and remove the lid. Add the cold food and stir well to ensure that it is distributed evenly, then re-cover the pot and return it to the oven.

Cooking on a Barbecue

Moroccan tagines are sometimes placed on a barbecue, but they should not be too near the heat source. It is best to wait until the coals have all turned grey. Cover the coals with some sand, to make the heat less concentrated, and then allow the tagine to heat up slowly by initially placing it at the edge of the barbecue and gradually moving it to the hottest part.

Using a Clay Pot for Baking

Clay pots can be used for baking cakes, breads and sponge-based desserts. It is, however, best to keep a separate clay pot for sweet foods or, alternatively, use earthenware that is glazed inside.

If you use a clay pot for baking, it is a good idea to line the base of the clay pot with a piece of baking parchment, so that the food doesn't stick to the base and is easy to remove after baking.

SAFETY FIRST

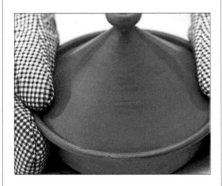

When you remove any type of clay pot from the oven, either to add extra ingredients or to serve the food, protect your hands with oven gloves. Place the pot on a folded towel, wooden board, heatproof mat or pot stand, as sudden contact with a cold surface could cause the pot to crack. Do the same with the lid, when you lift it off.

Clay pots should not be used under the grill (broiler) or in the freezer as the sudden change in temperature could cause the clay pot to crack or break.

Microwave Cooking

Clay pots can be used to cook foods in the microwave oven, as well as in a conventional oven. One of the advantages with using a clay pot for microwave cooking is that, because it is moist from soaking, it will absorb some of the microwave energy. This slows down the cooking process, which is perfect for protecting delicate foods, cooking foods more evenly and pot-roasting less tender cuts of meat, whole chickens or game birds.

Select a clay pot that will fit inside your microwave oven. The smaller, rectangular or round pots are ideal.

Prepare the pot as for oven cooking, by soaking it in water for 20 minutes. When setting the cooking time, refer to your microwave handbook for detailed instructions on using a clay pot, as each appliance is different. If you are adapting an existing microwave recipe, expect the food to take slightly longer to cook in a clay pot. The food is usually cooked on full (100%) power, but it may also be cooked on medium-high (70%) or medium (50%) settings so that the food simmers, rather than boils.

A safety note worth remembering is that because a clay pot is moist and absorbs microwave energy it will become hot; hotter, in fact, than many other types of microwave cookware. Make sure you use oven gloves to lift the clay pot out of the microwave, and always place the pot on a pot stand, wooden board or mat, or folded dishtowel when removing it from the oven, both for your own safety, and to avoid subjecting the pot to severe temperature changes.

ADAPTING RECIPES FOR CLAY-POT COOKING

A wide range of foods can be cooked in a clay pot, and you may wish to try using it for some of your favourite dishes. Find a clay-pot recipe in this book that is similar to the one you want to make, and use it as a blueprint. The main differences in cooking techniques that need to be observed are these:

• When an unglazed or partially glazed clay pot is used, the oven must not be preheated.

• When the pot is put into the cold oven, it is heated gradually until it reaches the required cooking temperature. If the dish contains liquid, it must be heated until it boils. This is likely to be at a higher temperature than when cooking in another type of container, because the pot forms an insulating layer between the heat of the oven and the food. When the liquid boils, the oven temperature may then be reduced, so that the contents of the pot simmer.

• If you are using a gas stove, it is essential that you increase the temperature gradually or the transition from cold to blasting heat may cause the pot to crack.

• You will probably have to extend the cooking time to take into account the fact that the ingredients, including any liquids, are cold when put into the oven, which also starts off cold. When foods are roasted with little or no liquid, however, the cooking time stays about the same because the higher cooking temperature compensates for the insulation of the clay pot.

• Because of the moist environment, food cooked in a clay pot doesn't overcook quickly when the lid is on, however, it is important to check the food frequently if the lid is removed towards the end of cooking to promote browning as the top of the food can easily scorch.

Cleaning and Storing Clay Pots

Before using a clay pot for the first time, brush it thoroughly inside and out to remove any loose clay particles left from the manufacturing process. Rinse the pot after brushing, then drain it. If you intend to cook in it straight away, then soak it thoroughly in cold water first.

After using the pot a few times, you may notice a colour change. This is completely natural and is part of the character of a clay pot. As with a well-seasoned frying pan or wok, this effect is due to a protective layer that builds up with use and enhances the cooking qualities of the pot.

Washing the Pot

1 Wash a clay pot promptly after every use, using a brush and hot water. A soft-bristled brush is fine if the pot is not too dirty, otherwise use a firm-bristled washing-up brush, Add washing-up liquid to the water if this is recommended in your handbook, as this helps to get rid of stubborn stains. Avoid using abrasive cleaning materials as detergents, as these may affect the porous nature of the clay and may impair its cooking qualities.

2 Having washed the pot, rinse it under hot water, then stand it upside down on kitchen paper to drain thoroughly.

Using a Dishwasher

Most glazed earthenware dishes can be used in the dishwasher, but some manufacturers do not recommend washing clay pots that way. Check your manufacturer's handbook.

Removing Food Residue

Sometimes food may bake on to the surface of a clay pot, especially if it has been used for cooking without the cover. Soaking the pot in hot water to which a little washing-up liquid has been added is usually sufficient to release the residue. Leave the pot to soak overnight if the residue is particularly stubborn. Some earthenware dishes can be filled with hot water to remove baked-on food, but do not leave them immersed in hot soapy water.

1 If an unglazed clay pot becomes tainted with residual flavours, soak it overnight in cold water containing bicarbonate of soda (baking soda). If the problem is severe, or if smells still linger, fill the pot with water, add bicarbonate of soda and place it in a cold oven.

2 Set the oven to 180°C/350°F/Gas 4 and leave the clay pot to heat in the oven for about 20 minutes. Increase the temperature of the oven to 200°C/400°F/Gas 6 and heat for another 20 minutes, then increase the oven temperature again to 230°C/450°F/Gas 8 and leave the pot at this temperature for 30 minutes to 1 hour.

3 Carefully lift the pot out of the oven using oven gloves and then discard the contents. Scrub the interior of the pot gently before rinsing it thoroughly with very hot water. Turn the pot and lid upside-down on a rack and leave to dry at room temperature. It is worth following this cleaning procedure after about a hundred uses, to clean the pores of your clay pot. This will allow it to take up water with the same efficiency as when it was brand new.

Storing the Pot

Before you put a clay pot away, make sure that it is not only completely clean but also thoroughly dried.

Invert the lid into the base. This is not only for safety and so that it takes up less room in your storecupboard, but also because placing the lid on the pot as for cooking could encourage moulds and mildew to grow on the inside surface of the pot and lid.

It is for this reason that the pot must also be stored somewhere dry and airy. Do not leave it in a damp place. It is the nature of a clay pot to absorb moisture, so it is important to keep it completely dry during storage. Do not wrap the clay pot or seal it in a plastic bag during storage.

SOUPS

There's something supremely comforting about hot soup, and when you prepare it yourself, the aroma ensures that the pleasure starts long before you lift the ladle. Nourishing, easy to digest, quick to cook and convenient, soup provides the perfect meal-in-a-bowl at lunchtime or a warming after-school snack, and when served as a first course, it gives guests a real sense of welcome. Mediterranean Leek and Fish Soup with Tomatoes and Garlic, Italian Farmhouse Soup, Seafood Chowder, and Bean and Pistou Soup are just some of the treats in store.

BOUILLABAISSE

*Perhaps the most famous of all Mediterranean fish soups, this recipe, originating from
Marseilles in the south of France, is a rich and colourful mixture of fish and shellfish,
flavoured with tomatoes, saffron and orange.*

SERVES 4–6

1.3–1.6kg/3–3½lb mixed fish and shellfish,
    such as red mullet, John Dory, monkfish,
    large prawns (shrimp) and clams
1.2 litres/2 pints/5 cups water
225g/8oz tomatoes
pinch of saffron threads
90ml/6 tbsp olive oil
1 onion, sliced
1 leek, sliced
1 celery stick, sliced
2 garlic cloves, crushed
bouquet garni
1 strip pared orange rind
2.5ml/½ tsp fennel seeds
15ml/1 tbsp tomato purée (paste)
10ml/2 tsp Pernod
4–6 thick slices French bread
45ml/3 tbsp chopped fresh parsley
salt and ground black pepper

1 Remove the heads, tails and fins from
the fish and put in a large pan, with the
water. Bring to the boil, and simmer for
15 minutes. Strain, and reserve the liquid.

2 Cut the fish into large chunks. Leave
the shellfish in their shells.

3 Scald the tomatoes, then drain and
refresh in cold water. Peel and chop them.
Soak the saffron in 15–30ml/1–2 tbsp
hot water. Heat the oil in the cleaned
pan, add the onion, leek and celery and
cook until softened. Add the garlic,
bouquet garni, orange rind, fennel seeds
and tomatoes, then stir in the saffron
and liquid and the fish stock. Season with
salt and pepper, then bring to the boil
and simmer for 30–40 minutes.

4 Add the shellfish and boil for about
6 minutes. Discard any clams that remain
closed. Add the fish and cook for a
further 6–8 minutes until it flakes easily.
Using a slotted spoon, transfer the fish
to a warmed serving platter. Keep the
liquid boiling and add the tomato purée
and Pernod, then check the seasoning.
Place a slice of bread in each soup bowl,
pour the broth over and serve the fish
separately, sprinkled with the parsley.

MEDITERRANEAN LEEK and FISH SOUP with TOMATOES

This chunky soup, which is almost a stew, makes a robust and wonderfully aromatic meal in a bowl. Serve it with crisp-toasted croûtes spread with a spicy garlic mayonnaise.

SERVES 4

30ml/2 tbsp olive oil
2 large thick leeks, white and green
    parts separated
5ml/1 tsp crushed coriander seeds
good pinch of dried red chilli flakes
300g/11oz small salad potatoes,
    thickly sliced
200g/7oz can chopped tomatoes
600ml/1 pint/2½ cups fish stock
150ml/¼ pint/⅔ cup fruity white wine
1 fresh bay leaf
1 star anise
1 strip pared orange rind
good pinch of saffron threads
450g/1lb white fish fillets, such as sea bass,
    monkfish, cod or haddock, skinned
450g/1lb small squid, cleaned
250g/9oz uncooked peeled
    prawns (shrimp)
30–45ml/2–3 tbsp chopped fresh parsley
salt and ground black pepper

For the garlic croûtes
1 short French loaf, sliced and toasted
spicy garlic mayonnaise

1 Gently heat the olive oil in a pan, then thinly slice the green part of the leeks. Add with the crushed coriander seeds and the dried red chilli flakes, and cook for 5 minutes, stirring occasionally.

2 Add the thickly sliced potatoes and chopped tomatoes and pour in the fish stock and white wine. Add the bay leaf, star anise, pared orange rind and saffron threads to the pan and stir well.

3 Bring to the boil, then reduce the heat and partly cover the pan. Simmer for about 20 minutes until the potatoes are tender. Taste and adjust the seasoning.

4 Cut the fish into chunks. Cut the squid sacs into rectangles and score a criss-cross pattern into them without cutting right through.

5 Add the fish to the soup, cook gently for 4 minutes, then add the prawns and cook for 1 minute. Add the squid and the thinly sliced white part of the leek and cook, stirring occasionally, for 2 minutes.

6 Stir in the chopped parsley and serve with the toasted croûtes topped with spicy garlic mayonnaise.

CHINESE CHICKEN and CHILLI SOUP

Ginger and lemon grass add an aromatic note to this tasty, refreshing soup, which can be served as a light lunch or appetizer.

2 Place the Chinese sand pot in an unheated oven. Set the temperature to 200°C/400°F/Gas 6 and cook the soup for 30–40 minutes, or until the stock is simmering and the chicken and vegetables are tender.

3 Add the spring onions and mushrooms, cover and return the pot to the oven for 10 minutes. Meanwhile place the noodles in a large bowl and cover with boiling water – soak for the required time, following the packet instructions.

4 Drain the noodles and divide among four warmed serving bowls. Stir the soy sauce into the soup and season with salt and pepper. Divide the soup between the bowls and serve immediately.

COOK'S TIP

Rice noodles are available in a variety of thicknesses and can be bought in straight lengths or in coils or loops. They are a creamy white colour and very brittle in texture. Rice noodles are pre-cooked so they only require a very short soaking time – check the packet for exact timings. Vermicelli rice noodles are very fine and will only need to be soaked for a few minutes.

SERVES 4

150g/5oz boneless chicken breast portion, cut into thin strips
2.5cm/1in piece fresh root ginger, finely chopped
5cm/2in piece lemon grass stalk, finely chopped
1 red chilli, seeded and thinly sliced
8 baby corn cobs, halved lengthwise
1 large carrot, cut into thin sticks
1 litre/1¾ pints/4 cups hot chicken stock
4 spring onions (scallions), thinly sliced
12 small shiitake mushrooms, sliced
115g/4oz/1 cup vermicelli rice noodles
30ml/2 tbsp soy sauce
salt and ground black pepper

1 Place the chicken strips, chopped ginger, chopped lemon grass and sliced chilli in a Chinese sand pot. Add the halved baby corn and the carrot sticks. Pour over the hot chicken stock and cover the pot.

COCONUT and SEAFOOD SOUP
with GARLIC CHIVES

*The long list of ingredients in this Thai-inspired recipe could mislead you into thinking that
this soup is complicated. In fact, it is very easy to put together.*

SERVES 4

600ml/1 pint/2½ cups fish stock
5 thin slices fresh root ginger
2 lemon grass stalks, chopped
3 kaffir lime leaves, shredded
25g/1oz garlic chives (1 bunch), chopped
15g/½oz fresh coriander (cilantro)
15ml/1 tbsp vegetable oil
4 shallots, chopped
400ml/14fl oz can coconut milk
30–45ml/2–3 tbsp Thai fish sauce
45–60ml/3–4 tbsp Thai green curry paste
450g/1lb uncooked large prawns (jumbo
    shrimp), peeled and deveined
450g/1lb prepared squid
a little lime juice (optional)
salt and ground black pepper
60ml/4 tbsp fried shallot slices, to serve

4 Stir in the curry paste and the peeled
prawns and cook for 3 minutes. Add the
squid, cook for a further 2 minutes. Add
the lime juice, if using, and season.

5 Stir in the remaining fish sauce, chopped
chives and the chopped coriander
leaves. Serve in warmed, shallow bowls
sprinkled with fried shallots.

VARIATIONS
• Instead of squid, you could add 400g/
14oz firm white fish, such as monkfish,
cut into small pieces.
• You could also replace the squid with
fresh mussels. Steam 675g/1½lb closed
mussels in a tightly covered pan for about
3 minutes, or until the shells have
opened. Discard any that remain shut, then
remove the mussels from their shells.

1 Pour the stock into a pan and add the
slices of fresh ginger, the chopped lemon
grass and half the lime leaves.

2 Add half the chopped chives to the
pan with the coriander stalks. Bring to
the boil, then reduce the heat. Cover the
pan, then simmer gently for 20 minutes.
Strain the stock.

3 Rinse the pan, then add the oil and
shallots. Cook over a medium heat for
5–10 minutes, stirring occasionally, until
the shallots are just beginning to brown.
Stir in the stock, coconut milk, the
remaining lime leaves and half the fish
sauce. Heat gently until the soup is just
simmering and cook over a low heat for
5–10 minutes.

MEDITERRANEAN SAUSAGE and PESTO SOUP

This hearty soup makes a satisfying one-pot meal that brings the summery flavour of basil to midwinter meals. Thick slices of warm crusty bread make the perfect accompaniment.

SERVES 4

oil, for deep-frying
450g/1lb smoked pork sausages
a handful of fresh basil leaves
15ml/1 tbsp olive oil
1 red onion, chopped
225g/8oz/1 cup red lentils
400g/14oz can chopped tomatoes
  with herbs
1 litre/1¾ pints/4 cups chicken stock
  or water
salt and ground black pepper
60ml/4 tbsp pesto, to serve

COOK'S TIP
The flavour of smoked sausages is very good in this soup, but you could use ordinary fresh sausages if you like. Choose course-textured sausages, such as Toulouse.

1 Heat the oil for deep-frying to 190°C/375°F or until a cube of day-old bread browns in about 60 seconds. Slice one of the sausages diagonally and deep-fry for 2–3 minutes, or until brown and crisp. Add the basil leaves and fry for a few seconds until crisp. Lift out the sausage slices and basil leaves using a slotted spoon and drain them on kitchen paper. Strain the oil into a bowl.

2 Heat the olive oil in the pan, add the chopped red onion and cook until softened. Coarsely chop the remaining sausages and add them to the pan. Cook for about 5 minutes, stirring, or until the sausages are cooked.

3 Stir in the lentils, tomatoes and stock or water and bring to the boil. Reduce the heat, cover and simmer for about 20 minutes. Cool the soup slightly before puréeing it in a blender. Return the soup to the rinsed-out pan.

4 Reheat the soup, add seasoning to taste, then ladle into warmed individual soup bowls. Sprinkle the soup with the deep-fried sausage slices and basil and swirl a little pesto through each portion just before serving. Serve with plenty of warm crusty bread.

MOROCCAN SPICED LAMB SOUP

Classic north African spices – ginger, turmeric and cinnamon – are combined with chickpeas and lamb to make this hearty, warming soup.

SERVES 6

75g/3oz/½ cup chickpeas, soaked overnight
15g/½oz/1 tbsp butter
225g/8oz lamb, cut into cubes
1 onion, chopped
450g/1lb tomatoes, peeled and chopped
a few celery leaves, chopped
30ml/2 tbsp chopped fresh parsley
15ml/1 tbsp chopped fresh
    coriander (cilantro)
2.5ml/½ tsp ground ginger
2.5ml/½ tsp ground turmeric
5ml/1 tsp ground cinnamon
1.75 litres/3 pints/7½ cups water
75g/3oz/scant ½ cup green lentils
75g/3oz vermicelli or soup pasta
2 egg yolks
juice of ½–1 lemon
salt and ground black pepper
fresh coriander (cilantro), to garnish
lemon wedges, to serve

1 Drain the chickpeas, rinse under cold water and set aside. Melt the butter in a large flameproof casserole or pan and fry the lamb and onion for 2–3 minutes, stirring, until the lamb is just browned.

2 Add the chopped tomatoes, celery leaves, herbs and spices and season well with ground black pepper. Cook for about 1 minute, then stir in the water and add the green lentils and the soaked, drained and rinsed chickpeas.

3 Slowly bring to the boil and skim the surface to remove the froth. Boil rapidly for 10 minutes, then reduce the heat and simmer very gently for 2 hours, or until the chickpeas are very tender.

4 Season with salt and pepper, then add the vermicelli or soup pasta to the pan and cook for 5–6 minutes until it is just tender. If the soup is very thick at this stage, add a little more water.

5 Beat the egg yolks with the lemon juice and stir into the simmering soup. Immediately remove the soup from the heat and stir until thickened. Pour into warmed serving bowls and garnish with plenty of fresh coriander. Serve the soup with lemon wedges.

COOK'S TIP
If you have forgotten to soak the chickpeas overnight, place them in a pan with about four times their volume of cold water. Bring very slowly to the boil, then cover the pan, remove it from the heat and leave to stand for 45 minutes before using as described in the recipe.

CATALAN POTATO and BROAD BEAN SOUP

While they are in season fresh broad beans are perfect, but canned or frozen are just as good in this creamy, richly flavoured soup.

SERVES 6

30ml/2 tbsp olive oil
2 onions, chopped
3 large floury potatoes, diced
450g/1lb fresh shelled broad
    (fava) beans
1.75 litres/3 pints/7½ cups vegetable or
    chicken stock
1 bunch coriander (cilantro),
    finely chopped
150ml/¼ pint/⅔ cup single (light) cream
salt and ground black pepper
coriander (cilantro) leaves, to garnish

COOK'S TIP
Broad beans sometimes have a tough outer skin, particularly if they are large. To remove this, first cook the beans briefly in boiling water, then peel off the skin, and add the tender, bright green centre part to the soup.

1 Heat the olive oil in a large pan, add the chopped onions and fry, stirring occasionally with a wooden spoon, for about 5 minutes until they are just softened but not brown.

2 Add the diced potatoes, shelled broad beans (reserving a few for garnishing) and vegetable or chicken stock to the pan. Bring to the boil, then simmer for 5 minutes.

3 Stir in the finely chopped coriander and simmer for a further 10 minutes.

4 Process the soup in batches in a food processor or blender, then return the soup to the rinsed-out pan.

5 Stir in the cream (reserving a little for garnishing), season, and bring to a simmer. Serve garnished with more coriander leaves, beans and cream.

SPANISH POTATO and GARLIC SOUP

Traditionally served in shallow earthenware dishes, this delicious, classic Spanish soup is a great choice for vegetarians.

SERVES 6

30ml/2 tbsp olive oil
1 large onion, finely sliced
4 garlic cloves, crushed
1 large potato, halved and cut
    into thin slices
5ml/1 tsp paprika
400g/14oz can chopped tomatoes, drained
5ml/1 tsp thyme leaves, plus extra chopped
    thyme leaves, to garnish
900ml/1½ pints/3¾ cups vegetable stock
5ml/1 tsp cornflour (cornstarch)
salt and ground black pepper

COOK'S TIP
Paprika is a popular spice in many Spanish dishes. It is made from red peppers that are dried and powdered into a coarse-grained spice. It has a slightly sweet, mild flavour and a rich red colour.

1 Heat the oil in a large, heavy pan, add the onion, garlic, potato and paprika and cook, stirring occasionally, for about 5 minutes, or until the onions have softened, but not browned.

2 Add the chopped tomatoes, thyme leaves and vegetable stock to the pan and simmer for 15–20 minutes until the potatoes have cooked through.

3 In a small bowl, mix the cornflour with a little water to form a smooth paste, then stir into the soup. Bring to the boil, stirring, then simmer for about 5 minutes until the soup has thickened.

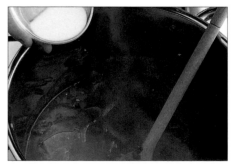

4 Using a wooden spoon, break up the potatoes slightly, then season to taste. Serve the soup garnished with the extra chopped thyme leaves.

CHICKEN and LEEK SOUP with PRUNES and BARLEY

This recipe is based on the traditional Scottish soup, Cock-a-leekie. The unusual combination of leeks and prunes is surprisingly delicious.

3 Bring the stock to the boil, then reduce the heat and cover the pan. Simmer gently for 1 hour. Skim off any scum when the water first starts to boil and occasionally during simmering.

4 Add the chicken breast portions to the pan and continue to cook for another 30 minutes until they are just cooked. Leave until cool enough to handle, then strain the stock. Reserve the chicken breast portions and the meat from the carcass. Discard all the skin, bones, cooked vegetables and herbs. Skim as much fat as you can from the stock, then return it to the pan.

5 Add the pearl barley to the stock. Bring to the boil over a medium heat, then lower the heat and cook very gently for 15–20 minutes, until the barley is just cooked and tender. Season the soup with 5ml/1 tsp each salt and ground black pepper.

6 Add the ready-to-eat prunes to the pan, then thinly slice the remaining leeks and add them to the pan. Bring to the boil, then cover the pan and simmer gently for about 10 minutes, or until the leeks are just cooked.

7 Slice the chicken breast portions and then add them to the soup with the remaining chicken meat from the carcass, sliced or cut into neat pieces. Reheat the soup, if necessary, then ladle it into warm, deep soup plates and sprinkle with plenty of chopped parsley to serve.

SERVES 6

115g/4oz/⅔ cup pearl barley
1 chicken, weighing about 2kg/4¼lb
900g/2lb leeks
1 fresh bay leaf
a few fresh parsley stalks and
    thyme sprigs
1 large carrot, thickly sliced
2.4 litres/4 pints/10 cups chicken or
    beef stock
400g/14oz ready-to-eat prunes
salt and ground black pepper
chopped fresh parsley, to garnish

1 Rinse the pearl barley thoroughly in a sieve under cold running water, then cook it in a large pan of boiling water for about 10 minutes. Drain the barley, rinse well again and drain thoroughly. Set aside in a cool place.

2 Cut the breast portions off the chicken and set aside, then place the remaining chicken carcass in the pan. Cut half the leeks into 5cm/2in lengths and add them to the pan. Tie the herbs together into a bouquet garni and add to the pan with the carrot and stock.

CLAM, MUSHROOM and POTATO CHOWDER

The delicate, sweet taste of clams and the soft earthiness of wild mushrooms combine
with potatoes to make this a great meal on its own – fit for any occasion.

SERVES 4

48 clams, scrubbed
50g/2oz/¼ cup unsalted (sweet)
  butter
1 large onion, chopped
1 celery stick, sliced
1 carrot, sliced
225g/8oz assorted wild and
  cultivated mushrooms
225g/8oz floury potatoes,
  thickly sliced
1.2 litres/2 pints/5 cups boiling light
  chicken or vegetable stock
1 thyme sprig
4 parsley stalks
salt and ground black pepper
thyme sprigs, to garnish

1 Place the clams in a large, heavy pan, discarding any that are open. Add 1cm/½in of water to the pan, then cover and bring to the boil. Cook over a medium heat for 6–8 minutes, shaking the pan occasionally, until the clams open (discard any clams that do not open).

2 Drain the clams over a bowl and remove most of the shells, leaving some in the shells as a garnish. Strain the cooking juices into the bowl, add all the clams and set aside.

3 Add the butter, onion, celery and carrot to the pan and cook gently until softened but not coloured. Add the mushrooms and cook for 3–4 minutes until their juices begin to appear. Add the potato slices, the clams and their juices, the stock, thyme and parsley stalks.

4 Bring to the boil, then reduce the heat, cover and simmer for 25 minutes. Season to taste, ladle into soup bowls, and garnish with thyme sprigs.

SEAFOOD CHOWDER

Chowder takes its name from the French word for cauldron – chaudière – the type of pot once traditionally used for soups and stews. Like most chowders, this is a substantial dish, which is good served with crusty bread for a lunch or supper.

SERVES 4–6

200g/7oz/generous 1 cup drained, canned sweetcorn
600ml/1 pint/2½ cups milk
15g/½oz/1 tbsp butter
1 small leek, sliced
1 small garlic clove, crushed
2 rindless smoked streaky (fatty) bacon rashers (strips), finely chopped
1 small green or red (bell) pepper, seeded and diced
1 celery stick, chopped
115g/4oz/generous ½ cup white long grain rice
5ml/1 tsp plain (all-purpose) flour
about 450ml/¾ pint/scant 2 cups hot chicken or vegetable stock
4 large scallops
115g/4oz white fish fillet, such as monkfish, plaice or flounder
15ml/1 tbsp finely chopped fresh flat leaf parsley
good pinch of cayenne pepper
30–45ml/2–3 tbsp single (light) cream (optional)
salt and ground black pepper
crusty bread, to serve

1 Place half the drained sweetcorn in a food processor or blender. Add a little of the milk and then process until the mixture is thick and creamy. Set aside.

COOK'S TIP
If you don't have a food processor, then simply chop the sweetcorn finely and transfer to a bowl. Beat in the milk a little at time until the mixture is thick and creamy.

2 Melt the butter in a large, heavy pan. add the leek, garlic and bacon and gently fry for 4–5 minutes until the leek has softened but not browned.

3 Add the diced green or red pepper and the chopped celery and cook over a very gentle heat for 3–4 minutes more, stirring frequently, until the pepper and celery have softened slightly.

4 Stir in the rice and cook for a few minutes, stirring occasionally, until the grains begin to swell, then sprinkle the flour evenly over the top of the rice and vegetables. Cook for about 1 minute, stirring all the time, then gradually stir in the remaining milk and the hot stock.

VARIATIONS
You can use other shellfish in place of the scallops if you prefer – try fresh or frozen prawns (shrimp), or mussels or clams, which are equally good in or out of their shells. Allow frozen shellfish to thaw at room temperature before adding to the chowder. Undyed, naturally smoked haddock or cod would make a delicious alternative fish.

5 Bring the mixture to the boil over a medium heat, then lower the heat and stir in the creamed sweetcorn mixture, with the whole sweetcorn. Season well.

6 Cover the pan and simmer very gently for about 20 minutes, or until the rice is tender, stirring occasionally. Add a little more chicken or vegetable stock or water to the pan if the mixture thickens too quickly or if the rice begins to stick to the base of the pan.

7 Cut the corals away from the scallops and set them aside, slice the white flesh into 5mm/¼in pieces. Cut the white fish fillet into bitesize chunks.

8 Add the scallops and chunks of fish to the chowder. Stir gently, then cook for 4 minutes.

9 Stir in the scallop corals, chopped parsley and cayenne pepper. Cook for a few minutes more until the scallops are just cooked and heated through, then stir in the cream, if using. Adjust the seasoning and serve the chowder with thick slices of crusty bread.

LENTIL and PASTA SOUP

This rustic vegetarian soup makes a warming winter meal and goes especially well with Granary or crusty Italian bread.

SERVES 4–6

175g/6oz/¾ cup brown lentils
3 garlic cloves, unpeeled
1 litre/1¾ pints/4 cups water
45ml/3 tbsp olive oil
25g/1oz/2 tbsp butter
1 onion, finely chopped
2 celery sticks, finely chopped
30ml/2 tbsp sun-dried tomato
 purée (paste)
1.75 litres/3 pints/7½ cups vegetable stock
a few fresh marjoram leaves
a few fresh basil leaves
leaves from 1 fresh thyme sprig
50g/2oz/½ cup dried small pasta shapes,
 such as macaroni or tubetti
salt and ground black pepper
tiny fresh herb leaves, to garnish

1 Put the lentils in a large pan. Smash one of the garlic cloves using the blade of a large knife (there's no need to peel it first), then add it to the lentils. Pour in the water and bring to the boil. Simmer for about 20 minutes, or until the lentils are tender. Tip the lentils into a sieve, remove the garlic and set it aside. Rinse the lentils under the cold tap and leave to drain.

2 Heat 30ml/2 tbsp of the oil with half the butter in the pan. Add the onion and celery and cook gently for 5 minutes.

3 Crush the remaining garlic, then peel and mash the reserved garlic. Add to the pan with the remaining oil, the tomato purée and the lentils. Stir, then add the stock, herbs and salt and pepper. Bring to the boil, stirring. Simmer for 30 minutes, stirring occasionally.

4 Add the pasta and bring the soup back to the boil, stirring. Reduce the heat and simmer until the pasta is just tender. Add the remaining butter to the pan and stir until melted. Taste the soup for seasoning, then serve hot in warmed bowls, sprinkled with herb leaves.

ITALIAN FARMHOUSE SOUP

Root vegetables form the base of this chunky, minestrone-style main meal soup. You can
vary the vegetables according to what you have to hand.

SERVES 4

30ml/2 tbsp olive oil
1 onion, roughly chopped
3 carrots, cut into large chunks
175–200g/6–7oz turnips, cut into
    large chunks
about 175g/6oz swede (rutabaga), cut into
    large chunks
400g/14oz can chopped Italian tomatoes
15ml/1 tbsp tomato purée (paste)
5ml/1 tsp dried mixed herbs
5ml/1 tsp dried oregano
50g/2oz dried (bell) peppers, washed and
    thinly sliced (optional)
1.5 litres/2½ pints/6¼ cups vegetable stock
    or water
50g/2oz/½ cup dried small macaroni
    or conchiglie
400g/14oz can red kidney beans, rinsed
    and drained
30ml/2 tbsp chopped fresh flat leaf parsley
salt and ground black pepper
freshly grated Parmesan cheese, to serve

1 Heat the olive oil in a large pan, add
the onion and cook over a low heat for
about 5 minutes until softened. Add the
carrot, turnip and swede chunks, canned
chopped tomatoes, tomato purée, dried
mixed herbs, dried oregano and dried
peppers, if using. Stir in salt and pepper
to taste.

2 Pour in the vegetable stock or water
and bring to the boil. Stir well, cover the
pan, then lower the heat and simmer for
30 minutes, stirring occasionally.

3 Add the pasta to the pan and bring
quickly to the boil, stirring. Lower the
heat and simmer, uncovered, for about
5 minutes until the pasta is only just
tender, or according to the instructions
on the packet. Stir frequently.

4 Stir in the kidney beans. Heat through
for 2–3 minutes, then remove the pan
from the heat and stir in the parsley.
Taste the soup for seasoning. Serve hot
in warmed soup bowls, with grated
Parmesan cheese handed separately.

BROCCOLI, ANCHOVY and PASTA SOUP

This wonderfully chunky and flavourful soup is from Puglia in the south of Italy, where anchovies and broccoli are often used together.

SERVES 4

30ml/2 tbsp olive oil
1 small onion, finely chopped
1 garlic clove, finely chopped
¼–⅓ fresh red chilli, seeded and
   finely chopped
2 drained canned anchovies
200ml/7fl oz/scant 1 cup passata (bottled
   strained tomatoes)
45ml/3 tbsp dry white wine
1.2 litres/2 pints/5 cups vegetable or light
   chicken stock
300g/11oz broccoli florets
200g/7oz/1¾ cups dried orecchiette pasta
   or other medium-size pasta shapes
salt and ground black pepper
freshly grated Pecorino cheese, to serve

1 Heat the oil in a large pan. Add the onion, garlic, chilli and anchovies and cook over a low heat, stirring constantly, for 5–6 minutes.

2 Add the passata and wine, with salt and pepper to taste. Bring to the boil, cover, then cook over a low heat, stirring occasionally, for 12–15 minutes.

3 Pour in the stock. Bring to the boil, then add the broccoli and simmer for about 5 minutes. Add the pasta and bring back to the boil, stirring. Simmer, stirring frequently for 7–8 minutes until the pasta is just tender, or according to the packet instructions. Taste for seasoning. Serve hot, in warmed bowls. Hand around grated Pecorino separately.

PASTA SQUARES and PEAS in BROTH

This thick, filling Italian soup, flavoured with pancetta or bacon and prosciutto, is traditionally made with home-made pasta and fresh peas. In this modern, more convenient version, ready-made fresh lasagne sheets are used with frozen peas, to save time.

SERVES 4–6

25g/1oz/2 tbsp butter
50g/2oz pancetta or rindless smoked
   streaky (fatty) bacon, roughly chopped
1 small onion, finely chopped
1 celery stick, finely chopped
400g/14oz/3½ cups frozen peas
5ml/1 tsp tomato purée (paste)
5–10ml/1–2 tsp finely chopped fresh flat
   leaf parsley
1 litre/1¾ pints/4 cups chicken stock
300g/11oz fresh lasagne sheets
about 50g/2oz prosciutto, cut into cubes
salt and ground black pepper
freshly grated Parmesan cheese, to serve

1 Melt the butter in a large pan and add the pancetta or rindless smoked streaky bacon, with the chopped onion and chopped celery. Cook together over a low heat, stirring constantly, for 5 minutes.

2 Add the frozen peas to the pan and cook, stirring, for 3–4 minutes. Stir in the tomato purée and finely chopped parsley, then add the chicken stock, with salt and pepper to taste. Bring to the boil. Cover, lower the heat and simmer the soup for 10 minutes.

3 Meanwhile, using a large, sharp knife and a ruler, cut the lasagne sheets into 2cm/¾in squares.

4 Taste the soup for seasoning. Drop the pasta into the pan, then stir and bring to the boil. Simmer for 2 minutes, or until the pasta is just tender, then stir in the prosciutto. Serve hot with grated Parmesan handed around separately.

COOK'S TIP
Take care when seasoning the soup with salt, because of the saltiness of the pancetta and the prosciutto.

CORN and POTATO CHOWDER

This creamy yet chunky soup is rich with the sweet taste of corn. It's excellent served with thick, crusty bread and topped with some grated Cheddar cheese.

2 Heat until the oil and butter are sizzling, then reduce the heat to low. Cover the pan and cook gently for about 10 minutes until the vegetables are just softened, shaking the pan occasionally.

3 Pour in the stock, season with salt and pepper to taste and bring to the boil. Reduce the heat, cover the pan again and simmer gently, stirring occasionally, for about 15 minutes, or until the vegetables are tender.

SERVES 4

1 onion, chopped
1 garlic clove, crushed
1 medium baking potato, chopped
2 celery sticks, sliced
1 green (bell) pepper, seeded and sliced
30ml/2 tbsp sunflower oil
25g/1oz/2 tbsp butter
600ml/1 pint/2½ cups vegetable stock
300ml/½ pint/1¼ cups milk
200g/7oz can flageolet, cannellini or
    haricot (navy) beans
300g/11oz can sweetcorn
good pinch of dried sage
salt and ground black pepper
freshly grated Cheddar cheese, to serve

1 Put the onion, garlic, potato, celery and green pepper into a large, heavy pan with the sunflower oil and butter.

4 Add the milk, canned beans and sweetcorn – including their liquids. Stir in the dried sage and simmer, uncovered, for 5 minutes, then check the seasoning and adjust to taste. Serve hot in bowls, sprinkled with the grated Cheddar cheese.

BEAN and PISTOU SOUP

This hearty vegetarian soup is a typical Provençal-style soup, richly flavoured with a home-made garlic and fresh basil pistou sauce.

SERVES 4–6

150g/5oz/scant 1 cup dried haricot (navy) beans, soaked overnight in cold water
150g/5oz/scant 1 cup dried flageolet or cannellini beans, soaked overnight in cold water
1 onion, chopped
1.2 litres/2 pints/5 cups hot vegetable stock
2 carrots, roughly chopped
225g/8oz Savoy cabbage, shredded
1 large potato, about 225g/8oz, roughly chopped
225g/8oz French (green) beans, chopped
salt and ground black pepper
basil leaves, to garnish

For the pistou
4 garlic cloves
8 large sprigs basil leaves
90ml/6 tbsp olive oil
60ml/4 tbsp freshly grated Parmesan cheese

3 Add the chopped carrots, shredded cabbage, chopped potato and French beans to the bean pot. Season with salt and pepper, cover and return the pot to the oven. Reduce the oven temperature to 180°C/350°F/Gas 4 and cook for 1 hour, or until all the vegetables are cooked right through.

4 Meanwhile place the garlic and basil in a mortar and pound with a pestle, then gradually beat in the oil. Stir in the grated Parmesan. Stir half the pistou into the soup and then ladle into warmed soup bowls. Top each bowl of soup with a spoonful of the remaining pistou and serve garnished with basil.

1 Soak a bean pot in cold water for 20 minutes then drain. Drain the soaked haricot and flageolet or cannellini beans and place in the bean pot. Add the chopped onion and pour over sufficient cold water to come 5cm/2in above the beans. Cover and place the pot in an unheated oven. Set the oven to 200°C/400°F/Gas 6 and cook for about 1½ hours, or until the beans are tender.

2 Drain the beans and onions. Place half the beans and onions in a food processor or blender and process to a paste. Return the drained beans and the bean paste to the bean pot. Add the hot vegetable stock.

FIRST COURSES AND LIGHT MEALS

When you are cooking a first course, appetizer or snack for family or friends, the most successful dishes are often the simplest, so anything that can be cooked in one pot is a sure winner. Whether you opt for a simple pasta dish such as Linguine with Rocket, a hot and spicy clay pot treat such as Potato Wedges with Tomato and Chilli Salsa, or Pork Ribs with Ginger and Chilli, or use your wok to make a stunning stir-fry, everyone will be glad you chose the easy option.

BRAISED BABY LEEKS in RED WINE with AROMATICS

Coriander seeds and oregano lend a Greek flavour to this dish of braised leeks. Serve it as part of a mixed hors d'oeuvre or as a partner for baked white fish.

SERVES 6

12 baby leeks or 6 thick leeks
15ml/1 tbsp coriander seeds,
    lightly crushed
5cm/2in piece of cinnamon stick
120ml/4fl oz/½ cup olive oil
3 fresh bay leaves
2 strips pared orange rind
5–6 fresh or dried oregano sprigs
5ml/1 tsp sugar
150ml/¼ pint/⅔ cup fruity red wine
10ml/2 tsp balsamic or
    sherry vinegar
30ml/2 tbsp coarsely chopped fresh
    oregano or marjoram
salt and ground black pepper

1 If using baby leeks, simply trim the ends, but leave them whole. Cut thick leeks into 5–7.5cm/2–3in lengths.

2 Place the coriander seeds and cinnamon in a pan wide enough to take all the leeks in a single layer. Cook over a medium heat for 2–3 minutes, until the spices give off a fragrant aroma, then stir in the olive oil, bay leaves, orange rind, fresh or dried oregano, sugar, wine and balsamic or sherry vinegar. Bring to the boil and simmer for 5 minutes.

3 Add the leeks to the pan. Bring back to the boil, reduce the heat and cover the pan. Cook the leeks gently for 5 minutes. Uncover and simmer gently for another 5–8 minutes, until the leeks are just tender when tested with the tip of a sharp knife.

4 Use a slotted spoon to transfer the leeks to a serving dish. Boil the pan juices rapidly until reduced to about 75–90ml/5–6 tbsp. Add salt and pepper to taste and pour the liquid over the leeks. Leave to cool.

5 The leeks can be left to stand for several hours. If you chill them, bring them back to room temperature again before serving. Sprinkle the chopped herbs over the leeks just before serving.

COOK'S TIP
Genuine balsamic vinegar from Modena in northern Italy has been produced for over 1,000 years. It has a high sugar content and wonderfully strong bouquet. It is a very dark brown colour and has a deep, rich flavour with hints of herbs and port. Nowadays you can find quite good balsamic vinegar in supermarkets. It is expensive, but the flavour is so rich that you only need to use a little.

POTATO WEDGES with TOMATO and CHILLI SALSA

This is a healthier version of traditionally baked potato skins; the clay pot keeps the potato flesh wonderfully moist and fluffy.

SERVES 4

6 potatoes, about 115g/4oz each
45ml/3 tbsp olive oil
salt and ground black pepper

For the tomato and chilli salsa
4 juicy ripe tomatoes
1 sun-dried tomato in olive
   oil, drained
3 spring onions (scallions)
1–2 red or green chillies, halved
   and seeded
15ml/1 tbsp extra virgin
   olive oil
10ml/2 tsp lemon juice

COOK'S TIP
Varieties of floury potatoes that produce a fluffy texture when baked are best for these wedges. Good types to use include Maris Piper, Désirée, King Edward and Pentland Squire.

1 Soak the clay pot or a potato pot in cold water for 20 minutes, then drain. Scrub the potatoes and dry with kitchen paper. Cut each potato lengthwise into four wedges. Brush with a little of the oil and sprinkle with salt and pepper.

2 Place the potatoes in the clay pot and cover with the lid. Place in an unheated oven, set the temperature to 200°C/ 400°F/Gas 6 and cook for 55–60 minutes, or until the potatoes are tender.

3 Meanwhile, finely chop the tomatoes, sun-dried tomato, spring onions and chilli and mix together with the olive oil and lemon juice. Cover and leave to stand to allow the flavours to mingle.

4 Uncover the potatoes, brush with the remaining olive oil and bake, uncovered, for a further 15 minutes until slightly golden. Divide the potato wedges and salsa among four serving bowls and plates, and serve immediately.

BRAISED VINE LEAVES

This popular eastern Mediterranean dish keeps moist when cooked slowly in a clay pot.

SERVES 4

12 fresh vine leaves
30ml/2 tbsp olive oil
1 small onion, chopped
30ml/2 tbsp pine nuts
1 garlic clove, crushed
115g/4oz cooked long grain rice
2 tomatoes, skinned, seeded and
    finely chopped
15ml/1 tbsp chopped fresh mint
1 lemon, sliced
150ml/¼ pint/⅔ cup dry white wine
200ml/7fl oz/scant 1 cup vegetable stock
salt and ground black pepper
lemon wedges, to serve

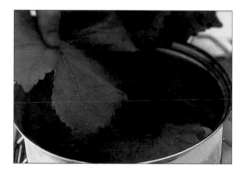

1 Soak the clay pot in cold water for 20 minutes, then drain. Blanch the vine leaves in a pan of boiling water for about 2 minutes or until they darken and soften. Rinse the leaves under cold running water and leave to drain.

2 Heat the oil in a frying pan, add the onion and fry for 5–6 minutes, stirring frequently, until softened. Add the pine nuts and crushed garlic and cook, stirring continuously until the onions and pine nuts are a golden brown colour.

3 Stir into the cooked rice, with the tomatoes, mint and seasoning, to taste.

4 Place a spoonful of the rice mixture at the stalk end of each vine leaf. Fold the sides over the filling and roll up tightly.

5 Place the stuffed vine leaves close together, seam side down in the clay pot. Place the lemon slices on top. Pour over the wine and sufficient stock to just cover the lemon slices.

6 Cover with the lid and place in an unheated oven. Set the oven to 200°C/400°F/Gas 6 and cook for 30 minutes. Reduce to 160°C/325°F/Gas 3 and cook for a further 30 minutes. Serve hot or cold, with lemon wedges.

PAN-FRIED HAM and VEGETABLES with EGGS

A perfect family supper dish, this is very easy to prepare. Serve with plenty of hot, crusty bread: Italian ciabatta is particularly good.

3 Add the courgettes and peppers to the onion and garlic and cook over a medium heat for 3–4 minutes.

4 Stir in the paprika, tomatoes, tomato purée, ham and seasoning. Bring to the boil and simmer gently for 15 minutes.

5 Reduce the heat to low. Make four wells in the tomato mixture, break an egg into each and season. Cook over a gentle heat until the white begins to set.

6 Preheat the grill (broiler). Sprinkle the cheese over the vegetables and grill (broil) for about 5 minutes until the eggs are set. Serve immediately with bread.

SERVES 4

30ml/2 tbsp olive oil
1 onion, roughly chopped
2 garlic cloves, crushed
175g/6oz cooked ham
225g/8oz courgettes (zucchini)
1 red (bell) pepper, seeded and
    thinly sliced
1 yellow (bell) pepper, seeded and
    thinly sliced
10ml/2 tsp paprika
400g/14oz can chopped tomatoes
15ml/1 tbsp sun-dried tomato purée (paste)
4 eggs
115g/4oz/1 cup coarsely grated
    Cheddar cheese
salt and ground black pepper
crusty bread, to serve

1 Heat the olive oil in a deep frying pan. Add the onion and garlic and cook for 4 minutes, stirring frequently, or until just beginning to soften.

2 While the onions and garlic are cooking, cut the ham and courgettes into 5cm/2in long batons. Set the ham aside.

WILD MUSHROOM and SUN-DRIED TOMATO SOUFFLES

These impressive little soufflés are baked in individual earthenware pots. They are packed with rich, Italian flavours and are remarkably easy to prepare and cook.

SERVES 4

25g/1oz/½ cup dried cep mushrooms
40g/1½oz/3 tbsp butter, plus extra
    for greasing
20ml/4 tsp grated Parmesan cheese
40g/1½oz/⅓ cup plain (all-purpose) flour
250ml/8fl oz/1 cup milk
50g/2oz/½ cup grated mature (sharp)
    Cheddar cheese
4 eggs, separated
2 sun-dried tomatoes in oil, drained
    and chopped
15ml/1 tbsp chopped fresh chives
salt and ground black pepper

1 Place the ceps in a bowl, pour over enough warm water to cover and leave to soak for 15 minutes. Grease four individual earthenware soufflé dishes with a little butter. Sprinkle the grated Parmesan cheese into the soufflé dishes and rotate each dish to coat the sides with cheese. Preheat the oven to 190°C/375°F/Gas 5.

2 Melt the 40g/1½oz/3 tbsp of butter in a large pan, remove from the heat and stir in the flour. Cook over a low heat for 1 minute, stirring constantly. Remove the pan from the heat and gradually stir in the milk. Return to the heat and bring to the boil, stirring constantly, until the sauce has thickened.

COOK'S TIP
A variety of different dried mushrooms are available — any can be used instead of the ceps.

3 Remove the sauce from the heat, then stir in the grated Cheddar cheese and plenty of seasoning. Beat in the egg yolks, one at a time, then stir in the chopped sun-dried tomatoes and the chives. Drain the soaked mushrooms, then coarsely chop them and add them to the cheese sauce.

4 Whisk the egg whites until they stand in soft peaks. Mix one spoonful into the sauce then carefully fold in the remainder. Divide the mixture among the soufflé dishes and bake for 25 minutes, or until the soufflés are golden brown on top, well risen and just firm to the touch. Serve immediately – before they sink.

LINGUINE with ROCKET

This is a first course that you will find in many a fashionable restaurant in Italy. It is very quick and easy to make at home and is worth trying for yourself.

SERVES 4

350g/12oz fresh or dried linguine
120ml/4fl oz/½ cup extra virgin olive oil
1 large bunch rocket (arugula), about
   150g/5oz, stalks removed, shredded
   or torn
75g/3oz/1 cup freshly grated
   Parmesan cheese
salt and ground black pepper

VARIATION
Oil-based pasta sauces such as this one are best served with fine, long pastas such as linguine. Spaghetti, capelli d'angelo, bucatini or fettucine would work just as well in this recipe.

1 Cook the pasta in a large pan of salted boiling water for 8–10 minutes until it is just tender, or according to the instructions on the packet. As soon as the pasta is cooked, drain thoroughly.

2 Heat about 60ml/4 tbsp of the olive oil in the pasta pan, then add the drained pasta, followed by the rocket. Toss over a medium to high heat for 1–2 minutes or until the rocket is just wilted, then remove the pan from the heat.

3 Tip the pasta and rocket into a warmed, large serving bowl. Add half the freshly grated Parmesan cheese and the remaining olive oil. Add a little salt and black pepper to taste.

4 Toss the mixture quickly to mix and serve immediately. Hand round the remaining Parmesan cheese.

COOK'S TIP
Buy rocket by the bunch from the greengrocer. The type sold in small cellophane packets in supermarkets is usually very expensive. Always check when buying rocket that all the leaves are bright green. In hot weather, rocket leaves quickly turn yellow.

SPAGHETTI with GARLIC and OIL

This simple Roman pasta dish can be made in less than 15 minutes. Use fresh chillies if you prefer and, since the oil is so important, the very best extra virgin olive oil.

SERVES 4

400g/14oz fresh or dried spaghetti
90ml/6 tbsp extra virgin olive oil
2–4 garlic cloves, crushed
1 dried red chilli
1 small handful fresh flat leaf parsley,
 roughly chopped
salt

COOK'S TIP

Don't use salt when you are preparing the hot oil, garlic and chilli mixture, because the salt will not dissolve sufficiently. This is why plenty of salt is recommended for cooking the pasta.

1 Cook the pasta in a large pan of salted boiling water, according to the packet instructions, until it is just tender, adding plenty of salt to the water (see Cook's Tip).

2 When the pasta is just tender, drain it by tipping it into a large colander, then transfer it to a warmed, large serving bowl. Rinse out the pasta pan and dry.

3 Heat the olive oil in the pan. Add the crushed garlic and the whole dried chilli and stir over a low heat for a minute or two until the garlic is just beginning to brown. Remove the chilli and discard.

4 Pour the hot olive oil and cooked garlic mixture over the pasta, add the roughly chopped fresh flat leaf parsley and toss vigorously until the pasta glistens, then serve immediately.

SPAGHETTI with BUTTER and HERBS

This is a versatile recipe. You can use just one favourite herb or several – basil, flat leaf parsley, rosemary, thyme, marjoram or sage would all work well.

SERVES 4

400g/14oz fresh or dried spaghetti
    alla chitarra
2 good handfuls mixed fresh herbs,
    plus extra herb leaves and flowers
    to garnish
115g/4oz/½ cup butter, diced
salt and ground black pepper
freshly grated Parmesan cheese, to serve

1 Cook the pasta in a large pan of salted boiling water for 10–12 minutes until just tender or according to the instructions on the packet.

2 Using a large sharp knife, chop the fresh herbs roughly or finely, whichever you prefer.

COOK'S TIP
Square-shaped chitarra spaghetti is the traditional type for this sauce, but you can use any type of long thin pasta, such as ordinary spaghetti or spaghettini, or even linguine.

VARIATION
If you like the flavour of garlic, add one or two crushed cloves to the pan when melting the butter.

3 Drain the pasta in a colander and then return the pasta to the pan. Add the butter and heat until it melts and sizzles, then add the chopped herbs and salt and pepper to taste.

4 Toss the pasta over a medium heat until it is thoroughly coated in the butter and herbs.

5 Serve the pasta immediately in warmed shallow bowls, sprinkled with some extra herb leaves and flowers. Hand around a bowl of freshly grated Parmesan separately.

SPAGHETTI with CHEESE and BLACK PEPPER

This dish is very quick and easy to cook, perfect for a midweek supper. The flavours are very simple, so choose a strong-tasting cheese and a good extra virgin olive oil. Pecorino is traditional in this dish, but Parmesan could also be used.

SERVES 4

400g/14oz fresh or
    dried spaghetti
115g/4oz/1 cup freshly grated
    Pecorino cheese
about 5ml/1 tsp coarsely ground
    black pepper
extra virgin olive oil, to taste
salt

1 Cook the fresh or dried pasta in a large pan of salted boiling water until it is just tender, or according to the instructions on the packet.

2 As soon as the spaghetti is cooked, drain it, leaving it a little moister than usual, then tip the spaghetti straight into a large warmed serving bowl.

3 Add the freshly grated cheese, lots of black pepper, and salt to taste. Toss the pasta well to mix, then moisten with as much olive oil as you like. Serve the pasta immediately.

DEVILLED KIDNEYS on BRIOCHE CROUTES

The expression "devilled" dates from the 18th century. It was used to describe dishes or foods that were seasoned with hot spices giving a fiery flavour that was associated with the devil and the heat of hell – in this case, cayenne pepper and Worcestershire sauce provide the "fire".

SERVES 4

8 mini brioche slices
25g/1oz/2 tbsp butter
1 shallot, finely chopped
2 garlic cloves, finely chopped
115g/4oz/1½ cups mushrooms, halved
1.5ml/¼ tsp cayenne pepper
15ml/1 tbsp Worcestershire sauce
8 lamb's kidneys, halved and trimmed
150ml/¼ pint/⅔ cup double (heavy) cream
30ml/2 tbsp chopped fresh parsley,
   to garnish

1 Preheat the grill (broiler) to high and toast the brioche slices until they are a golden brown colour on both sides, and keep warm.

2 Melt the butter in a large frying pan until it is just foaming. Add the finely chopped shallot, finely chopped garlic and halved mushrooms, then cook for about 5 minutes, or until the shallot is just beginning to soften. Stir in the cayenne pepper and the Worcestershire sauce and allow the mixture to simmer for about 1 minute, stirring continuously with a wooden spoon.

3 Add the kidneys to the pan and cook for 3–5 minutes on each side. Finally, stir in the cream and simmer for about 2 minutes, or until the sauce is heated through and slightly thickened.

4 Remove the brioche croûtes from the wire rack and place on warmed plates. Top with the kidneys. Sprinkle with the chopped parsley and serve immediately.

COOK'S TIPS
• If you can't find mini brioches, you can use a large brioche instead. Slice it thickly and stamp out croûtes using a 5cm/2in round cutter.
• If you prefer, the brioche croûtes can be fried rather than toasted. Melt 25g/1oz/ 2 tbsp butter in the frying pan and fry the croûtes until crisp and golden on both sides. Remove from the pan and drain on kitchen paper.

PORK RIBS with GINGER and CHILLI

Ginger, garlic and chilli are used to flavour the sweet-and-sour sauce that coats these ribs. Cook the pork ribs in a covered clay pot first to tenderize the meat, then uncover the dish so the ribs become deliciously sticky and brown.

SERVES 4

16–20 small meaty pork ribs, about
  900g/2lb total weight
1 onion, finely chopped
5cm/2in piece fresh root ginger, peeled
  and grated
2 garlic cloves, crushed
2.5–5ml/½–1 tsp chilli powder
60ml/4 tbsp soy sauce
45ml/3 tbsp tomato purée (paste)
45ml/3 tbsp clear honey
30ml/2 tbsp red wine vinegar
45ml/3 tbsp dry sherry
60ml/4 tbsp water
salt and ground black pepper

1 Soak the clay pot in cold water for 20 minutes, then drain. Place the ribs in the clay pot, arranging them evenly.

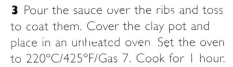

2 Mix together the onion, ginger, garlic, chilli powder, soy sauce, tomato purée, honey, wine vinegar, sherry and water.

3 Pour the sauce over the ribs and toss to coat them. Cover the clay pot and place in an unheated oven. Set the oven to 220°C/425°F/Gas 7. Cook for 1 hour.

4 Remove the lid, baste the ribs and season with salt and pepper. Cook uncovered for 15–20 minutes, basting the ribs two to three times during the cooking. Serve with steamed rice or baked potatoes.

COOK'S TIPS
• For a stronger flavour, place the ribs in a shallow dish, coat them evenly with the sauce and leave to marinate in a cool place for 1–2 hours before cooking in the clay pot.
• If you cannot get hold of fresh root ginger, ginger in sunflower oil (sold in small jars) is available from major supermarkets. It is in a paste form and can simply be added when the flavour of fresh root ginger is required. Use 10ml/ 2 tsp instead of 5cm/2in of fresh ginger.

LAMB'S LIVER and BACON CASSEROLE

The trick when cooking liver is to seal it quickly, then simmer it gently and briefly. Prolonged and/or fierce cooking makes liver hard and grainy. Boiled new potatoes tossed in lots of butter go well with this simple casserole.

SERVES 4

30ml/2 tbsp extra virgin olive oil or
   sunflower oil
225g/8oz rindless unsmoked lean bacon
   rashers (strips), cut into pieces
2 onions, halved and sliced
175g/6oz/2 cups chestnut
   mushrooms, halved
450g/1lb lamb's liver, trimmed
   and sliced
25g/1oz/2 tbsp butter
15ml/1 tbsp soy sauce
30ml/2 tbsp plain (all-purpose) flour
150ml/¼ pint/⅔ cup hot, well-flavoured
   chicken stock
salt and ground black pepper

1 Heat the oil in a frying pan, add the bacon and fry until crisp. Add the sliced onions to the pan and cook for about 10 minutes, stirring frequently, or until softened. Add the mushrooms to the pan and fry for a further 1 minute.

2 Use a slotted spoon to remove the bacon and vegetables from the pan and keep warm. Add the liver to the fat remaining in the pan and cook over a high heat for 3–4 minutes, turning once to seal the slices on both sides. Remove the liver from the pan and keep warm.

3 Melt the butter in the pan, add the soy sauce and flour and blend together. Stir in the stock and bring to the boil, stirring until thickened. Return the liver, bacon and vegetables to the pan and heat through for 1 minute. Season with salt and pepper to taste, and serve immediately with new potatoes and lightly cooked green beans.

FILLET of BEEF STROGANOFF

Legend has it that this Russian recipe was devised by Count Paul Stroganov's cook to use beef frozen by the Siberian climate. The only way that it could be prepared was cut into very thin strips. The strips of lean beef were served in a brandy-flavoured cream sauce.

3 Cook the onion and garlic over a low heat, stirring occasionally until the onion has softened. Add the mushrooms and stir-fry over a high heat for 1–2 minutes. Transfer the vegetables and their juices to a dish and set aside.

4 Wipe the pan, then add and heat the remaining oil. Coat a batch of meat with flour, then fry over a high heat until well browned. Remove from the pan, then coat and fry another batch. When the last batch is cooked, replace all the meat and vegetables. Add the brandy and simmer until it has almost evaporated.

5 Stir in the beef stock or consommé and seasoning and cook for 10–15 minutes, stirring frequently with a wooden spoon, or until the meat is tender and the sauce is thick and glossy. Add the sour cream, stir well and sprinkle with the chopped fresh flat leaf parsley. Serve immediately with plain boiled rice and a simple salad.

COOK'S TIP
If you do not have a very large frying pan, it may be easier to cook this dish in a large, flameproof casserole.

SERVES 8

1.2kg/2½lb beef fillet (tenderloin)
30ml/2 tbsp plain (all-purpose) flour
large pinch each of cayenne pepper
    and paprika
75ml/5 tbsp sunflower oil
1 large onion, chopped
3 garlic cloves, finely chopped
450g/1lb/6½ cups chestnut
    mushrooms, sliced
75ml/5 tbsp brandy
300ml/½ pint/1¼ cups beef stock
    or consommé
300ml/½ pint/1¼ cups sour cream
45ml/3 tbsp chopped fresh flat leaf parsley
salt and ground black pepper

1 Thinly slice the beef fillet across the grain, then cut it into fine strips. Season the flour with the cayenne and paprika.

2 Heat half the oil in a large frying pan and add the chopped onion and garlic.

SWEET-and-SOUR PORK STIR-FRY

This is a great idea for a quick family supper. Remember to cut the carrots into thin matchstick strips so that they cook in time.

SERVES 4

450g/1lb pork fillet (tenderloin)
30ml/2 tbsp plain (all-purpose) flour
45ml/3 tbsp oil
1 onion, roughly chopped
1 garlic clove, crushed
1 green (bell) pepper, seeded and sliced
350g/12oz carrots, cut into thin strips
225g/8oz can bamboo shoots, drained
15ml/1 tbsp white wine vinegar
15ml/1 tbsp soft brown sugar
10ml/2 tsp tomato purée (paste)
30ml/2 tbsp light soy sauce
salt and ground black pepper

1 Thinly slice the pork. Season the flour and toss the pork in it to coat.

2 Heat the oil in a wok or large frying pan and cook the pork over a medium heat for about 5 minutes, until golden and cooked through. Remove the pork with a slotted spoon and drain on kitchen paper. You may need to do this in several batches.

3 Add the onion and garlic to the pan and cook for 3 minutes. Stir in the pepper and carrots and stir-fry over a high heat for 6–8 minutes, or until beginning to soften slightly.

4 Return the meat to the pan with the bamboo shoots. Add the remaining ingredients with 120ml/4fl oz/½ cup water and bring to the boil. Simmer gently for 2–3 minutes, or until piping hot. Adjust the seasoning, if necessary, and serve immediately.

VARIATION
Finely sliced strips of skinless chicken breast fillet can be used in this recipe instead of the pork.

PORK CHOW MEIN

This is a very speedy dish to cook, but make sure that you prepare all the ingredients before you start to cook. If you don't have a wok, use a very large frying pan instead.

SERVES 4

175g/6oz medium egg noodles
350g/12oz pork fillet (tenderloin)
30ml/2 tbsp sunflower oil
15ml/1 tbsp sesame oil
2 garlic cloves, crushed
8 spring onions (scallions), sliced
1 red (bell) pepper, seeded and
  roughly chopped
1 green (bell) pepper, seeded and
  roughly chopped
30ml/2 tbsp dark soy sauce
45ml/3 tbsp dry sherry
175g/6oz/¾ cup beansprouts
45ml/3 tbsp chopped fresh flat leaf parsley
15ml/1 tbsp toasted sesame seeds

1 Soak the noodles according to the packet instructions, then drain well.

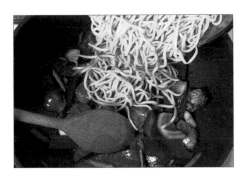

2 Thinly slice the pork fillet. Heat the sunflower oil in a wok or large frying pan and cook the pork over a high heat until golden brown and cooked through.

3 Add the sesame oil to the pan, with the garlic, spring onions and peppers. Cook over a high heat for 3–4 minutes, or until beginning to soften.

4 Reduce the heat slightly, then stir in the soaked noodles, with the dark soy sauce and dry sherry. Stir-fry for about 2 minutes. Add the beansprouts and cook for a further 1–2 minutes. If the noodles begin to stick to the pan, add a splash of water. Stir in the chopped parsley and serve the chow mein sprinkled with the toasted sesame seeds.

MINTED LAMB STIR-FRY

Lamb and mint have a long-established partnership that works particularly well in this full-flavoured stir-fry. Serve with plenty of crusty bread.

SERVES 2

275g/10oz lamb neck fillet or boneless
  leg steaks
30ml/2 tbsp sunflower oil
10ml/2 tsp sesame oil
1 onion, roughly chopped
2 garlic cloves, crushed
1 red chilli, seeded and
  finely chopped
75g/3oz fine green beans, halved
225g/8oz fresh spinach, shredded
30ml/2 tbsp oyster sauce
30ml/2 tbsp Thai fish sauce (*nam pla*)
15ml/1 tbsp lemon juice
5ml/1 tsp sugar
45ml/3 tbsp chopped fresh mint
salt and ground black pepper
mint sprigs, to garnish
noodles or rice, to serve

1 Trim the lamb of any excess fat and cut into thin slices. Heat the sunflower and sesame oils in a wok or large frying pan and cook the lamb over a high heat until browned. Remove with a slotted spoon and drain on kitchen paper.

2 Add the onion, garlic and chilli to the wok, cook for 2–3 minutes, then add the beans and stir-fry for 3 minutes.

3 Stir in the shredded spinach with the browned meat, oyster sauce, Thai fish sauce, lemon juice and sugar. Stir-fry for a further 3–4 minutes, or until the lamb is cooked through.

4 Sprinkle in the chopped mint and toss lightly, then adjust the seasoning. Serve piping hot, garnished with mint sprigs and accompanied by noodles or rice.

STIR-FRIED CRISPY DUCK

This stir-fry would be delicious wrapped in flour tortillas or steamed Chinese pancakes,
with a little extra warm plum sauce.

2 Heat the oil in a wok or large frying pan and cook the duck over a high heat until golden and crisp. Keep stirring to prevent the duck from sticking. Remove the duck with a slotted spoon and drain on kitchen paper. You may need to cook the duck in several batches.

3 Add the spring onions to the pan and cook for 2 minutes. Stir in the cabbage and cook for 5 minutes, or until it is softened and golden.

SERVES 2

275–350g/10–12oz boneless duck breast
30ml/2 tbsp plain (all-purpose) flour
60ml/4 tbsp oil
1 bunch spring onions (scallions), halved
    lengthwise and cut into 5cm/2in strips,
    plus extra to garnish
275g/10oz/2½ cups finely shredded
    green cabbage
225g/8oz can water chestnuts, drained
    and sliced
50g/2oz/½ cup unsalted cashew nuts
115g/4oz cucumber, cut into strips
45ml/3 tbsp plum sauce
15ml/1 tbsp light soy sauce
salt and ground black pepper

1 Remove any skin from the duck breast, then trim off a little of the fat. Thinly slice the meat into even-size pieces. Season the flour with plenty of salt and pepper and use it to completely coat each piece of duck.

4 Return the duck to the pan with the water chestnuts, cashews and cucumber. Stir-fry for 2 minutes. Add the plum sauce and soy sauce and season to taste, then heat for 2 minutes. Serve garnished with the sliced spring onions.

MUSSELS and CLAMS with LEMON GRASS and COCONUT CREAM

Lemon grass has an incomparable flavour and aroma and is widely used in Thai cooking, especially with seafood. If you have difficulty obtaining fresh baby clams for this recipe, then use a few extra mussels instead.

SERVES 6

1.8–2kg/4–4½lb mussels
450g/1lb baby clams
120ml/4fl oz/½ cup dry white wine
1 bunch spring onions (scallions), chopped
2 lemon grass stalks, chopped
6 kaffir lime leaves, chopped
10ml/2 tsp Thai green curry paste
200ml/7fl oz/scant 1 cup coconut cream
30ml/2 tbsp chopped fresh
   coriander (cilantro)
salt and ground black pepper
garlic chives, to garnish

1 Clean the mussels by pulling off the beards, scrubbing the shells well and removing any barnacles. Discard any broken mussels or any that do not close when tapped sharply. Wash the clams.

COOK'S TIP
The kaffir lime tree is native to South-east Asia and both the leaves and fruit rind are used in cooking. Dried kaffir lime leaves, available from supermarkets, can be used in place of fresh – add them at the beginning of the cooking time and remove and discard just before serving.

2 Put the white wine in a large, heavy pan with the spring onions, chopped lemon grass stalks, kaffir lime leaves and Thai green curry paste. Simmer all the ingredients together until the wine has almost evaporated.

3 Add the mussels and clams to the pan, cover tightly and steam the shellfish over a high heat for 5–6 minutes, or until they open.

4 Using a slotted spoon, transfer the cooked mussels and clams to a heated serving bowl and keep hot. At this stage discard any shellfish that remain closed. Strain the cooking liquid into the clean pan and gently simmer until it is reduced to about 250ml/8fl oz/1 cup.

5 Stir in the coconut cream and fresh coriander, with plenty of salt and pepper to taste. Increase the heat and simmer gently until the sauce is piping hot. Pour the sauce over the mussels and clams and serve immediately, garnished with garlic chives.

SAFFRON MUSSELS with WHITE WINE and GARLIC

Mussels are easy to cook in a clay pot and they stay deliciously moist. The saffron adds a lovely pungent flavour as well as its characteristic yellow colour to the creamy sauce.

SERVES 4

few threads of saffron
1kg/2¼lb mussels in their shells
25g/1oz/2 tbsp butter
2 shallots, finely chopped
2 garlic cloves, finely chopped
200ml/7fl oz/scant 1 cup dry white wine
60ml/4 tbsp double (heavy) cream or
    crème fraîche
30ml/2 tbsp chopped fresh parsley
salt and ground black pepper
French bread, to serve

1 Soak a large clay pot in cold water for about 20 minutes, then drain. Put the saffron in a small bowl, add 15ml/1 tbsp boiling water and leave to soak.

2 Scrub the mussels, pull off the beards and discard any open mussels that don't close when tapped. Place all the closed mussels in the soaked clay pot.

3 Melt the butter in a frying pan, add the shallots and garlic and cook gently for 5 minutes, to soften. Stir in the wine and saffron water and bring to the boil. Pour the liquid over the mussels.

4 Cover the clay pot and place in an unheated oven. Set the oven to 220°C/425°F/Gas 7. Cook the mussels for 15 minutes, then remove the pot from the oven and, firmly holding the lid on, shake the pot. Return the pot to the oven and cook for another 10 minutes, or until the mussels have opened.

COOK'S TIP
Saffron is the stigma of a type of crocus. It is an expensive spice and is sold as thin, wiry threads. It has a mild aroma and adds a slightly pungent flavour to both sweet and savoury dishes, and also to buns, cakes and breads. However, the main characteristic of saffron is the distinctive yellow colour it imparts once diluted in a liquid.

5 Using a slotted spoon, transfer the mussels to four warmed serving bowls (discard any that have not opened). Mix the cream or crème fraîche and parsley into the cooking liquid and season to taste. Pour the cooking liquid over the mussels and serve immediately with French bread to soak up the sauce.

PENNE with CREAM and SMOKED SALMON

This modern way of serving pasta is popular all over Italy. The three essential ingredients combine together beautifully, and the dish is very quick and easy to make. Accompany with a green salad, ciabatta bread and some sparkling wine for an easy but impressive meal.

SERVES 4

350g/12oz/3 cups dried penne
115g/4oz thinly sliced
    smoked salmon
2–3 fresh thyme sprigs
25g/1oz/2 tbsp unsalted (sweet)
    butter, diced
150ml/¼ pint/⅔ cup extra-thick single
    (light) cream
salt and ground black pepper

VARIATION
Although penne is the traditional pasta to serve with this sauce, it also goes very well with fresh ravioli stuffed with spinach and ricotta.

COOK'S TIP
This dish can be served as an appetizer or a main course.

1 Cook the dried pasta in a large pan of lightly salted boiling water for 10 minutes until it is just tender or according to the instructions on the packet.

2 Meanwhile, using sharp kitchen scissors, cut the smoked salmon slices into thin strips, about 5mm/¼in wide. Strip the leaves from the thyme sprigs and rinse in cold water.

3 Drain the pasta and return it to the pan. Add the butter and heat gently until melted, then stir in the cream with about one-quarter of the smoked salmon and thyme leaves, then season with pepper. Heat gently for 3–4 minutes, stirring all the time. Check the seasoning. Divide among four warmed bowls, top with the remaining salmon and thyme leaves and serve immediately.

PRAWNS with BAKED GARLIC and ROASTED TOMATOES

Packed full of wonderful Mediterranean flavours, this simple, gutsy dish makes a marvellous first course for a dinner party.

SERVES 4

4 small garlic bulbs
60–75ml/4–5 tbsp olive oil
500g/1¼lb baby plum tomatoes on the vine
16 raw large prawns (jumbo shrimp), in their shells
a few sprigs of fresh thyme
salt and ground black pepper
lemon wedges and warm crusty bread, to serve

COOK'S TIPS

• If you can't find small garlic bulbs use one large one and bake it in the oven for about 50 minutes, or until the cloves are soft and creamy.
• Spread a little of the baked garlic on the bread and drizzle with olive oil.

1 Cut a small cross in the top of each bulb of garlic. Place the bulbs in a garlic baker, brush with half the olive oil and sprinkle with a little salt and ground black pepper.

2 Place the garlic baker in an unheated oven, set the temperature to 200°C/400°F/Gas 6 and bake the garlic for about 40 minutes. The garlic cloves should be soft and creamy – if not, bake for a further 10 minutes.

3 Place the tomatoes and prawns in a shallow earthenware baking dish. Drizzle over the remaining olive oil, sprinkle with thyme sprigs and season. Place the dish in the oven after the garlic has been cooking for 30 minutes; turn the prawns after 7 minutes.

4 Arrange the garlic, tomatoes and prawns on a warmed serving plate and serve with lemon wedges and plenty of crusty bread.

COD and PRAWN GREEN COCONUT CURRY

This quick curry takes just minutes to make. If you can't find green masala curry paste at your local supermarket, simply substitute another variety — the curry will be just as good.

SERVES 4

675g/1½lb cod fillets, skinned
90ml/6 tbsp green masala curry paste
175ml/6fl oz/¾ cup canned coconut
    milk or 200ml/7fl oz/scant 1 cup
    coconut cream
175g/6oz raw or cooked, peeled
    prawns (shrimp)
fresh coriander (cilantro), to garnish
basmati rice, to serve

VARIATION
Any firm fish, such as monkfish, can be used instead of cod. Whole fish steaks can be cooked in the sauce, but allow an extra 5 minutes' cooking time and baste them with the sauce from time to time.

1 Using a sharp knife, cut the skinned cod fillets into 4cm/1½in pieces.

2 Put the green masala curry paste and the coconut milk or cream into a frying pan. Heat to simmering and simmer gently for 5 minutes, stirring occasionally.

3 Add the cod pieces and prawns (if raw) to the cream mixture and cook gently for 5 minutes. If using cooked prawns, then add them after this time and heat through. Garnish the curry with fresh coriander and serve immediately with basmati rice.

FISH STEW with LEMON GRASS

Lemon grass and ginger give this delicate stew of fish, prawns, new potatoes and broccoli an appetizing aromatic flavour.

SERVES 4

25g/1oz/2 tbsp butter
175g/6oz onions, chopped
20ml/4 tsp plain (all-purpose) flour
400ml/14fl oz/1⅔ cups light fish stock
150ml/¼ pint/⅔ cup white wine
2.5cm/1in piece fresh root ginger, peeled
    and finely chopped
2 lemon grass stalks, trimmed and
    finely chopped
450g/1lb new potatoes, scrubbed and
    halved if necessary
450g/1lb white fish fillets
175g/6oz large, cooked, peeled
    prawns (shrimp)
275g/10oz small broccoli florets
150ml/¼ pint/⅔ cup double (heavy) cream
60ml/4 tbsp chopped fresh garlic chives
salt and ground black pepper
crusty bread, to serve

3 Remove the skin from the fish fillets and cut the fillets into large chunks. Add the chunks of fish to the pan with the prawns, broccoli and cream. Stir gently.

4 Simmer gently for 5 minutes, taking care not to break up the fish. Adjust the seasoning and sprinkle in the chives. Serve with plenty of crusty bread.

1 Melt the butter in a large pan. Add the onions and cook for 3–4 minutes. Stir in the flour and cook for 1 minute.

2 Stir in the stock, wine, ginger, lemon grass and potatoes. Season and bring to the boil. Cover and cook for 15 minutes, or until the potatoes are almost tender.

GINGERED SEAFOOD STIR-FRY

This would make a lovely summer supper. Serve with lots of bread to mop up the juices and some chilled dry white wine. It would also be good as a first course for four.

SERVES 2

15ml/1 tbsp sunflower oil
5ml/1 tsp sesame oil
2.5cm/1in piece fresh root ginger, peeled
    and finely chopped
1 bunch spring onions (scallions), sliced
1 red (bell) pepper, seeded and
    finely chopped
115g/4oz small "queen" scallops
8 large, raw prawns (shrimp), peeled
115g/4oz squid rings
15ml/1 tbsp lime juice
15ml/1 tbsp light soy sauce
60ml/4 tbsp coconut milk
salt and ground black pepper
mixed salad leaves and crusty bread,
    to serve

1 Heat the sunflower and sesame oils in a wok or large frying pan and cook the chopped ginger and sliced spring onions for 2–3 minutes, stirring frequently, until golden brown. Add the chopped red pepper and cook, stirring constantly, for a further 3 minutes.

2 Add the scallops, prawns and squid rings to the wok or frying pan and cook over a medium heat for about 3 minutes stirring occasionally with a wooden spoon, until all the seafood is opaque and just cooked through. Add the lime juice and light soy sauce.

3 Pour in the coconut milk and mix well, then simmer the sauce, uncovered, for 2 minutes, until the sauce begins to thicken slightly.

4 Season the stir-fry well. Arrange the mixed salad leaves on two individual serving plates and spoon over the seafood mixture with the juices. Serve the seafood with plenty of crusty bread to mop up the juices.

TUNA FRITTATA

This is the ultimate meal in a pan – easy to prepare and easy to serve. For a stronger cheese flavour, try a creamy goat's cheese in place of the soft white cheese.

SERVES 2–3

25g/1oz/2 tbsp butter
15ml/1 tbsp olive oil
1 onion, finely chopped
175g/6oz courgettes (zucchini), halved
 lengthwise and sliced
75g/3oz/1¼ cups brown cap (cremini)
 mushrooms, sliced
50g/2oz asparagus tips
4 eggs, beaten
75g/3oz/⅜ cup soft white (farmer's) cheese
 or ricotta cheese
30ml/2 tbsp chopped fresh thyme
200g/7oz can tuna, in olive oil, drained and
 roughly flaked
115g/4oz cooked, peeled
 prawns (shrimp)
salt and ground black pepper

1 Heat the butter and oil in a non-stick frying pan. Add the chopped onion and cook for 3 minutes, then add the sliced courgettes, mushrooms and asparagus tips and cook for a further 10 minutes, or until beginning to soften and brown.

2 Beat together the eggs, soft or ricotta cheese, chopped thyme and plenty of seasoning until they are well combined.

3 Stir the tuna into the pan, add the prawns and season well. Heat through gently. Pour over the egg mixture and cook over a gentle heat for 5 minutes.

4 Push the egg away from the sides to allow the uncooked egg to run on to the pan. Preheat the grill (broiler) to medium and grill (broil) the omelette to set and brown the surface. Serve cut in wedges.

SIDE DISHES

With the modern emphasis on eating plenty of vegetables, serving several side dishes makes sense, but it can present logistical problems. Space on top of the stove is often limited, so use the oven as well. Choose something quick and simple, such as Cauliflower with Tomatoes and Cumin, Courgettes in Tomato Sauce or Roasted Tomatoes and Garlic. Or go for a dish that's a little out-of-the-ordinary, such as Baked Fennel with a Crumb Crust, Braised Red Cabbage with Beetroot, or Roasted Potatoes with Garlic and Red Onions.

CAULIFLOWER with TOMATOES and CUMIN

This makes an excellent side dish to serve with grilled meat or fish.

SERVES 4

30ml/2 tbsp sunflower or olive oil
1 onion, chopped
1 garlic clove, crushed
1 small cauliflower, broken into florets
5ml/1 tsp cumin seeds
good pinch of ground ginger
4 tomatoes, peeled, seeded
    and quartered
175ml/6fl oz/¾ cup water
15–30ml/1–2 tbsp lemon juice (optional)
salt and ground black pepper
30ml/2 tbsp chopped fresh coriander
    (cilantro) (optional)

VARIATIONS
• Use a 200g/7oz can of chopped
tomatoes instead of the fresh tomatoes.
• Broccoli florets can be used in place of
the cauliflower, if you prefer.

1 Heat the oil in a flameproof casserole, add the onion and garlic and stir-fry for 2–3 minutes until the onion is softened. Add the cauliflower and stir-fry for a further 2–3 minutes until the cauliflower is flecked with brown. Add the cumin seeds and ginger, and fry briskly for 1 minute, then add the peeled, seeded and quartered tomatoes, the water and some salt and pepper to taste.

2 Bring to the boil, then reduce the heat, cover with a plate or with foil and simmer for 6–7 minutes, or until the cauliflower is just tender.

3 Stir in a little lemon juice to sharpen the flavour, if you like, and adjust the seasoning if necessary. Sprinkle over the chopped fresh coriander, if using, and serve immediately.

ROAST VEGETABLES with FRESH HERBS and CHILLI SAUCE

Oven roasting brings out all the flavours of these classic Mediterranean vegetables. Serve them hot with grilled or roast meat or fish.

SERVES 4

2–3 courgettes (zucchini)
1 large onion
1 red (bell) pepper
16 cherry tomatoes
2 garlic cloves, chopped
pinch of cumin seeds
5ml/1 tsp fresh thyme or 4–5 torn
    basil leaves
60ml/4 tbsp olive oil
juice of ½ lemon
5–10ml/1–2 tsp harissa
fresh thyme sprigs, to garnish

COOK'S TIP
Harissa is a spicy paste made from a base of beetroot (beets) and carrots and flavoured with chillies, coriander seeds, caraway, garlic, salt and olive oil. It is a popular ingredient in northern African cooking and is sold in small pots – look out for its distinctive orangey red colour.

1 Preheat the oven to 220°C/425°F/ Gas 7. Trim the courgettes and then cut them into long thin strips. Cut the onion into thin wedges and cut the pepper into fairly large chunks, discarding the seeds and core.

VARIATION
Other vegetables would work well in this dish. Add wedges of red and yellow (bell) peppers in place of one of the courgettes, or add chunks of aubergine (eggplant).

2 Place the vegetables in a large roasting pan, add the tomatoes, chopped garlic, cumin seeds and thyme or basil. Sprinkle with the olive oil and toss to coat. Cook in the oven for 25–30 minutes until the vegetables are very soft and slightly charred at the edges.

3 Blend the lemon juice with the harissa and stir into the roasted vegetables just before serving, garnished with the fresh thyme sprigs.

ROASTED TOMATOES and GARLIC

These are so simple to prepare yet taste absolutely wonderful. Use a large, shallow earthenware dish that will allow the tomatoes to sear and char in a very hot oven.

SERVES 4

8 well-flavoured tomatoes (see Cook's Tip), halved
12 garlic cloves, unpeeled
60ml/4 tbsp extra virgin olive oil
3–4 bay leaves
salt and ground black pepper
45ml/3 tbsp fresh oregano leaves, to garnish

COOK'S TIP
If possible use ripe plum tomatoes for this recipe as they not only keep their shape and their delicious flavour, but also do not fall apart when roasted at such a high temperature. Leave the stalks on the tomatoes, if you like.

1 Preheat the oven to 230°C/450°F/ Gas 8. Select a large, shallow ovenproof dish that will hold all the tomato halves snugly in a single layer. Arrange the tomatoes in the dish and tuck the whole, unpeeled garlic cloves evenly in among the tomatoes.

2 Brush the tomatoes with the oil, add the bay leaves and sprinkle black pepper over the top. Bake for about 45 minutes, or until the tomatoes have softened and are sizzling in the dish. Season with salt and more black pepper, if needed. Garnish with oregano leaves and serve.

SLOW-COOKED SPICED ONIONS

Onions marinated and baked in a spicy sauce are delicious with grilled or roasted meats.
Choose a good, extra virgin olive oil for a rich, peppery flavour.

SERVES 4

675g/1½lb Spanish or red onions
90ml/6 tbsp olive or sunflower oil or a
    mixture of both
pinch of saffron threads
2.5ml/½ tsp ground ginger
5ml/1 tsp ground black pepper
5ml/1 tsp ground cinnamon
15ml/1 tbsp sugar

1 Slice the onions very thinly and place
them in a shallow dish. Blend together
the olive and/or sunflower oil, saffron,
ground ginger, black pepper, cinnamon
and sugar, and pour over the onions. Stir
gently to mix, then set the onions aside
for about 2 hours.

2 Preheat the oven to 160°C/325°F/Gas 3
and pour the onions and the marinade
into a casserole or ovenproof dish.

COOK'S TIP
Onions grown in warmer climates are
milder than those from cooler regions.
Consequently Spanish onions have a mild,
sweet flavour. Their skins are a rich
golden colour and they are one of the
largest varieties available.

3 Fold a large piece of foil into three
and place over the top of the casserole
or ovenproof dish, securing it with a lid.

4 Cook in the oven for 45 minutes,
or until the onions are very soft, then
increase the oven temperature to
200°C/400°F/Gas 6. Remove the lid and
foil and cook for a further 5–10 minutes,
or until the onions are lightly glazed.
Serve immediately.

COOK'S TIP
When slicing onions, chop off the neck
and just a little of the base to help the
onion stay together. Score a line down
the side of the onion and peel away the
outer skin and first layer of flesh.

OVEN-ROASTED RED ONIONS

The wonderful taste of these sweet red onions is enhanced still further with the powerful flavours of fresh rosemary and juniper berries, and the added tangy sweetness from the balsamic vinegar.

SERVES 4

4 large or 8 small red onions
45ml/3 tbsp olive oil
6 juniper berries, crushed
8 small rosemary sprigs
30ml/2 tbsp balsamic vinegar
salt and ground black pepper

VARIATION
Add a similar quantity of long, thin potato wedges to the onion. Use a larger dish so that the vegetables are still in one layer.

COOK'S TIP
To help hold back the tears during preparation, chill the onions first for about 30 minutes and then remove the root end last. The root contains the largest concentration of the sulphuric compounds that make the eyes water.

I Soak a clay onion baker in cold water for 15 minutes, then drain. If the base of the baker is glazed, only the lid will need to be soaked.

2 Trim the roots from the onions and remove the skins, if you like. Cut the onions from the tip to the root, cutting the large onions into quarters and the small onions in half.

3 Rub the onions with olive oil, salt and pepper and the juniper berries. Place the onions in the baker, inserting the rosemary in among the onions. Pour the remaining olive oil and vinegar over.

4 Cover and place in an unheated oven. Set the oven to 200°C/400°F/Gas 6 and cook for 40 minutes. Remove the lid and cook for a further 10 minutes.

ROASTED SWEET POTATOES, ONIONS and BEETROOT in COCONUT and GINGER PASTE

Sweet potatoes and beetroot take on a wonderful sweetness when roasted, and are delicious with savoury onions and aromatic coconut, ginger and garlic paste.

SERVES 4

30ml/2 tbsp groundnut (peanut) or mild
   olive oil
450g/1lb sweet potatoes, peeled and cut
   into thick strips or chunks
4 beetroot (beets), cooked, peeled and cut
   into wedges
450g/1lb small onions, halved
5ml/1 tsp coriander seeds, lightly crushed
3–4 small whole fresh red chillies
salt and ground black pepper
chopped fresh coriander (cilantro), to garnish

For the paste
2 large garlic cloves, chopped
1–2 green chillies, seeded and chopped
15ml/1 tbsp chopped fresh root ginger
45ml/3 tbsp chopped fresh coriander (cilantro)
75ml/5 tbsp coconut milk
30ml/2 tbsp groundnut (peanut) or mild
   olive oil
grated rind of ½ lime
2.5ml/½ tsp soft light brown sugar

1 To make the paste, process the garlic, chillies, ginger, coriander and coconut milk in a food processor or blender.

2 Tip the spicy paste into a small bowl and beat in the oil, grated lime rind and light brown sugar. Preheat the oven to 200°C/400°F/Gas 6.

3 Heat the oil in a large roasting pan in the oven for 5 minutes. Add the sweet potatoes, beetroot, onions and coriander seeds, tossing them in the hot oil. Roast the vegetables for 10 minutes.

4 Stir in the spicy paste and the whole red chillies. Season the vegetables well with salt and pepper, and shake the roasting pan to toss the vegetables and coat them thoroughly with the paste.

5 Return the vegetables to the oven and cook for a further 25–35 minutes, or until both the sweet potatoes and onions are fully cooked and tender. During cooking, stir the mixture two or three times with a wooden spoon to prevent the coconut and ginger paste from sticking to the roasting pan. Serve the vegetables immediately, sprinkled with a little chopped fresh coriander.

COOK'S TIP
Try to buy orange-fleshed sweet potatoes for this dish – they not only look more attractive than white-fleshed ones in this dish, they are also more nutritious.

COURGETTES in TOMATO SAUCE

*This rich-flavoured Mediterranean dish can be served hot or cold, either as a side dish or
as part of a tapas meal. Cut the courgettes into fairly thick slices, so that they retain
their texture and stay slightly crunchy.*

SERVES 4

15ml/1 tbsp olive oil
1 onion, chopped
1 garlic clove, chopped
4 courgettes (zucchini), thickly sliced
400g/14oz can chopped tomatoes,
    drained
2 tomatoes, peeled, seeded and chopped
5ml/1 tsp vegetable bouillon powder
15ml/1 tbsp tomato purée (paste)
salt and ground black pepper

VARIATION
Add 1 or 2 sliced and seeded red, green
or yellow (bell) peppers with the
courgettes in step 1.

1 Heat the olive oil in a heavy pan, add
the chopped onion and garlic and sauté
for about 5 minutes, or until the onion is
softened, stirring occasionally. Add the
thickly sliced courgettes and cook for a
further 5 minutes.

2 Add the canned and fresh tomatoes,
bouillon powder and tomato purée. Stir
well, then simmer for 10–15 minutes
until the sauce is thickened and the
courgettes are just tender. Season
to taste and serve.

BAKED FENNEL with a CRUMB CRUST

*The delicate aniseed flavour of baked fennel makes it a very good accompaniment to all
kinds of dishes, from pasta and risotto to roast chicken.*

SERVES 4

3 fennel bulbs, cut lengthwise
    into quarters
30ml/2 tbsp olive oil
1 garlic clove, chopped
50g/2oz/1 cup day-old wholemeal
    (whole wheat) breadcrumbs
30ml/2 tbsp chopped fresh flat
    leaf parsley
salt and ground black pepper
a few fronds of fennel leaves, to
    garnish (optional)

COOK'S TIPS
• When buying fennel, look for compact,
unblemished white-green bulbs. The
leaves should look fresh and green.
Tougher specimens will have bulbs that
spread at the top.
• Fennel has a distinctive liquorice flavour,
which particularly complements fish
dishes. All parts of the plant are edible
including the bulb, the celery-like stalks
and the feathery leaves.

1 Cook the fennel in a pan of boiling
salted water for 10 minutes. Preheat the
oven to 190°C/375°F/Gas 5.

2 Drain the fennel and place in a large
earthenware baking dish or baking tray,
then brush with half of the olive oil.

VARIATION
To make a cheese-topped version, add
60ml/4 tbsp finely grated strong-flavoured
cheese, such as mature (sharp) Cheddar,
Red Leicester or Parmesan, to the
breadcrumb mixture in step 3.

3 In a small bowl, mix together the
chopped garlic, wholemeal breadcrumbs
and chopped fresh flat leaf parsley, then
stir in the rest of the olive oil. Sprinkle
the mixture evenly over the fennel, then
season well with salt and pepper.

4 Bake the fennel for about 30 minutes,
or until it is tender and the breadcrumb
topping is crisp and golden brown. Serve
the baked fennel hot, garnished with a
few fronds of fennel leaves, if you like.

BRAISED LETTUCE and PEAS with MINT

Based on the traditional French way of braising peas with lettuce in butter, this dish is delicious with simply cooked fish or roast or grilled duck.

2 Toss the vegetables in the butter, then sprinkle in the sugar, 2.5ml/½ tsp salt and plenty of black pepper. Cover, then cook very gently for 5 minutes, stirring once.

3 Add the peas and mint sprigs to the pan. Toss the peas in the buttery juices, then pour in the light stock or water.

4 Cover the pan and cook over a gentle heat for a further 5 minutes until the peas are almost tender, then remove the lid from the pan. Increase the heat to high and cook, stirring occasionally, until the cooking liquid has reduced to a few tablespoons.

5 Stir in the remaining butter and adjust the seasoning. Transfer to a warmed serving dish and garnish with the extra mint. Serve immediately.

VARIATIONS
• Braise about 250g/9oz baby carrots with the lettuce.
• Use 1 lettuce, shredding it coarsely, and omit the fresh mint. Towards the end of cooking, stir in about 150g/5oz rocket (arugula) – preferably the slightly stronger-flavoured, wild variety – and cook briefly until just wilted.
• Fry 115g/4oz chopped smoked bacon or pancetta with 1 small chopped red or white onion in the butter. Use 1 bunch of spring onions and omit the mint. Stir in some chopped fresh flat leaf parsley before serving. This version is also very good with small, white summer turnips, braised with the lettuce.

SERVES 4

50g/2oz/¼ cup butter
4 Little Gem (Bibb) lettuces,
    halved lengthwise
2 bunches spring onions (scallions)
5ml/1 tsp sugar
400g/14oz shelled peas (about
    1kg/2¼lb in pods)
a few sprigs of mint, plus extra fresh mint
    to garnish
120ml/4fl oz/½ cup light vegetable or
    chicken stock or water
salt and ground black pepper

1 Melt half the butter in a wide, heavy pan over a low heat. Add the lettuces and spring onions.

BRAISED LEEKS with CARROTS

Sweet carrots and leeks go well together and are good finished with a little chopped mint, chervil or parsley. This is a good accompaniment to roast beef, lamb or chicken.

SERVES 4

65g/2½oz/5 tbsp butter
675g/1½lb carrots, thickly sliced
2 fresh bay leaves
75ml/5 tbsp water
675g/1½lb leeks, cut into 5cm/2in lengths
120ml/4fl oz/½ cup white wine
30ml/2 tbsp chopped fresh mint, chervil
   or parsley
a pinch of sugar
salt and ground black pepper

1 Melt 25g/1oz/2 tbsp of the butter in a wide, heavy pan and cook the carrots without allowing them to brown, for about 5 minutes. Add the bay leaves, seasoning, sugar and the water. Bring to the boil, cover and cook for 10 minutes, or until the carrots are just tender.

2 Uncover the pan and boil until the juices have evaporated, leaving the carrots moist and glazed. Remove the carrots from the pan and set aside.

3 Melt 25g/1oz/2 tbsp of the remaining butter in the pan. Add the leeks and fry them over a low heat for 4–5 minutes, without allowing them to brown.

4 Add seasoning, a good pinch of sugar, the wine and half the chopped herbs. Heat until simmering, then cover and cook gently for 5–8 minutes, until the leeks are tender, but not collapsed.

5 Uncover the leeks and turn them in the buttery juices. Increase the heat and then boil the liquid rapidly until it is reduced to a few tablespoons.

6 Add the carrots to the leeks and reheat them gently, stirring occasionally, then add the remaining butter. Adjust the seasoning, if necessary. Transfer to a warmed serving dish and serve sprinkled with the remaining chopped herbs.

VARIATION
Braised leeks in tarragon cream
Cook 900g/2lb leeks, cut into 5cm/2in lengths, in 40g/1½oz/3 tbsp butter as step 3. Season with salt and pepper, add a pinch of sugar, 45ml/3 tbsp tarragon vinegar, 6 fresh tarragon sprigs or 5ml/ 1 tsp dried tarragon and 60ml/4 tbsp white wine. Cover and cook as step 4. Add 150ml/¼ pint/⅔ cup double (heavy) cream and allow to bubble and thicken. Adjust the seasoning and serve sprinkled with plenty of finely chopped fresh tarragon leaves. A spoonful of tarragon-flavoured mustard is good stirred into these creamy leeks. Serve with fish or chicken dishes.

BRAISED RED CABBAGE with BEETROOT

The moist, gentle cooking of the clay pot finishes this vegetable dish to perfection.
Serve with casseroles and roast meats – it is especially delicious with roast pork.

SERVES 6–8

675g/1½lb red cabbage
1 Spanish onion, thinly sliced
30ml/2 tbsp olive oil
30ml/2 tbsp light muscovado (brown) sugar
2 tart eating apples, peeled, cored
   and sliced
300ml/½ pint/1¼ cups vegetable stock
60ml/4 tbsp red wine vinegar
375g/13oz raw beetroot (beet), peeled
   and coarsely grated
salt and ground black pepper

COOK'S TIP
When buying cabbage, choose one that
is firm and heavy for its size. The leaves
should look healthy – avoid any with
curling leaves or blemishes. These
guidelines apply to any type of cabbage –
red, green or white.

1 Soak a large clay pot or bean pot in
cold water for 20 minutes, then drain.
Finely shred the red cabbage and place
in the clay pot.

2 Place the onion and olive oil in a
frying pan and sauté until soft and
transparent. Stir in the sugar and fry the
onion gently until it is caramelized and
golden. Take care not to overcook.

3 Stir in the apple slices, vegetable stock
and wine vinegar, then transfer to the
clay pot. Season with salt and pepper.

4 Cover and place in an unheated oven.
Set the oven temperature to 190°C/
375°F/Gas 5 and cook for 1 hour. Stir in
the beetroot, re-cover the pot and cook
for a further 20–30 minutes, or until the
cabbage and beetroot are tender.

SPINACH BRAISED with SWEET POTATOES

Sweet potatoes make an interesting alternative to the ordinary variety. Here the garlic and ginger subtly compliment the flavours of the potatoes and spinach.

SERVES 4

30ml/2 tbsp sunflower oil
I onion, chopped
I garlic clove, finely chopped
2.5cm/Iin piece fresh root ginger,
    peeled and grated
2.5ml/½ tsp cayenne pepper
675g/I½lb sweet potatoes
150ml/¼ pint/⅔ cup vegetable or
    chicken stock
225g/8oz spinach
45ml/3 tbsp pine nuts, toasted
salt and ground black pepper

I Soak a clay potato pot in cold water for 20 minutes, then drain. Heat the oil in a large frying pan, add the onion, garlic, ginger and cayenne pepper and fry gently, stirring occasionally, for about 8 minutes, or until the onion is softened.

2 Peel the sweet potatoes and cut them into 2.5cm/Iin chunks. Add the chunks to the frying pan and stir to coat them in the oil and spices.

COOK'S TIP
To toast pine nuts, heat a heavy frying pan and add the nuts, cook them for 3–4 minutes or until they turn a golden brown colour, stirring occasionally. Watch the nuts carefully – they will scorch and burn quickly if toasted for too long.

VARIATIONS
• Add a drained, 400g/14oz can chickpeas to the potato mixture after 30 minutes cooking and stir well.
• Use baby new potatoes in place of the sweet potatoes.

3 Transfer the potato mixture to the clay pot and add the stock. Cover the pot and place in an unheated oven. Set the oven to 220°C/425°F/Gas 7 and cook for 50–60 minutes, or until the potatoes are just tender, stirring halfway through cooking.

4 Wash the spinach and shred roughly. Stir into the potatoes with the toasted pine nuts, re-cover the clay pot and cook for a further 5 minutes in the oven. Remove from the oven and leave to stand for 5 minutes. Adjust the seasoning and serve immediately.

ROOT VEGETABLE GRATIN with INDIAN SPICES

Subtly spiced with curry powder, turmeric, coriander and mild chilli powder, this rich gratin is substantial enough to serve on its own for lunch or supper. It also makes a good accompaniment to a vegetable or bean curry.

2 Preheat the oven to 180°C/350°F/ Gas 4. Heat half the butter in a heavy pan, add the curry powder, ground turmeric and coriander and half the chilli powder. Cook for 2 minutes, then leave to cool slightly. Drain the vegetables, then pat them dry with kitchen paper. Place in a bowl, add the spice mixture and the shallots and mix well.

3 Arrange the vegetables in a shallow baking dish, seasoning well with salt and pepper between the layers. Mix together the cream and milk, pour the mixture over the vegetables, then sprinkle the remaining chilli powder on top.

4 Cover the dish with baking parchment and bake for 45 minutes. Remove the baking parchment, dot the vegetables with the remaining butter and bake for a further 50 minutes, or until the top is golden brown. Serve the gratin garnished with chopped parsley.

SERVES 4

2 large potatoes, about 450g/1lb
   total weight
2 sweet potatoes, about 275g/10oz
   total weight
175g/6oz celeriac
15ml/1 tbsp unsalted (sweet) butter
5ml/1 tsp curry powder
5ml/1 tsp ground turmeric
2.5ml/½ tsp ground coriander
5ml/1 tsp mild chilli powder
3 shallots, chopped
150ml/¼ pint/⅔ cup single (light) cream
150ml/¼ pint/⅔ cup milk
salt and ground black pepper
chopped fresh flat leaf parsley, to garnish

1 Cut the potatoes, sweet potatoes and celeriac into thin, even slices using a sharp knife or the slicing attachment on a food processor. Immediately place the vegetables in a bowl of cold water to prevent them from discolouring.

COOK'S TIP
The cream adds a delicious richness to this gratin; use semi-skimmed (low-fat) milk, if you prefer a lighter meal.

ROASTED POTATOES with GARLIC and RED ONIONS

These mouthwatering potatoes are a fine accompaniment to just about anything. The key is to use small firm potatoes; the smaller they are cut, the quicker they will cook.

SERVES 4

675g/1½lb small firm potatoes
25g/1oz/2 tbsp butter
30ml/2 tbsp olive oil
2 large or 4 small red onions, cut
   into wedges
8 garlic cloves, unpeeled
30ml/2 tbsp chopped fresh rosemary or
   10ml/2 tsp dried
salt and ground black pepper

COOK'S TIP
Choose waxy or new potatoes that will hold their shape for this dish. You can peel them, or simply scrub them well and leave the skins on.

1 Preheat the oven to 230°C/450°F/ Gas 8. Peel and quarter the potatoes, rinse them and pat dry on kitchen paper.

2 Put the butter and oil in a roasting pan and heat in the oven. When the butter has melted and is foaming, add the potatoes, onion wedges and garlic cloves to the roasting pan.

3 Sprinkle over the rosemary, toss well then spread out the vegetables.

4 Place the pan in the oven and roast for about 25 minutes until the potatoes are golden and tender when tested with a fork. Shake the pan from time to time to redistribute the vegetables. When cooked, season with salt and pepper.

POTATO GRATIN

Potatoes, layered with mustard butter and baked until golden, are perfect to serve with a green salad, or as an accompaniment to a vegetable or nut roast.

SERVES 4

4 large potatoes, about 900g/2lb
   total weight
30ml/2 tbsp butter
15ml/1 tbsp olive oil
2 large garlic cloves, crushed
30ml/2 tbsp Dijon mustard
15ml/1 tbsp lemon juice
15ml/1 tbsp fresh thyme leaves, plus
   extra to garnish
50ml/2fl oz/¼ cup vegetable stock
salt and ground black pepper

1 Thinly slice the potatoes using a knife, mandolin or a slicing attachment on a food processor. Place the potato slices in a bowl of cold water to prevent them from discolouring.

2 Preheat the oven to 200°C/400°F/ Gas 6. Heat the butter and oil in a deep, flameproof frying pan. Add the garlic and cook gently for 2–3 minutes until light golden, stirring constantly. Stir in the mustard, lemon juice and thyme. Remove from the heat and pour the mixture into a jug (pitcher).

3 Drain the potatoes and pat dry with kitchen paper. Place a layer of potatoes in the frying pan, season and pour over one-third of the butter mixture. Arrange another layer of potatoes on top, pour over half of the remaining butter mixture and season. Arrange a final layer of potatoes on top, pour over the remainder of butter mixture and the stock. Season and sprinkle with the reserved thyme.

4 Cover the potatoes with baking parchment and bake for 1 hour, then remove the paper, return to the oven and cook for 15 minutes, or until golden.

VARIATION
Any root vegetables can be used: try sweet potatoes, parsnips or turnips.

NEW POTATOES with THYME and LEMON

These potatoes are the perfect accompaniment to meat or poultry. You can even use old potatoes, cut into chunks, ideal for serving as an alternative with a traditional roast.

SERVES 4

675g/1½lb small new potatoes
4 garlic cloves, sliced
8 thyme sprigs
4 strips finely pared lemon rind
75ml/5 tbsp olive oil
coarsely ground black pepper
coarse sea salt

COOK'S TIPS
• Thyme is an aromatic, woody herb that goes particularly well with lemon. It has a strong aroma and pungent flavour and grows wild in most warm climates. Thyme is often associated with dishes from the Mediterranean.
• You could easily make this dish with older potatoes – simply peel them, if you like, then cut them into even-size chunks or wedges before adding them to the pot.

1 Soak a clay potato pot in cold water for 20 minutes, then drain. Scrub the new potatoes and rinse thoroughly in cold water. Place the potatoes in the pot.

2 Add the sliced garlic cloves, thyme sprigs and pared lemon rind to the pot, tucking them in among the potatoes. Sprinkle over plenty of coarsely ground black pepper and coarse sea salt.

3 Drizzle over the olive oil. Cover with the lid and place in an unheated oven. Set the oven to 200°C/400°F/Gas 6 and cook for 1 hour, or until just tender.

4 If wished, remove the lid and bake for a further 15–20 minutes, until slightly golden. If you prefer to keep the skins soft, remove the potatoes from the oven and leave to stand for 10 minutes.

POTATOES BAKED with FENNEL, ONIONS, GARLIC and SAFFRON

Potatoes, fennel and onions flavoured with garlic, saffron and spices make a sophisticated and attractive accompaniment to fish or chicken or egg-based main-course dishes.

SERVES 4–6

500g/1¼lb small waxy potatoes, cut into
  chunks or wedges
good pinch of saffron threads
  (12–15 threads)
1 head of garlic, separated into
  individual cloves
12 small red or yellow onions, peeled
  but left whole
3 fennel bulbs, cut into wedges, feathery
  tops reserved for garnish (optional)
4–6 fresh bay leaves
6–9 fresh thyme sprigs
175ml/6fl oz/¾ cup fish, chicken or
  vegetable stock
30ml/2 tbsp sherry or
  balsamic vinegar
2.5ml/½ tsp sugar
5ml/1 tsp fennel seeds, lightly crushed
2.5ml/½ tsp paprika
45ml/3 tbsp olive oil
salt and ground black pepper

1 Boil the potato chunks or wedges in a pan of boiling salted water for 8–10 minutes. Drain. Preheat the oven to 190°C/375°F/Gas 5. Soak the saffron threads in 30ml/2 tbsp warm water for 10 minutes.

2 Peel and finely chop two of the garlic cloves and set aside. Place the potato chunks or wedges, whole red or yellow onions, remaining unpeeled garlic cloves, fennel wedges, fresh bay leaves and fresh thyme sprigs in a large roasting pan or dish. Mix together the stock and the saffron and its soaking liquid in a jug (pitcher) or measuring cup.

3 Add the vinegar and sugar to the stock mixture, then pour the liquid over the vegetables. Stir in the fennel seeds, paprika, chopped garlic and oil, and season with salt and pepper.

4 Cook the vegetables in the oven for 1–1¼ hours, stirring occasionally, until they are just tender. Chop the reserved fennel tops, if using, and sprinkle them over the vegetables to garnish. Season the vegetables with more salt and pepper and serve immediately .

COOK'S TIP
Sherry vinegar has a rich, mellow flavour and it makes a good addition to a variety of sauces and dressings. It can be used simply to add extra piquancy to a dish. Try sprinkling a little over oven-roasted vegetables or add a teaspoon or two to soups, sauces or stews.

LENTIL DHAL with ROASTED GARLIC and WHOLE SPICES

This spicy lentil dhal makes a sustaining and comforting meal when served with rice or Indian breads and any dry-spiced dish, particularly a cauliflower or potato dish. It's a bit of a cheat to have in a one-pot cookbook, since there's a spicy garnish that needs to be cooked – in a small frying pan – at the end.

SERVES 4–6

40g/1½oz/3 tbsp butter or ghee
1 onion, chopped
2 green chillies, seeded and chopped
15ml/1 tbsp chopped fresh root ginger
225g/8oz/1 cup yellow or red lentils
900ml/1½ pints/3¾ cups water
45ml/3 tbsp roasted garlic purée
5ml/1 tsp ground cumin
5ml/1 tsp ground coriander
200g/7oz tomatoes, peeled and diced
a little lemon juice
salt and ground black pepper
30–45ml/2–3 tbsp coriander (cilantro)
   sprigs, to garnish

For the spicy garnish
30ml/2 tbsp groundnut (peanut) oil
4–5 shallots, sliced
2 garlic cloves, thinly sliced
15g/½oz/1 tbsp butter or ghee
5ml/1 tsp cumin seeds
5ml/1 tsp mustard seeds
3–4 small dried red chillies
8–10 fresh curry leaves

1 First begin the spicy garnish. Heat the oil in a large, heavy pan. Add the shallots and fry them over a medium heat, stirring occasionally, until they are crisp and browned. Add the garlic and cook, stirring frequently, for a moment or two until the garlic colours slightly. Use a slotted spoon to remove the mixture from the pan and set aside.

COOK'S TIP
Ghee is type of clarified butter that has had all the milk solids removed by heating – it was originally made to extend the keeping qualities of butter in India. It is the main cooking fat used in Indian cooking. Because the milk solids have been removed, ghee has a high smoking point and can therefore be cooked at higher temperatures than ordinary butter. Look for it in Indian and Asian stores.

2 Melt the butter or ghee in the pan and cook the onion, chillies and ginger for 10 minutes, until golden.

3 Stir in the lentils and water, then bring to the boil, reduce the heat and part-cover the pan. Simmer, stirring occasionally, for 50–60 minutes, until similar to a very thick soup.

4 Stir in the roasted garlic purée, cumin and ground coriander, then season with salt and pepper to taste. Cook for a further 10–15 minutes, uncovered, stirring frequently.

5 Stir in the tomatoes and then adjust the seasoning, adding a little lemon juice to taste if necessary.

6 To make the spicy garnish: melt the butter or ghee in a frying pan. Add the cumin and mustard seeds and fry until the mustard seeds pop. Stir in the chillies, curry leaves and the shallot mixture, then immediately swirl the mixture into the cooked dhal. Garnish with coriander, spicy fried shallots and garlic and serve.

RICE with DILL and BROAD BEANS

This is a favourite rice dish in Iran. The combination of broad beans, plenty of fresh dill and warm spices works very well, and the saffron rice adds a splash of bright colour.

SERVES 4

275g/10oz/1½ cups basmati rice,
    soaked in cold water and drained
750ml/1¼ pints/3 cups water
40g/1½oz/3 tbsp butter
175g/6oz/1½ cups frozen baby broad (fava)
    beans, thawed and peeled
90ml/6 tbsp finely chopped fresh dill, plus
    fresh dill sprigs to garnish
5ml/1 tsp ground cinnamon
5ml/1 tsp ground cumin
2–3 saffron threads, soaked in
    15ml/1 tbsp boiling water
salt

1 Tip the rice into a large pan with the water. Add a little salt. Bring to the boil, then simmer very gently for 5 minutes. Drain, rinse in warm water and drain again.

2 Melt the butter in the rinsed-out pan. Pour two-thirds of the melted butter into a bowl and set aside. Spoon enough rice into the pan to cover the base. Add one-quarter of the beans and a little dill.

3 Spread over another layer of rice, then a layer of beans and dill. Repeat the layers until all the beans and dill have been used, ending with a layer of rice. Cook over a gentle heat for 8 minutes until nearly tender.

4 Pour the reserved melted butter evenly over the rice, then sprinkle the ground cinnamon and cumin over the top. Cover the pan with a clean dishtowel or cloth and a tight-fitting lid, lifting the corners of the towel or cloth back over the lid. Cook over a low heat for 25–30 minutes.

5 Spoon about 45ml/3 tbsp of the cooked rice into the bowl of saffron water and then mix the rice and liquid together. Spoon the remaining rice mixture on to a large serving plate and spoon the saffron rice on one side to garnish. Serve immediately, decorated with fresh sprigs of dill.

BASMATI RICE with VEGETABLES

Serve this tasty dish with roast chicken, grilled lamb cutlets or pan-fried fish. Add the vegetables near the end of cooking so that they remain crisp.

2 Heat the oil in a large pan and fry the onion for a few minutes over a medium heat until it starts to soften.

3 Add the rice to the pan and fry for about 10 minutes, stirring constantly to prevent the rice sticking to the base of the pan. Stir in the crushed garlic.

4 Pour in the water or stock and stir well. Bring to the boil, then lower the heat. Cover and simmer for 10 minutes.

SERVES 4

350g/12oz/1¾ cups basmati rice
45ml/3 tbsp vegetable oil
1 onion, chopped
2 garlic cloves, crushed
750ml/1¼ pints/3 cups water or
   vegetable stock
115g/4oz/⅔ cup fresh or drained canned
   sweetcorn kernels
1 red or green (bell) pepper, seeded
   and chopped
1 large carrot, grated
fresh chervil sprigs, to garnish

1 Rinse the rice in a sieve under cold water, then leave to drain thoroughly for about 15 minutes.

5 Sprinkle the corn over the rice, spread the chopped pepper on top and sprinkle over the grated carrot. Cover tightly and steam over a low heat until the rice is tender, then mix with a fork. Pile on to a serving plate and garnish with chervil.

SAFFRON RICE with ONION and CARDAMOM

This delightfully fragrant, buttery pilaff is wonderful with both Indian and Middle-eastern dishes, especially ones featuring fish, shellfish, chicken or lamb.

2 Toast the saffron threads in a dry, heavy frying pan over a low heat for about 2 minutes, then place in a small bowl and add 30ml/2 tbsp warm water. Leave to soak for 10–15 minutes.

3 Melt the butter in the pan, then cook the onion with the cardamom pods very gently for 8–10 minutes, until soft and buttery yellow.

4 Add the drained rice to the pan and stir well to coat the grains in the butter. Add the salt and bay leaves, followed by the stock and saffron with its liquid. Bring the rice to the boil, stir, then reduce the heat to very low and cover tightly. Cook the rice for 10–12 minutes, until it has absorbed all the liquid.

5 Lay a clean, folded dishtowel over the pan under the lid and press on the lid to wedge it firmly in place. Leave the rice to stand for 10–15 minutes to continue cooking in its own heat.

6 Fluff up the grains of cooked rice with a fork. Tip it into a warmed serving dish and serve immediately as an accompaniment to a spicy main course.

SERVES 4

350g/12oz/1¾ cups basmati rice
good pinch of saffron threads (about 15 threads)
25g/1oz/2 tbsp butter
1 onion, finely chopped
6 green cardamom pods, lightly crushed
5ml/1 tsp salt
2–3 fresh bay leaves
600ml/1 pint/2½ cups well-flavoured chicken or vegetable stock or water

1 Put the rice into a sieve and rinse well under cold running water. Tip it into a bowl, add cold water to cover and set aside to soak for 30–40 minutes. Drain in the sieve.

COOK'S TIP
After boiling, when all the liquid has been absorbed, basmati rice is set aside to finish cooking in its own heat and become tender. Wedging a folded dishtowel under the pan lid ensures the heat is not lost and the steam is absorbed.

GARLIC CHIVE RICE with MUSHROOMS

Rice is readily infused with the pungent aroma and taste of garlic chives, creating a dish with an excellent flavour. Serve with vegetarian dishes, fish or chicken.

SERVES 4

60ml/4 tbsp groundnut (peanut) oil
250g/9oz mixed mushrooms,
  thickly sliced
25g/1oz garlic chives, chopped
350g/12oz/1¾ cups long grain rice
1 small onion, finely chopped
2 green chillies, seeded and finely chopped
15g/½oz fresh coriander (cilantro)
600ml/1 pint/2½ cups vegetable or
  mushroom stock
5ml/1 tsp salt
50g/2oz toasted cashew nuts
ground black pepper

5 Add the rice to the onions and fry over a low heat, stirring frequently, for 4–5 minutes until the onion is softened. Pour in the stock mixture, then stir in the salt and plenty of black pepper.

6 Bring to the boil, stir and reduce the heat to very low. Cover tightly and cook for 15–20 minutes, until the rice has absorbed all the liquid. Lay a clean, folded dishtowel over the pan under the lid and press on the lid to wedge it firmly in place. Leave to stand in a warm place for 10 minutes, allowing the towel to absorb the steam while the rice becomes completely tender.

7 Add the cooked mushroom and chive mixture to the rice and mix well. Stir in the chopped fresh coriander leaves, then adjust the seasoning. Serve immediately, sprinkled with the toasted cashew nuts.

1 Heat half the oil in a large frying pan and cook the thickly sliced mushrooms for 5–6 minutes, stirring occasionally, until they are tender and browned.

2 Add half of the garlic chives to the pan and cook for 1–2 minutes. Remove from the pan using a slotted spoon and set aside. Wash and drain the rice.

3 Add the remaining oil to the frying pan, add the chopped onion and chillies and cook over a gentle heat, stirring occasionally, for 10–12 minutes, until the onions have softened.

4 Set half the remaining garlic chives aside. Cut the stalks off the coriander and set the leaves aside. Purée the remaining chives and the coriander stalks with the stock in a food processor or blender.

COOK'S TIP
You'll find garlic chives in Asian and Thai food stores.

STOVE-TOP MEAT, POULTRY AND GAME

This chapter lifts the lid on delicious main courses made effortlessly on top of the stove or in a free-standing electric cooker. You'll be reminded of old favourites like Coq au Vin and Hunter's Chicken and invited to try some exciting new flavours, such as Ostrich Stew with Sweet Potatoes and Chickpeas, or Grouse with Orchard Fruit Stuffing. For a wonderful experience you'll be sure to repeat, try Pancetta and Broad Bean Risotto.

CALFS' LIVER with SLOW-COOKED ONIONS, MARSALA and SAGE

Liver and onions are an international favourite, from British liver with onion gravy to the famous Venetian dish of Fegato alla Veneziana. *Inspired by Italian cooking, this dish is good served with polenta, either soft or set and grilled.*

3 Add the remaining oil to the pan and fry the remaining sage leaves for about 30 seconds, then leave them to drain on kitchen paper.

4 Add the remaining butter and extra oil to the pan and increase the heat to high. Season the flour, then dip the liver in it and fry quickly for about 2 minutes on each side until browned, but still pink in the middle. Use a slotted spoon or metal spatula to transfer the liver to warm plates and keep warm.

5 Immediately add the Marsala to the pan and let it bubble fiercely until reduced to a few tablespoons of sticky glaze. Distribute the onions over the liver and spoon over the Marsala juices. Sprinkle with the fried sage leaves and extra parsley and serve immediately.

VARIATION
Chicken liver and onion bruschetta
Cook the onions as above, replacing the sage with 5ml/1 tsp chopped fresh thyme. Fry 400g/14oz chicken livers in 25g/1oz/ 2 tbsp butter and 15ml/1 tbsp olive oil until browned but still pink in the centre. Flame the chicken livers with 45ml/3 tbsp cognac, and add 150g/5oz seeded, skinned grapes (optional). Heat the grapes through, then toss them into the cooked onions. Heap the mixture on to thick slices of toasted country bread rubbed with oil and garlic or on to thick slices of grilled (broiled) polenta. Serve sprinkled with chopped fresh parsley.

SERVES 4

45ml/3 tbsp olive oil, plus extra for
    shallow frying
25g/1oz/2 tbsp butter
500g/1¼lb mild onions, thinly sliced
small bunch of fresh sage leaves
30ml/2 tbsp chopped fresh parsley, plus a
    little extra to garnish
2.5ml/½ tsp sugar
15ml/1 tbsp balsamic vinegar
30ml/2 tbsp plain (all-purpose) flour
675g/1½lb calfs' liver, thinly sliced
150ml/¼ pint/⅔ cup Marsala
salt and ground black pepper

1 Heat half the oil with half the butter in a large, wide, heavy pan and cook the onions, covered, over a very gentle heat for 30 minutes. Stir once or twice.

2 Chop five of the sage leaves and add them to the pan with the chopped parsley, a pinch of salt, the sugar and balsamic vinegar. Cook, uncovered and stirring frequently with a wooden spoon, until the onions are very tender and a golden brown colour. Taste for seasoning and add salt and pepper as necessary. Tip the onions into a heatproof dish and keep warm.

OSSO BUCCO with RISOTTO MILANESE

Two one-pot dishes in one recipe, both so utterly delicious that it seemed churlish to omit them from this collection. Osso Bucco is a traditional Milanese veal stew and is classically accompanied by this saffron-scented risotto.

SERVES 4

50g/2oz/¼ cup butter
15ml/1 tbsp olive oil
1 large onion, chopped
1 leek, finely chopped
45ml/3 tbsp plain (all-purpose) flour
4 large portions of veal shin, hind cut
600ml/1 pint/2½ cups dry white wine
salt and ground black pepper

For the risotto
25g/1oz/2 tbsp butter
1 onion, finely chopped
350g/12oz/1¾ cups risotto rice
1 litre/1¾ pints/4 cups chicken stock
2.5ml/½ tsp saffron threads
60ml/4 tbsp white wine
50g/2oz/⅔ cup freshly grated
    Parmesan cheese

For the gremolata
grated rind of 1 lemon
30ml/2 tbsp chopped fresh parsley
1 garlic clove, finely chopped

1 Heat the butter and oil until sizzling in a large heavy frying pan. Add the onion and leek, and cook gently for about 5 minutes. Season the flour and toss the veal in it, then add to the pan and cook over a high heat until it browns.

2 Gradually stir in the wine and heat until simmering. Cover the pan and simmer for 1½ hours, stirring occasionally. Use a slotted spoon to transfer the veal to a warmed serving dish, then boil the sauce over a high heat until it is reduced and thickened to the required consistency.

3 Make the risotto about 30 minutes before the end of the cooking time for the stew. Melt the butter in a large pan and cook the onion until softened.

4 Stir in the rice to coat all the grains in butter. Add a ladleful of boiling chicken stock and mix well. Continue adding the boiling stock a ladleful at a time, allowing each portion to be completely absorbed before adding the next.

5 Pound the saffron threads in a mortar, then stir in the wine. Add the saffron-scented wine to the risotto and cook for a final 5 minutes. Remove the pan from the heat and stir in the Parmesan.

6 Mix the lemon rind, chopped parsley and garlic together for the gremolata. Spoon some risotto on to each plate, then add some veal. Sprinkle each with a little gremolata and serve immediately.

CITRUS BEEF CURRY

This superbly aromatic Thai-style curry is not too hot but full of flavour. For a special meal, it goes perfectly with fried noodles.

SERVES 4

450g/1lb rump (round) steak
30ml/2 tbsp sunflower oil
30ml/2 tbsp medium curry paste
2 bay leaves
400ml/14fl oz/1⅔ cups coconut milk
300ml/½ pint/1¼ cups beef stock
30ml/2 tbsp lemon juice
45ml/3 tbsp Thai fish sauce
    (*nam pla*)
15ml/1 tbsp sugar
115g/4oz baby (pearl) onions, peeled but
    left whole
225g/8oz new potatoes, halved
115g/4oz/1 cup unsalted roasted peanuts,
    roughly chopped
115g/4oz fine green beans, halved
1 red (bell) pepper, seeded and
    thinly sliced
unsalted roasted peanuts, to
    garnish (optional)

1 Trim any fat off the beef and cut the beef into 5cm/2in strips.

2 Heat the sunflower oil in a large, heavy pan, add the curry paste and cook over a medium heat for 30 seconds, stirring constantly.

3 Add the beef and cook, stirring, for 2 minutes until it is beginning to brown and is thoroughly coated with the spices.

4 Stir in the bay leaves, coconut milk, stock, lemon juice, fish sauce and sugar, and bring to the boil, stirring.

5 Add the onions and potatoes, then bring back to the boil, reduce the heat and simmer, uncovered, for 5 minutes.

6 Stir in the peanuts, beans and pepper and simmer for a further 10 minutes, or until the beef and potatoes are tender. Serve in shallow bowls, with a spoon and fork, to enjoy all the rich and creamy juices. Sprinkle with extra unsalted roasted peanuts, if you like.

SPICED LAMB with TOMATOES and PEPPERS

Select lean tender lamb from the leg for this lightly spiced curry with juicy peppers and wedges of onion. Serve warm naan bread to mop up the tomato-rich juices.

3 Cut two of the onions into wedges (six from each onion) and add to the oil remaining in the pan. Fry the onions over a medium heat for 10 minutes, or until they are beginning to colour. Add the peppers and cook for 5 minutes. Use a slotted spoon to remove the vegetables from the pan and set aside.

4 Meanwhile, chop the remaining onion. Add it to the oil remaining in the pan with the chopped garlic, chilli and ginger, and cook for 4–5 minutes, stirring frequently, until the onion has softened.

5 Stir in the curry paste and canned tomatoes with the reserved yogurt. Return the lamb to the pan, season and stir well. Bring to the boil, then reduce the heat and simmer for 30 minutes.

SERVES 6

1.5kg/3¼lb lean boneless lamb, cubed
250ml/8fl oz/1 cup natural (plain) yogurt
30ml/2 tbsp sunflower oil
3 onions
2 red (bell) peppers, seeded and cut
   into chunks
3 garlic cloves, finely chopped
1 red chilli, seeded and chopped
2.5cm/1in piece fresh root ginger, peeled
   and chopped
30ml/2 tbsp mild curry paste
2 × 400g/14oz cans chopped tomatoes
large pinch of saffron threads
800g/1¾lb plum tomatoes, halved, seeded
   and cut into chunks
salt and ground black pepper
chopped fresh coriander (cilantro),
   to garnish

1 Mix the lamb with the yogurt in a bowl. Cover and chill for about 1 hour.

2 Heat the oil in a large pan. Drain the lamb and reserve the yogurt, then cook the lamb in batches until it is golden on all sides – this will take about 15 minutes in total. Remove the lamb from the pan using a slotted spoon and set aside.

6 Pound the saffron to a powder in a mortar, then stir in a little boiling water to dissolve the saffron. Add this liquid to the curry and stir well. Return the onion and pepper mixture to the pan, then stir in the fresh tomatoes. Bring the curry back to simmering point and cook for 15 minutes. Garnish with chopped fresh coriander to serve.

BRAISED SHOULDER of LAMB with PEARL BARLEY and BABY VEGETABLES

In this wonderful, slow-cooked stew, the pearl barley absorbs all the rich meat juices and stock to become full-flavoured and nutty in texture when cooked.

SERVES 4

60ml/4 tbsp olive oil
1 large onion, chopped
2 garlic cloves, chopped
2 celery sticks, sliced
a little plain (all-purpose) flour
675g/1½lb boned shoulder of lamb, cut
  into cubes
900ml–1 litre/1½–1¾ pints/3¾–4 cups
  lamb stock
115g/4oz/⅔ cup pearl barley
225g/8oz baby carrots
225g/8oz baby turnips
salt and ground black pepper
30ml/2 tbsp chopped fresh marjoram,
  to garnish

1 Heat 45ml/3 tbsp of the oil in a flameproof casserole. Cook the onion and garlic until softened, add the celery, then cook until the vegetables brown.

2 Season the flour and toss the lamb in it. Use a slotted spoon to remove the vegetables from the casserole.

3 Add and heat the remaining oil with the juices in the casserole. Brown the lamb in batches until golden. When all the meat is browned, return it to the casserole with the onion mixture. Stir in 900ml/1½ pints/3¾ cups of the stock. Add the pearl barley. Cover, then bring to the boil, reduce the heat and simmer for 1 hour, or until the pearl barley and lamb are tender.

4 Add the baby carrots and turnips to the casserole for the final 15 minutes of cooking. Stir the meat occasionally during cooking and add the remaining stock, if necessary. Stir in seasoning to taste, and serve piping hot, garnished with marjoram. Warm, crusty bread would make a good accompaniment.

IRISH STEW

Simple and delicious, this is the quintessential Irish main course. Traditionally, mutton chops are used, but as they are harder to find these days you can use lamb instead.

SERVES 4

1.3kg/3lb boneless lamb chops, cut into large chunks
15ml/1 tbsp vegetable oil
3 onions
4 large carrots
900ml/1½ pints/3¾ cups water
4 large potatoes, cut into large chunks
1 large fresh thyme sprig
15g/½oz/1 tbsp unsalted (sweet) butter
15ml/1 tbsp chopped fresh parsley
salt and ground black pepper

1 Trim any fat from the lamb. Heat the oil in a large, flameproof casserole and brown the meat on all sides. Remove from the casserole.

2 Cut the onions into quarters and thickly slice the carrots. Add them to the casserole and cook for 5 minutes, stirring, or until the onions are browned. Return the meat to the pan with the water. Bring to the boil, reduce the heat, cover and simmer for 1 hour.

3 Add the potatoes to the pan with the thyme and cook for a further 1 hour.

4 Leave the stew to settle for a few minutes. Remove the fat from the liquid with a spoon, then stir in the butter and the parsley. Season well before serving.

LAMB and PUMPKIN COUSCOUS

*Pumpkin is a very popular Moroccan ingredient and this is a traditional couscous recipe,
with echoes of the very early vegetable couscous dishes made by the Berbers.*

SERVES 4–6

75g/3oz/½ cup chickpeas, soaked overnight
   and drained
675g/1½lb lean lamb
2 large onions, sliced
pinch of saffron threads
1.5ml/¼ tsp ground ginger
2.5ml/½ tsp ground turmeric
5ml/1 tsp ground black pepper
1.2 litres/2 pints/5 cups water
450g/1lb carrots
675g/1½lb pumpkin
75g/3oz/⅔ cup raisins
400g/14oz/2¼ cups couscous
salt
sprigs of fresh parsley, to garnish

2 Cut the lamb into bitesize pieces and place in the pan with the sliced onions, and add the saffron, ginger, turmeric, pepper and salt. Pour in the water and stir well, then slowly bring to the boil. Cover the pan and simmer for about 1 hour until the meat is tender.

3 Peel or scrape the carrots and cut them into large chunks. Cut the pumpkin into 2.5cm/1in cubes, discarding the skin, seeds and pith.

I Place the chickpeas in a large pan of boiling water. Boil for 10 minutes, then reduce the heat and cook for 1–1½ hours until tender. Place in cold water and remove the skins by rubbing with your fingers. Discard the skins and drain.

4 Stir the carrots, pumpkin and raisins into the meat mixture with the chickpeas, cover the pan and simmer for 30–35 minutes more, stirring occasionally, until the vegetables and meat are completely tender.

5 Meanwhile, prepare the couscous according to the instructions on the packet and steam on top of the stew, then fork lightly to fluff up. Spoon the couscous on to a warmed serving plate, add the stew and stir the stew into the couscous. Extra gravy can be served separately. Sprinkle some tiny sprigs of fresh parsley over the top and serve immediately.

NOISETTES of PORK with CREAMY CALVADOS and APPLE SAUCE

This dish gives the impression of being far more difficult to prepare than it really is, so it is ideal as part of a formal menu to impress guests. Buttered gnocchi or griddled polenta and red cabbage are suitable accompaniments.

SERVES 4

30ml/2 tbsp plain (all-purpose) flour
4 noisettes of pork, about 175g/6oz each,
    firmly tied
25g/1oz/2 tbsp butter
4 baby leeks, finely sliced
5ml/1 tsp mustard seeds,
    coarsely crushed
30ml/2 tbsp Calvados
150ml/¼ pint/⅔ cup dry white wine
2 eating apples, peeled, cored
    and sliced
150ml/¼ pint/⅔ cup double (heavy) cream
30ml/2 tbsp chopped fresh flat
    leaf parsley
salt and ground black pepper

1 Place the flour in a bowl and add plenty of seasoning. Turn the noisettes in the flour mixture to coat them lightly.

2 Melt the butter in a heavy frying pan and cook the noisettes until golden on both sides. Remove from the pan and set aside.

3 Add the leeks to the fat remaining in the pan and cook for 5 minutes. Stir in the mustard seeds and pour in the Calvados, then carefully ignite it to burn off the alcohol. When the flames have died down pour in the wine and replace the pork. Cook gently for 10 minutes, turning the pork frequently.

4 Add the sliced apples to the pan and pour in the cream. Simmer for about 5 minutes, or until the apples are tender and the sauce is thick and creamy. Taste for seasoning, then stir in the chopped fresh parsley and serve immediately.

OSTRICH STEW with SWEET POTATOES and CHICKPEAS

Lean and firm, ostrich meat marries well with the soft-textured sweet potatoes and chickpeas in this quick and easy, rich-flavoured stew.

SERVES 4

45ml/3 tbsp olive oil
1 large onion, chopped
2 garlic cloves, finely chopped
675g/1½lb ostrich fillet, cut into
    short strips
450g/1lb sweet potatoes, peeled
    and diced
2 × 400g/14oz cans chopped tomatoes
400g/14oz can chickpeas, drained
salt and ground black pepper
fresh oregano, to garnish

COOK'S TIP
Steamed couscous is a quick and easy accompaniment to this healthy stew, but it would also be good served with rice, or simply some warm, crusty bread.

1 Heat half the oil in a flameproof casserole. Add the chopped onion and garlic, and cook for about 5 minutes, or until softened but not coloured, stirring occasionally. Remove from the casserole using a slotted spoon and set aside. Add the remaining oil to the casserole and heat.

2 Fry the meat in batches over a high heat until browned. When the last batch is cooked, replace the meat and onions and stir in the potatoes, tomatoes and chickpeas. Bring to the boil, reduce the heat and simmer for 25 minutes, or until the meat is tender. Season and serve, garnished with the fresh oregano.

PANCETTA and BROAD BEAN RISOTTO

This delicious risotto makes a healthy and filling meal, when served with a mixed green salad. Use smoked bacon instead of pancetta, if you like.

SERVES 4

225g/8oz frozen baby broad (fava) beans
15ml/1 tbsp olive oil
1 onion, chopped
2 garlic cloves, finely chopped
175g/6oz smoked pancetta, diced
350g/12oz/1¾ cups risotto rice
1.2 litres/2 pints/5 cups chicken stock
30ml/2 tbsp chopped fresh mixed herbs,
    such as parsley, thyme and oregano
salt and ground black pepper
coarsely chopped fresh parsley, to garnish
shavings of Parmesan cheese, to serve
    (see Cook's Tip)

1 First, cook the broad beans in a large flameproof casserole of lightly salted boiling water for about 3 minutes until tender. Drain and set aside.

2 Heat the olive oil in the casserole. Add the chopped onion, chopped garlic and diced pancetta and cook gently for about 5 minutes, stirring occasionally.

3 Add the rice to the pan and cook for 1 minute, stirring. Add 300ml/½ pint/ 1¼ cups of the stock and simmer, stirring frequently until it has been absorbed.

4 Continue adding the stock, a ladleful at a time, stirring frequently until the rice is just tender and creamy, and almost all of the liquid has been absorbed. This will take 30–35 minutes. It may not be necessary to add all the stock.

5 Stir the beans, mixed herbs and seasoning into the risotto. Heat gently, then serve garnished with the chopped fresh parsley and sprinkled with shavings of Parmesan cheese.

COOK'S TIP
To make thin Parmesan cheese shavings, take a rectangular block or long wedge of Parmesan and firmly scrape a vegetable peeler down the side of the cheese to make shavings. The swivel-bladed type of peeler is best for this job.

RISOTTO with CHICKEN

This is a classic risotto combination of creamy rice and tender cubes of chicken, flavoured with aromatic saffron, prosciutto, white wine and Parmesan cheese.

SERVES 6

30ml/2 tbsp olive oil
225g/8oz skinless, boneless chicken breast
    portions, cut into 2.5cm/1in cubes
1 onion, finely chopped
1 garlic clove, finely chopped
450g/1lb/2¼ cups risotto rice
120ml/4fl oz/½ cup dry white wine
1.5ml/¼ tsp saffron threads
1.75 litres/3 pints/7½ cups simmering
    chicken stock
50g/2oz prosciutto, cut into
    thin strips
25g/1oz/2 tbsp butter, diced
25g/1oz/⅓ cup freshly grated Parmesan
    cheese, plus extra to serve
salt and ground black pepper
sprigs of flat leaf parsley, to garnish

1 Heat the olive oil in a large frying pan over a medium-high heat. Add the cubes of chicken and cook, stirring occasionally with a wooden spoon, until they start to turn white.

2 Reduce the heat to low and add the chopped onion and garlic. Cook, stirring occasionally, until the onion is soft. Stir in the risotto rice, then sauté for 2 minutes, stirring constantly, until all the rice grains are coated in oil.

3 Add the dry white wine to the rice mixture and cook, stirring constantly, until the wine has been absorbed. Add the saffron threads to the simmering stock and stir well, then add ladlefuls of hot stock to the rice mixture, allowing each ladleful to be fully absorbed before adding the next.

4 When the rice is about three-quarters cooked, add the strips of prosciutto and stir well. Continue cooking, stirring occasionally, until the rice is just tender and the risotto is creamy.

5 Add the butter and the Parmesan and stir in well. Season with salt and pepper to taste. Serve the risotto hot, sprinkled with a little more Parmesan, and garnish with flat leaf parsley.

CHICKEN CASSEROLE with WINTER VEGETABLES

A casserole of wonderfully tender chicken, root vegetables and lentils, finished with crème fraîche, mustard and tarragon.

SERVES 4

350g/12oz onions
350g/12oz leeks
225g/8oz carrots
450g/1lb swede (rutabaga)
30ml/2 tbsp oil
4 chicken portions, about 900g/2lb
   total weight
115g/4oz/½ cup green lentils
475ml/16fl oz/2 cups chicken stock
300ml/½ pint/1¼ cups apple juice
10ml/2 tsp cornflour (cornstarch)
45ml/3 tbsp crème fraîche
10ml/2 tsp wholegrain mustard
30ml/2 tbsp chopped fresh tarragon
salt and ground black pepper
fresh tarragon sprigs, to garnish

1 Preheat the oven to 190°C/375°F/ Gas 5. Prepare the onions, leeks, carrots and swede and roughly chop them.

COOK'S TIP
Chop the vegetables into similarly sized pieces so that they cook evenly.

2 Heat the oil in a large flameproof casserole. Season the chicken portions with plenty of salt and pepper and brown them in the hot oil until golden. Drain on kitchen paper.

3 Add the onions to the casserole and cook for 5 minutes, stirring, until they begin to soften and colour. Add the leeks, carrots, swede and lentils to the casserole and stir over a medium heat for 2 minutes.

4 Return the chicken to the pan, then add the stock, apple juice and seasoning. Bring to the boil and cover tightly. Cook in the oven for 50–60 minutes, or until the chicken and lentils are tender.

5 Place the casserole on the stove-top over a medium heat. In a small bowl, blend the cornflour with about 30ml/ 2 tbsp water to make a smooth paste and add to the casserole with the crème fraîche, wholegrain mustard and chopped tarragon. Adjust the seasoning, then simmer gently for about 2 minutes, stirring, until thickened slightly, before serving, garnished with tarragon sprigs.

COQ au VIN

This French country casserole was traditionally made with an old boiling bird, marinated overnight in red wine, then simmered gently until tender. Modern recipes use tender roasting birds to save time and because boiling fowl are not readily available.

SERVES 6

45ml/3 tbsp light olive oil
12 shallots
225g/8oz rindless streaky (fatty) bacon
   rashers (strips), chopped
3 garlic cloves, finely chopped
225g/8oz small mushrooms, halved
6 boneless chicken thighs
3 boneless chicken breast
   portions, halved
1 bottle red wine
salt and ground black pepper
45ml/3 tbsp chopped fresh parsley,
   to garnish

For the bouquet garni
3 sprigs each parsley, thyme and sage
1 bay leaf
4 peppercorns

For the beurre manié
25g/1oz/2 tbsp butter, softened
25g/1oz/¼ cup plain (all-purpose) flour

1 Heat the oil in a large, flameproof casserole and cook the shallots for about 5 minutes, or until golden. Increase the heat, then add the chopped bacon, garlic and mushrooms and cook for a further 10 minutes, stirring frequently.

2 Use a slotted spoon to transfer the cooked ingredients to a plate, then brown the chicken portions in the oil remaining in the pan, turning them until they are golden brown all over. Return the cooked shallots, garlic, mushrooms and bacon to the casserole and pour in the red wine.

3 Tie the ingredients for the bouquet garni in a bundle in a small piece of muslin (cheesecloth) and add to the casserole. Bring to the boil, reduce the heat and cover the casserole with a tightly fitting lid, then simmer for 30–40 minutes.

4 To make the beurre manié, cream the butter and flour together in a small bowl using your fingers or a spoon to make a smooth paste.

5 Add small lumps of the beurre manié paste to the bubbling casserole, stirring well until each piece has melted into the liquid before adding the next. When all the paste has been added, bring the casserole back to the boil and simmer for 5 minutes.

6 Season the casserole to taste with salt and pepper and serve garnished with chopped fresh parsley and accompanied by boiled potatoes.

CHICKEN with CHICKPEAS and ALMONDS

The almonds in this tasty Moroccan-style recipe are pre-cooked until soft, adding an interesting texture and flavour to the chicken.

SERVES 4

75g/3oz/½ cup blanched almonds
75g/3oz/½ cup chickpeas, soaked overnight
   and drained
4 part-boned chicken breast portions, skinned
50g/2oz/4 tbsp butter
2.5ml/½ tsp saffron threads
2 Spanish onions, finely sliced
900ml/1½ pints/3¾ cups chicken stock
1 small cinnamon stick
60ml/4 tbsp chopped fresh flat leaf
   parsley, plus extra to garnish
lemon juice, to taste
salt and ground black pepper

1 Place the blanched almonds and the soaked and drained chickpeas in a large flameproof casserole of water and bring to the boil. Boil for 10 minutes, then reduce the heat. Simmer for 1–1½ hours until the chickpeas are soft. Drain the chickpeas and almonds and set aside.

2 Place the skinned chicken pieces in the casserole, together with the butter, half of the saffron, and salt and plenty of black pepper. Heat gently, stirring, until the butter has melted.

3 Add the onions and stock, bring to the boil, then add the reserved cooked almonds, chickpeas and cinnamon stick. Cover with a tightly fitting lid and cook very gently for 45–60 minutes until the chicken is completely tender.

4 Transfer the cooked chicken to a serving plate and keep warm. Bring the sauce to the boil and cook over a high heat until it is well reduced, stirring frequently with a wooden spoon.

5 Add the chopped parsley and remaining saffron to the casserole and cook for a further 2–3 minutes. Sharpen the sauce with a little lemon juice, then pour the sauce over the chicken and serve, garnished with extra fresh parsley.

CHICKEN with TOMATOES and HONEY

A thick tomato and honey sauce coats chicken pieces in this subtly spiced dish.

SERVES 4

30ml/2 tbsp sunflower oil
25g/1oz/2 tbsp butter
4 chicken quarters
1 onion, grated or very finely chopped
1 garlic clove, crushed
5ml/1 tsp ground cinnamon
good pinch of ground ginger
1.3–1.6kg/3–3½lb tomatoes, peeled,
   cored and roughly chopped
30ml/2 tbsp clear honey
50g/2oz/⅓ cup blanched almonds
15ml/1 tbsp sesame seeds
salt and ground black pepper
chopped flat leaf parsley, to garnish

1 Place the oil and butter in a large, flameproof casserole. Add the chicken and cook over a medium heat for about 3 minutes until it is lightly browned.

2 Add the grated or chopped onion, garlic, cinnamon, ginger, tomatoes and plenty of seasoning, and heat gently until the tomatoes begin to bubble.

3 Lower the heat and then cover the casserole. Simmer very gently for about 1 hour, stirring and turning the chicken occasionally, or until it is completely cooked through.

4 Lift out the chicken pieces and transfer them to a plate. Increase the heat and cook the tomato sauce until it is reduced to a thick purée, stirring frequently. Stir in the honey, cook for 1 minute, then return the chicken pieces to the pan and cook for 2–3 minutes to heat through.

5 Transfer the chicken and sauce to a warmed serving dish and sprinkle with the blanched almonds and sesame seeds. Serve hot, garnished with parsley.

COOK'S TIP
To blanch whole almonds, place them in a strainer and lower it into boiling water. Cook the almonds for 2–3 minutes, then remove the strainer from the water. Pinch the softened almond skin between your thumb and finger to squeeze it off.

HUNTER'S CHICKEN

This traditional dish sometimes has strips of green pepper in the sauce instead of the mushrooms. Creamed potato or polenta makes a good accompaniment.

SERVES 4

15g/½oz/¼ cup dried porcini mushrooms
30ml/2 tbsp olive oil
15g/½oz/1 tbsp butter
4 chicken portions, on the bone, skinned
1 large onion, thinly sliced
400g/14oz can chopped tomatoes
150ml/¼ pint/⅔ cup red wine
1 garlic clove, crushed
leaves of 1 fresh rosemary sprg,
    finely chopped
115g/4oz/1¾ cups fresh field (portabello)
    mushrooms, thinly sliced
salt and ground black pepper
fresh rosemary sprigs, to garnish

2 Heat the oil and butter in a large, flameproof casserole until foaming. Add the chicken portions and sauté over a medium heat for 5 minutes, or until golden brown. Remove the pieces and drain on kitchen paper.

3 Add the sliced onion and chopped porcini mushrooms to the pan. Cook gently, stirring frequently, for about 3 minutes until the onion has softened but not browned. Stir in the chopped tomatoes, red wine and reserved mushroom soaking liquid, then add the crushed garlic and chopped rosemary, with salt and pepper to taste. Bring to the boil, stirring constantly.

4 Return the chicken to the casserole and turn to coat with the sauce. Cover with a tightly fitting lid and simmer gently for 30 minutes.

1 Put the porcini in a bowl, add 250ml/ 8fl oz/1 cup warm water and soak for 20 minutes. Squeeze the porcini over the bowl, strain the liquid and reserve. Finely chop the porcini.

5 Add the fresh mushrooms to the casserole and stir well to mix into the sauce. Continue simmering gently for 10 minutes, or until the chicken is tender. Taste for seasoning. Serve hot, with creamed potato or polenta, if you like. Garnish with the rosemary sprigs.

SEVILLE CHICKEN

*Oranges and almonds are a favourite ingredient in southern Spain, especially around
Seville, where the orange and almond trees are a familiar and wonderful sight.*

SERVES 4

1 orange
8 chicken thighs
plain (all-purpose) flour, seasoned with salt
   and pepper
45ml/3 tbsp olive oil
1 large Spanish onion, roughly chopped
2 garlic cloves, crushed
1 red (bell) pepper, seeded and sliced
1 yellow (bell) pepper, seeded
   and sliced
115g/4oz chorizo, sliced
50g/2oz/½ cup flaked (sliced) almonds
225g/8oz/generous 1 cup brown
   basmati rice
about 600ml/1 pint/2½ cups chicken or
   vegetable stock
400g/14oz can chopped tomatoes
175ml/6fl oz/¾ cup white wine
generous pinch of dried thyme
salt and ground black pepper
fresh thyme sprigs, to garnish

1 Pare a thin strip of peel from the
orange using a vegetable peeler and set
it aside. Peel the orange, then cut it into
even segments, working over a bowl to
catch any excess juice. Dust the chicken
thighs with plenty of seasoned flour.

2 Heat the olive oil in a large frying pan
and fry the chicken pieces on both sides
until nicely brown. Transfer the browned
chicken to a plate. Add the chopped
onion and crushed garlic to the pan and
fry for 4–5 minutes until the onion
begins to brown. Add the sliced red
and yellow peppers to the pan and fry,
stirring occasionally with a wooden
spoon, until they are slightly softened.

3 Add the chorizo, stir-fry for a few
minutes, then sprinkle over the almonds
and rice. Cook, stirring, for 1–2 minutes.

4 Pour in the chicken or vegetable stock,
chopped tomatoes and white wine, then
add the reserved orange peel and the
dried thyme. Season well. Bring the
sauce to simmering point, stirring, then
return the chicken to the pan.

5 Cover tightly and cook over a very
low heat for 1–1¼ hours until the rice
and chicken are tender. Just before
serving, add the orange segments and
juice, and allow to cook briefly to heat
through. Season to taste, garnish with
sprigs of fresh thyme and serve.

MEDITERRANEAN DUCK with HARISSA and SAFFRON

Harissa is a fiery chilli sauce from north Africa. Mixed with cinnamon, saffron and preserved lemon, it gives this colourful casserole an unforgettable flavour.

SERVES 4

15ml/1 tbsp olive oil
1.8–2kg/4–4½lb duck, quartered
1 large onion, thinly sliced
1 garlic clove, crushed
2.5ml/½ tsp ground cumin
400ml/14fl oz/1⅔ cups duck or
   chicken stock
juice of ½ lemon
5–10ml/1–2 tsp harissa
1 cinnamon stick
5ml/1 tsp saffron threads
50g/2oz/⅓ cup black olives
50g/2oz/⅓ cup green olives
peel of 1 preserved lemon, rinsed, drained
   and cut into fine strips
2–3 lemon slices
30ml/2 tbsp chopped fresh coriander
   (cilantro), plus extra leaves
    to garnish
salt and ground black pepper

1 Heat the oil in a flameproof casserole. Add the duck quarters and cook until browned all over. Remove the duck with a slotted spoon and set aside. Add the onion and garlic to the oil remaining in the casserole and cook for 5 minutes until soft. Add the ground cumin and cook, stirring, for 2 minutes.

COOK'S TIP
The term "duck" refers to birds over two months old. The rich flavour of duck is best appreciated when a duck reaches its full-grown size. Look for a duck with a supple, waxy skin with a dry appearance. It should have a long body with tender, meaty breasts.

2 Pour in the stock and lemon juice, then add the harissa, cinnamon and saffron. Bring to the boil. Return the duck to the casserole and add the olives, preserved lemon peel and lemon slices. Season with salt and pepper.

3 Lower the heat, partially cover the casserole and simmer gently for about 45 minutes, or until the duck is cooked through. Discard the cinnamon stick. Stir in the chopped coriander and garnish with the coriander leaves.

CHICKEN and PRAWN JAMBALAYA

*This colourful mixture of rice, peppers and tomatoes with chicken, gammon and prawns is
flavoured with garlic and fresh herbs and a few dashes of fiery Tabasco sauce. It's an
ideal dish for big family gatherings and celebrations.*

SERVES 10

2 chickens, each about 1.3–1.6kg/3–3½lb
450g/1lb piece raw smoked gammon
    (smoked or cured ham)
50g/2oz/⅓ cup lard or
    bacon fat
50g/2oz/½ cup plain (all-purpose) flour
3 onions, finely sliced
2 green (bell) peppers, seeded and sliced
675g/1½lb tomatoes, peeled and chopped
2–3 garlic cloves, crushed
10ml/2 tsp chopped fresh thyme or
    5ml/1 tsp dried thyme
24 raw Mediterranean prawns (jumbo
    shrimp), peeled with tails intact
500g/1¼lb/2½ cups white long grain rice
1.2 litres/2 pints/5 cups water
2–3 dashes Tabasco sauce
45ml/3 tbsp chopped fresh flat leaf parsley,
    plus tiny fresh parsley sprigs to garnish
salt and ground black pepper

4 Add the diced gammon, onions, green
peppers, tomatoes, garlic and thyme and
stir well to mix. Cook, stirring regularly,
for about 10 minutes, then add the
prawns and mix lightly.

5 Stir the rice into the frying pan and
pour in the water. Season well with salt,
black pepper and Tabasco sauce. Bring
to the boil, then cook gently, stirring
occasionally, until the rice is tender and
all the liquid has been fully absorbed.
Add a little extra boiling water if the rice
looks like drying out before it is cooked.
Check the seasoning and add salt,
pepper and more Tabasco if necessary.

6 Mix the chopped fresh flat leaf parsley
into the finished dish, garnish with tiny
sprigs of flat leaf parsley and serve the
jambalaya immediately with plenty of
crusty bread.

1 Cut each chicken into ten pieces and
season the pieces well with salt and
pepper. Dice the gammon, discarding
the rind and fat.

2 Melt the lard or bacon fat in a large,
heavy frying pan. Add the chicken pieces
in several batches, cook them until they
are golden brown all over, then lift
them out with a slotted spoon and
set them aside.

3 Reduce the heat. Sprinkle the flour
into the fat in the pan and stir with a
wooden spoon until the roux turns a
golden brown colour. Return the chicken
pieces to the pan.

GROUSE with ORCHARD FRUIT STUFFING

Tart apples, plums and pears make a fabulous orchard fruit stuffing that complements the rich gamey flavour of grouse perfectly.

SERVES 2

juice of ½ lemon
2 young grouse
50g/2oz/¼ cup butter
4 Swiss chard leaves
50ml/2fl oz/¼ cup Marsala
salt and ground black pepper

For the stuffing
2 shallots, finely chopped
1 tart cooking apple, peeled, cored
   and chopped
1 pear, peeled, cored and chopped
2 plums, halved, stoned (pitted)
   and chopped
large pinch of mixed (apple pie) spice

1 Sprinkle the lemon juice over the grouse and season well. Melt half the butter in a flameproof casserole, add the grouse and cook for 10 minutes, or until browned. Use tongs to remove the grouse from the casserole and set aside.

2 Add the shallots to the fat remaining in the casserole and cook until softened but not coloured. Add the apple, pear, plums and mixed spice, and cook for about 5 minutes, or until the fruits are just beginning to soften. Remove the casserole from the heat and spoon the hot fruit mixture into the body cavities of the birds.

3 Truss the birds neatly with string. Smear the remaining butter over the birds and wrap them in the chard leaves, then replace them in the casserole.

4 Pour in the Marsala and heat until simmering. Cover tightly and simmer for 20 minutes, or until the birds are tender, taking care not to overcook them. Leave to rest in a warm place for about 10 minutes before serving.

COOK'S TIP
There isn't a lot of liquid in the casserole for cooking the birds – they are steamed rather than boiled, so it is very important that the casserole has a heavy base and a tight-fitting lid, otherwise the liquid may evaporate and the chard will burn on the base of the pan.

SPICY VENISON CASSEROLE

Being low in fat but high in flavour, venison is an excellent choice for healthy, yet rich, casseroles. Cranberries and orange bring a festive fruitiness to this spicy recipe. Serve with small baked potatoes and green vegetables.

SERVES 4

15ml/1 tbsp olive oil
1 onion, chopped
2 celery sticks, sliced
10ml/2 tsp ground allspice
15ml/1 tbsp plain (all-purpose) flour
675g/1½lb stewing venison, cubed
225g/8oz fresh or frozen cranberries
grated rind and juice of 1 orange
900ml/1½ pints/3¾ cups beef or
    venison stock
salt and ground black pepper

1 Heat the oil in a flameproof casserole. Add the onion and celery and fry for about 5 minutes, or until softened.

2 Meanwhile, mix the ground allspice with the flour and either spread the mixture out on a large plate or place in a large plastic bag. Toss a few pieces of venison at a time (to prevent them becoming soggy) in the flour mixture until they are all lightly coated. Spread the floured venison out on a large plate until ready to cook.

3 When the onion and celery are just softened, remove them from the casserole using a slotted spoon and set aside. Add the venison pieces to the casserole in batches and cook until well browned and sealed on all sides.

COOK'S TIP
Freshly made stock is always best, but if you are short of time, look for cartons or tubs of fresh stock in the chilled food cabinets of large supermarkets.

4 Add the cranberries and the orange rind and juice to the casserole along with the stock, and stir well. Return the vegetables and the browned venison to the casserole and heat until simmering. Cover tightly and reduce the heat.

5 Simmer for about 45 minutes, or until the venison is tender, stirring occasionally. Season the venison casserole to taste with salt and pepper before serving.

VARIATIONS
Farmed venison is increasingly easy to find and is available from good butchers and many large supermarkets. It makes a rich and flavourful stew, but lean pork or braising steak could be used in place of the venison, if you prefer. You could also replace the cranberries with pitted and halved ready-to-eat prunes and, for extra flavour, use either ale or stout instead of about half the stock.

VENISON SAUSAGES with RED WINE GRAVY

Strongly flavoured, meaty sausages are delicious with a robust red wine gravy flavoured with assertive shiitake mushrooms. Serve with soft polenta, mashed potatoes or plenty of thickly sliced crusty bread to mop up the delicious gravy.

SERVES 4

15ml/1 tbsp sunflower oil (optional)
12 venison or wild boar sausages
2 leeks, sliced
2 plump garlic cloves, sliced
225g/8oz/3 cups shiitake
    mushrooms, quartered
15ml/1 tbsp plain (all-purpose) flour
600ml/1 pint/2½ cups red wine
30ml/2 tbsp chopped mixed fresh herbs,
    such as flat leaf parsley and marjoram
salt and ground black pepper

1 Pour the sunflower oil, if using, into a large frying pan, add the venison or wild boar sausages and cook over a medium heat for 15–20 minutes, turning frequently.

2 Add the leeks, garlic and mushrooms and mix well. Cook the vegetables for 10–15 minutes, or until the leeks are soft and beginning to brown.

3 Sprinkle in the flour and gradually pour in the red wine, stirring with a wooden spoon and pushing the sausages around to mix the flour and the liquid smoothly with the leeks.

4 Bring slowly to the boil, reduce the heat and simmer for 10–15 minutes, stirring occasionally, or until the gravy is smooth and glossy. Season the gravy with salt and pepper to taste and then sprinkle the mixed herbs over the sausages. Serve immediately with polenta or mashed potatoes.

COOK'S TIP
Shiitake mushrooms have a slightly floury-looking medium to dark grey-brown cap. They have a firm and meaty texture that becomes silky when cooked. The stalks can be tough so discard if necessary.

RABBIT with RED WINE and PRUNES

This is a favourite French dish and is often found on the menus of small country restaurants. It has a wonderfully rich flovour and the prunes add a delicious sweetness to the sauce. Serve with crisp, golden sautéed potatoes.

SERVES 4

8 rabbit portions
30ml/2 tbsp vegetable oil
2 onions, finely chopped
2 garlic cloves, finely chopped
60ml/4 tbsp Armagnac or brandy
300ml/½ pint/1¼ cups dry red wine
5ml/1 tsp soft light brown sugar
16 ready-to-eat prunes
150ml/¼ pint/⅔ cup double (heavy) cream
salt and ground black pepper

VARIATIONS
• Chicken can also be cooked in this way. Use 4 chicken drumsticks and 4 thighs in place of the rabbit portions.
• The prunes can be replaced with ready-to-eat dried apricots if you prefer – these go well with the rabbit and particularly well with chicken.

1 Season the rabbit portions liberally with salt and pepper. Heat the vegetable oil in a large, flameproof casserole and fry the rabbit portions in batches until they are golden brown on all sides.

2 Remove the browned rabbit portions from the casserole, add the chopped onion and garlic, and cook, stirring occasionally, until the onion is softened.

3 Return the rabbit to the casserole, add the Armagnac or brandy and ignite it. When the flames have died down, pour in the wine. Stir in the sugar and prunes, cover and simmer for 30 minutes.

4 Remove the rabbit from the casserole and keep warm. Add the cream to the sauce and simmer for 3–5 minutes, then season to taste and serve immediately.

OVEN-COOKED MEAT, POULTRY AND GAME

Nothing quite matches the flavour of meat that has

simmered in the oven for hours with tasty root

vegetables and aromatic herbs, especially when

a little beer or wine has been poured into the pot,

as in Pot-roast Beef with Guinness, Chicken with

Forty Cloves of Garlic, or Marinated Pigeon in Red

Wine. Equally delicious are sustaining stews, such as

Boeuf Bourguignon and Braised Lamb with Apricots

and Herb Dumplings.

SLOW-BAKED BEEF with a POTATO CRUST

*This recipe makes the most of braising beef by marinating it in red wine and topping it
with a cheesy grated potato crust that bakes to a golden, crunchy consistency.*

SERVES 4

675g/1½lb stewing beef, diced
300ml/½ pint/1¼ cups red wine
3 juniper berries, crushed
pared strip of orange peel
30ml/2 tbsp olive oil
2 onions, cut into chunks
2 carrots, cut into chunks
1 garlic clove, crushed
225g/8oz/3 cups button
   (white) mushrooms
150ml/¼ pint/⅔ cup beef stock
30ml/2 tbsp cornflour (cornstarch)
salt and ground black pepper

For the crust
450g/1lb potatoes, grated
15ml/1 tbsp olive oil
30ml/2 tbsp creamed horseradish
50g/2oz/½ cup grated mature (sharp)
   Cheddar cheese
salt and ground black pepper

1 Place the diced beef in a non-metallic
bowl. Add the wine, juniper berries and
orange peel and season with pepper. Mix
the ingredients together, then cover and
leave to marinate for at least 4 hours or
overnight if possible.

COOK'S TIP
Use a large-holed, coarse grater on the
food processor for the potatoes. They
will hold their shape better while being
blanched than if you use a finer blade.

2 Preheat the oven to 160°C/325°F/
Gas 3. Drain the diced stewing beef,
reserving the marinade.

3 Heat the oil in a large flameproof
casserole and fry the meat in batches for
5 minutes to brown and seal. Add the
onions, carrots and garlic and cook for
5 minutes. Stir in the mushrooms, red
wine marinade and beef stock.

4 Mix the cornflour with water to make
a smooth paste and stir into the beef
mixture. Season, cover and cook in the
oven for 1½ hours.

5 Prepare the crust about 45 minutes
before the end of the cooking time for
the beef. Start by blanching the grated
potatoes in boiling water for 5 minutes.
Drain well and then squeeze out all the
extra liquid.

6 Stir in the olive oil, horseradish, grated
cheese and seasoning, then sprinkle the
mixture evenly over the surface of the
beef. Increase the oven temperature
to 200°C/400°F/Gas 6 and cook for a
further 30 minutes until the potato crust
is crisp and lightly browned.

POT-ROAST BEEF with GUINNESS

This heart-warming, rich pot-roast is ideal for a winter supper. Brisket of beef has the best flavour but this dish works equally well with rolled silverside or topside.

SERVES 6

30ml/2 tbsp vegetable oil
900g/2lb rolled brisket of beef
275g/10oz onions, roughly chopped
2 celery sticks, thickly sliced
450g/1lb carrots, cut into large chunks
675g/1½lb potatoes, peeled and cut into
    large chunks
30ml/2 tbsp plain (all-purpose) flour
475ml/16fl oz/2 cups beef stock
300ml/½ pint/1¼ cups Guinness
1 bay leaf
45ml/3 tbsp chopped fresh thyme
5ml/1 tsp soft light brown sugar
30ml/2 tbsp wholegrain mustard
15ml/1 tbsp tomato purée (paste)
salt and ground black pepper

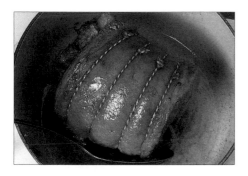

1 Preheat the oven to 180°C/350°F/ Gas 4. Heat the oil in a large flameproof casserole and brown the meat all over until golden.

3 Add the celery, carrot and potato to the casserole and cook over a medium heat for 2–3 minutes, or until they are just beginning to colour.

5 Add the bay leaf, thyme, sugar, mustard, tomato purée and plenty of seasoning. Place the meat on top, cover tightly and transfer to the oven.

2 Remove the meat from the pan and drain it on a double layer of kitchen paper. Add the chopped onions to the pan and cook for about 4 minutes, or until they are just beginning to soften and turn brown, stirring all the time.

4 Stir in the flour and cook for a further 1 minute stirring continuously. Pour in the beef stock and the Guinness and stir until well combined. Bring the sauce to the boil, stirring continuously with a wooden spoon.

6 Cook for about 2½ hours, or until the vegetables and meat are tender. Adjust the seasoning and add another pinch of sugar, if necessary. To serve, remove the meat and carve into thick slices. Serve with the vegetables and plenty of gravy.

CLAY-POT BEEF with RED PEPPERS

Using a clay pot to cook lean meat keeps it moist and juicy. Here it is cooked with sweet peppers and onion in a rich red wine sauce.

SERVES 6

1.2kg/2½lb top rump (round) steak
  or silverside (pot roast) of beef,
  neatly tied
2 garlic cloves
30ml/2 tbsp sunflower oil
1 large onion, chopped
300ml/½ pint/1¼ cups beef stock
15ml/1 tbsp tomato purée (paste)
150ml/¼ pint/⅔ cup red wine
bouquet garni
4 sweet romano red (bell) peppers, halved
  lengthwise and seeded
15ml/1 tbsp butter, softened
15ml/1 tbsp plain (all-purpose) flour
salt and ground black pepper

1 Soak the clay pot in cold water for 20 minutes, then drain. Using a sharp knife, make about 20 small incisions in the beef. Cut the garlic cloves into thin slivers and insert into the cuts.

2 Season the beef with salt and pepper. Heat the sunflower oil in a large frying pan, add the beef and cook, stirring frequently with a wooden spoon until browned on all sides. Remove the beef from the pan and set aside.

3 Add the onion to the frying pan and fry gently for 5–8 minutes, stirring occasionally, until light golden. Transfer the onion to the clay pot.

4 Place the beef on top of the onion in the clay pot, then mix together the beef stock, tomato purée and wine and pour over the beef.

5 Add the bouquet garni to the pot, then cover the pot and place it in an unheated oven. Set the oven to 200°C/400°F/Gas 6 and cook for 1 hour. Uncover, baste the meat and add the pepper halves, arranging them around the meat. Cook uncovered for a further 45 minutes until the beef is tender, basting occasionally.

6 To serve, transfer the beef to a large warmed serving dish with the peppers and onion. Drain the juices from the clay pot into a pan and heat gently.

7 Blend together the butter and flour to make a smooth paste, then gradually add small pieces of the paste to the sauce, whisking until well blended. Bring the sauce to the boil and simmer gently for about 1 minute, whisking all the time, until the sauce is thickened slightly. Pour into a sauce boat and serve with the beef and vegetables.

VARIATIONS
Romano peppers are an elongated variety that are available in large supermarkets. If you can't find them, use ordinary bell-shaped peppers instead – the dish will be just as good. If you prefer, use green, orange or yellow peppers in place of red.

COOK'S TIPS
• The butter and flour paste used in step 7 to thicken the sauce is known as a beurre manié. The paste is always made from equal quantities of plain flour and softened butter. It is used for thickening casseroles, sauces and occasionally soups.
• A bouquet garni is a selection of aromatic herbs used to flavour soups, stocks or casseroles. The most widely used herbs include thyme, parsley, rosemary and bay leaves. Fresh herbs can be tied together with string or dried herbs can be wrapped in a small muslin (cheesecloth) square and secured with string. Ready-made bouquet garnis of dried herbs are sold in many supermarkets.

BEEF CARBONADE

This rich, dark stew of beef cooked slowly with lots of onions, garlic and beer is a classic casserole from the north of France and neighbouring Belgium.

SERVES 6

45ml/3 tbsp vegetable oil or beef dripping
3 onions, sliced
45ml/3 tbsp plain (all-purpose) flour
2.5ml/½ tsp mustard powder
1kg/2¼lb stewing beef (shin, shank or chuck), cut into large cubes
2–3 garlic cloves, finely chopped
300ml/½ pint/1¼ cups dark beer or ale
150ml/¼ pint/⅔ cup water
5ml/1 tsp dark brown sugar
1 fresh thyme sprig
1 fresh bay leaf
1 celery stick
salt and ground black pepper

For the topping
50g/2oz/¼ cup butter
1 garlic clove, crushed
15ml/1 tbsp Dijon mustard
45ml/3 tbsp chopped fresh parsley
6–12 slices of French baguette

1 Preheat the oven to 160°C/325°F/Gas 3. Heat 30ml/2 tbsp of the oil or dripping in a pan and cook the onions over a low heat until softened. Remove from the pan and set aside.

2 Meanwhile, mix together the flour and mustard and season. Toss the beef in the flour. Add the remaining oil or dripping to the pan and heat over a high heat. Brown the beef all over, then transfer it to a deep, earthenware baking dish.

3 Reduce the heat and return the onions to the pan. Add the garlic, cook briefly, then add the beer or ale, water and sugar. Tie the thyme and bay leaf together and add to the pan with the celery. Bring to the boil, stirring, then season with salt and pepper.

4 Pour the sauce over the beef and mix well. Cover tightly, then place in the oven and cook for 2½ hours. Check the beef once or twice to make sure that it is not too dry, adding a little extra water, if necessary. Test for tenderness, allowing an extra 30–40 minutes' cooking time if necessary.

5 To make the topping, beat together the butter, crushed garlic, Dijon mustard and 30ml/2 tbsp of the chopped fresh parsley. Spread the flavoured butter thickly over the bread. Increase the oven temperature to 190°C/375°F/Gas 5. Taste and season the stew, then arrange the prepared bread slices, buttered side uppermost, on top. Bake for 20 minutes, or until the bread is browned and crisp. Sprinkle the remaining chopped fresh parsley over the top to garnish and serve immediately.

BOEUF BOURGUIGNON

The classic French dish of beef cooked in Burgundy style, with red wine, small pieces of bacon, shallots and mushrooms, is baked for several hours at a low temperature.

SERVES 6

175g/6oz rindless streaky (fatty) bacon
    rashers (strips), chopped
900g/2lb lean braising steak, such as top
    rump (round) steak
30ml/2 tbsp plain (all-purpose) flour
45ml/3 tbsp sunflower oil
25g/1oz/2 tbsp butter
12 shallots
2 garlic cloves, crushed
175g/6oz/2⅓ cups mushrooms, sliced
450ml/¾ pint/scant 2 cups robust
    red wine
150ml/¼ pint/⅔ cup beef stock
    or consommé
1 bay leaf
2 sprigs each of fresh thyme, parsley
    and marjoram
salt and ground black pepper

1 Preheat the oven to 160°C/325°F/ Gas 3. Heat a large flameproof casserole, then add the bacon and cook, stirring occasionally, until the pieces are crisp and golden brown.

2 Meanwhile, cut the beef into 2.5cm/ 1in cubes. Season the flour and use to coat the meat. Use a slotted spoon to remove the bacon from the casserole and set aside. Add and heat the oil, then brown the beef in batches and set aside with the bacon.

COOK'S TIP
Beef consommé, which can be used as an alternative to beef stock in this recipe, is a clear, light soup. It is sold in cans, or in cartons as a fresh soup. Fresh beef stock is also available in cartons.

3 Add the butter to the fat remaining in the casserole. Cook the shallots and garlic until they are just beginning to colour, then add the mushrooms and cook for a further 5 minutes. Return the bacon and beef to the casserole, and stir in the wine and stock or consommé. Tie the herbs together into a bouquet garni and add to the casserole.

4 Cover and cook in the oven for 1½ hours, or until the meat is tender, stirring once or twice during the cooking time. Season to taste and serve the casserole with creamy mashed root vegetables, such as celeriac and potatoes.

COOK'S TIP
Boeuf Bourguignon freezes very well. Transfer the mixture to a dish so that it cools quickly, then pour it into a rigid plastic container. Push all the cubes of meat down into the sauce or they will dry out. Freeze for up to 2 months. Thaw overnight in the refrigerator, then transfer to a flameproof casserole and add 150ml/ ¼ pint/⅔ cup water. Stir well, then bring to the boil, stirring occasionally, and simmer steadily for at least 10 minutes, or until the meat is piping hot.

BEEF HOTPOT with HERB DUMPLINGS

Tender chunks of beef braised in beer, flavoured with shallots and mushrooms and finished with parsley- and thyme-flavoured dumplings.

SERVES 4

20g/¾oz/⅓ cup dried porcini mushrooms
60ml/4 tbsp warm water
40g/1½oz/3 tbsp butter
30ml/2 tbsp sunflower oil
115g/4oz/⅔ cup lardons or cubed pancetta
900g/2lb lean braising steak, cut
   into chunks
45ml/3 tbsp plain (all-purpose) flour
450ml/¾ pint/scant 2 cups beer
450ml/¾ pint/scant 2 cups beef stock
bouquet garni
8 shallots
175g/6oz/2 cups button (white) mushrooms
salt and ground black pepper
sprigs of thyme, to garnish

For the herb dumplings
115g/4oz/1 cup self-raising
   (self-rising) flour
50g/2oz/scant ½ cup shredded suet
2.5ml/½ tsp salt
2.5ml/½ tsp mustard powder
15ml/1 tbsp chopped fresh parsley
15ml/1 tbsp chopped fresh thyme

1 Soak a clay pot in cold water for 20 minutes, then drain. Place the porcini mushrooms in a bowl, add the warm water and leave to soak. In a frying pan, melt half the butter with half the oil, add the lardons or pancetta and quickly brown. Remove with a slotted spoon and transfer to the clay pot.

2 Add the beef to the frying pan and brown in batches, then, using a slotted spoon, transfer to the clay pot. Sprinkle the flour into the fat remaining in the frying pan and stir well.

3 Stir the beer and stock into the flour and bring to the boil, stirring constantly. Strain the mushroom soaking liquid and add to the frying pan along with the porcini. Season well. Pour the sauce over the meat in the clay pot, then add the bouquet garni. Cover the pot and place in an unheated oven. Set the oven to 200°C/400°F/Gas 6. Cook for 30 minutes, then reduce the oven temperature to 160°C/325°F/Gas 3 and cook for a further 1 hour.

4 Heat the remaining butter and oil in a frying pan and cook the shallots until golden. Remove and set aside. Add the button mushrooms and sauté for 2–3 minutes. Stir the shallots and mushrooms into the pot and cook for 30 minutes.

5 In a bowl, mix together the dumpling ingredients with sufficient cold water to bind to a soft, sticky dough. Divide into 12 small balls and place on top of the hotpot. Cover and cook for 25 minutes.

BLACK BEAN CHILLI CON CARNE

Fresh green and dried red chillies add plenty of fire to this classic Tex-Mex dish of tender beef cooked in a spicy tomato sauce.

SERVES 6

225g/8oz/1¼ cups dried black beans
500g/1¼lb braising steak
30ml/2 tbsp vegetable oil
2 onions, chopped
1 garlic clove, crushed
1 fresh green chilli, seeded and
   finely chopped
15ml/1 tbsp paprika
10ml/2 tsp ground cumin
10ml/2 tsp ground coriander
400g/14oz can chopped tomatoes
300ml/½ pint/1¼ cups beef stock
1 dried red chilli, crumbled
5ml/1 tsp hot pepper sauce
1 fresh red (bell) pepper, seeded and chopped
salt
fresh coriander (cilantro), to garnish
boiled rice, to serve

1 Put the beans in a large pan. Add enough cold water to cover them, bring to the boil and boil vigorously for about 10 minutes. Drain, tip into a clean bowl, cover with cold water and leave to soak for about 8 hours or overnight.

2 Preheat the oven to 150°C/300°F/ Gas 2. Cut the braising steak into small dice. Heat the vegetable oil in a large, flameproof casserole. Add the chopped onion, crushed garlic and chopped green chilli and cook them gently for 5 minutes until soft, using a slotted spoon to transfer the mixture to a plate.

3 Increase the heat to high, add the meat to the casserole and brown on all sides, then stir in the paprika, ground cumin and ground coriander.

4 Add the tomatoes, beef stock, dried chilli and hot pepper sauce. Drain the beans and add them to the casserole, with enough water to cover. Bring to simmering point, cover and cook in the oven for 2 hours. Stir occasionally and add extra water, if necessary.

5 Season the casserole with salt and add the chopped red pepper. Replace the lid, return the casserole to the oven and cook for 30 minutes more, or until the meat and beans are tender. Sprinkle over the fresh coriander and serve with rice.

COOK'S TIP
Red kidney beans are traditionally used in chilli con carne, but in this recipe black beans are used instead. They are the same shape and size as red kidney beans but have a shiny black skin. They are also known as Mexican or Spanish black beans.

VARIATION
Use minced (ground) beef in place of the braising steak.

ROAST LAMB with BEANS and GREEN PEPPERCORNS

Roasting the lamb slowly on a bed of beans results in a dish that combines meltingly tender meat with vegetables all in one pot.

SERVES 6

8–10 garlic cloves, peeled
1.8–2kg/4–4½lb leg of lamb
30ml/2 tbsp olive oil
400g/14oz spinach leaves
400g/14oz can flageolet, cannellini or
   haricot (navy) beans, drained
400g/14oz can butter (lima) beans, drained
2 large, fresh rosemary sprigs, plus extra
   to garnish
15–30ml/1–2 tbsp drained, bottled
   green peppercorns

1 Preheat the oven to 150°C/300°F/ Gas 2. Set four garlic cloves aside and slice the rest lengthwise into three or four pieces. Make shallow slits in the skin of the lamb and insert a piece of garlic in each.

2 Heat the olive oil in a heavy, shallow flameproof casserole or a roasting pan that is large enough to hold the leg of lamb. Add the reserved garlic cloves and the fresh spinach leaves to the casserole or pan and cook over a medium heat, stirring occasionally, for 4–5 minutes, or until the spinach is wilted.

3 Add the beans and tuck the rosemary sprigs and peppercorns among them. Place the lamb on top, then cover the casserole or roasting pan with foil or a lid. Roast the lamb for 3–4 hours until it is cooked to your taste. Serve the lamb and beans hot, garnished with the remaining fresh rosemary sprigs.

MIDDLE-EASTERN ROAST LAMB and POTATOES

When the Eastern aroma of the garlic and saffron come wafting out of the oven, this deliciously garlicky lamb won't last very long.

SERVES 6–8

2.75kg/6lb leg of lamb
4 garlic cloves, halved
60ml/4 tbsp olive oil
juice of 1 lemon
2–3 saffron threads, soaked in
   15ml/1 tbsp boiling water
5ml/1 tsp mixed dried herbs, oregano
   or marjoram
450g/1lb small baking potatoes,
   thickly sliced
2 large or 4 small onions,
   thickly sliced
salt and ground black pepper
fresh thyme, to garnish

1 Make eight evenly-spaced incisions in the leg of lamb, press the halved garlic cloves into the slits and place the lamb in a large non-metallic dish.

2 Mix together the olive oil, lemon juice, saffron mixture and herbs. Rub over the lamb and marinate for 2 hours.

3 Preheat the oven to 180°C/350°F/ Gas 4. Layer the potato and onion slices in a large roasting pan. Lift the lamb out of the marinade and place it on top of the sliced potato and onions, fat side up and season well with plenty of salt and ground black pepper.

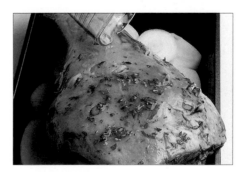

4 Pour the marinade over the lamb, then roast for 2 hours, basting occasionally. Remove from the oven and cover with foil, then rest for 10 minutes before carving. Garnish with thyme.

LAMB SHANKS with BEANS and HERBS

A hearty winter meal, the lamb shanks are slowly cooked in a clay pot until tender on a bed of tasty beans and vegetables.

SERVES 4

175g/6oz/1 cup dried cannellini beans,
   soaked overnight in cold water
150ml/¼ pint/⅔ cup water
45ml/3 tbsp olive oil
4 large lamb shanks, about 225g/8oz each
1 large onion, chopped
450g/1lb carrots, cut into thick chunks
2 celery sticks, cut into thick chunks
450g/1lb tomatoes, quartered
250ml/8fl oz/1 cup vegetable stock
4 fresh rosemary sprigs
2 bay leaves
salt and ground black pepper

1 Soak a large clay pot in cold water for 20 minutes, then drain. Drain and rinse the cannellini beans and place in a large pan of unsalted boiling water and boil rapidly for 10 minutes, then drain.

2 Place the 150ml/¼ pint/⅔ cup water in the soaked clay pot and then add the drained cannellini beans.

3 Heat 30ml/2 tbsp of the olive oil in a large frying pan, add the lamb shanks and cook over a high heat, turning the lamb shanks occasionally until brown on all sides. Remove the lamb shanks with a slotted spoon and set aside.

4 Add the remaining oil to the pan, then add the onion and sauté for 5 minutes, until soft and translucent.

5 Add the carrots and celery to the pan and cook for 2–3 minutes. Stir in the quartered tomatoes and vegetable stock and mix well. Transfer the vegetable mixture to the clay pot and season well with salt and pepper, then add the fresh rosemary and bay leaves and stir again to combine.

6 Place the lamb shanks on top of the beans and vegetables. Cover the clay pot and place it in an unheated oven. Set the oven to 220°C/425°F/Gas 7 and cook for about 30 minutes, or until the liquid is bubbling.

7 Reduce the oven temperature to 160°C/325°F/Gas 3 and cook for about 1½ hours, or until the meat is tender. Check the seasoning and serve on warmed plates, placing each lamb shank on a bed of beans and vegetables.

COOK'S TIP
Lamb shanks are small joints cut from the lower end of the leg. One shank is an ideal-sized portion for one. Until recently you would have had to order them from the butcher, but they are now becoming increasingly available from larger supermarkets. To obtain a tender result, shanks should be cooked for a long time at a low heat.

VARIATIONS
• Dried butter (lima) beans or the smaller haricot (navy) beans can be used in place of the cannellini beans.
• If you prefer, two 400g/14oz cans cannellini beans can be used in this dish – simply place the drained beans in the soaked clay pot with the water and continue from step 3.
• A variety of other root vegetables would work well in this recipe – try chopped swede (rutabaga), sweet potatoes, butternut squash, parsnips or celeriac instead of the carrots. In spring, a mixture of baby turnips and baby carrots would also be good.

BRAISED LAMB with APRICOTS and HERB DUMPLINGS

A rich and fruity lamb casserole, topped with light, herby dumplings, which is delicious served with baked potatoes and broccoli.

SERVES 6

30ml/2 tbsp sunflower oil
675g/1½lb lean lamb fillet, cut into
   2.5cm/1in cubes
350g/12oz baby (pearl) onions, peeled
1 garlic clove, crushed
225g/8oz/3 cups button
   (white) mushrooms
175g/6oz/¾ cup small ready-to-eat
   dried apricots
about 250ml/8fl oz/1 cup well-flavoured
   lamb or beef stock
250ml/8fl oz/1 cup red wine
15ml/1 tbsp tomato purée (paste)
salt and ground black pepper
fresh herb sprigs, to garnish

For the dumplings
115g/4oz/1 cup self-raising
   (self-rising) flour
50g/2oz/scant ½ cup shredded
   vegetable suet
15–30ml/1–2 tbsp chopped fresh
   mixed herbs

1 Preheat the oven to 160°C/325°F/ Gas 3. Heat the oil in a large, flameproof casserole, add the lamb and cook over a high heat until browned all over, stirring occasionally. Remove the meat from the casserole using a slotted spoon, then set aside and keep warm.

2 Reduce the heat slighty, then add the baby onions, crushed garlic and whole mushrooms to the oil remaining in the casserole and cook them gently for about 5 minutes, stirring occasionally with a wooden spoon.

3 Return the meat to the casserole, then add the dried apricots, stock, wine and tomato purée. Season to taste with salt and pepper and stir to mix.

4 Bring to the boil, stirring, then remove the casserole from the heat and cover. Transfer the casserole to the oven and cook for 1½–2 hours until the lamb is cooked and tender, stirring once or twice during the cooking time and adding a little extra stock, if necessary.

5 Meanwhile, make the dumplings. Place the flour, suet, herbs and seasoning in a bowl and stir to mix. Add enough cold water to make a soft, elastic dough. Divide the dough into small, marble-size pieces and, using lightly floured hands, roll each piece into a small ball.

6 Remove the lid from the casserole and place the dumplings on top of the braised lamb and vegetables.

7 Increase the oven temperature to 190°C/375°F/Gas 5. Return the casserole to the oven and cook for a further 20–25 minutes until the herb dumplings are cooked. Serve, garnished with the fresh herb sprigs.

VARIATIONS
Use lean beef or pork in place of the lamb and substitute shallots for the baby onions, if you prefer.

ITALIAN LAMB MEATBALLS with CHILLI TOMATO SAUCE

Serve these piquant Italian-style meatballs with pasta and a leafy salad. Sprinkle with a little grated Parmesan cheese for that extra Italian touch.

SERVES 4

450g/1lb lean minced (ground) lamb
1 large onion, grated
1 garlic clove, crushed
50g/2oz/1 cup fresh white breadcrumbs
15ml/1 tbsp chopped fresh parsley
1 small egg, lightly beaten
30ml/2 tbsp olive oil
salt and ground black pepper
60ml/4 tbsp finely grated Parmesan cheese
    and rocket (arugula) leaves, to serve

For the sauce
1 onion, finely chopped
400g/14oz can chopped tomatoes
200ml/7fl oz/scant 1 cup passata (bottled
    strained tomatoes)
5ml/1 tsp granulated sugar
2 green chillies, seeded and finely chopped
30ml/2 tbsp chopped fresh oregano
salt and ground black pepper

1 Soak a small clay pot in cold water for 15 minutes, then drain. Place the minced lamb, onion, garlic, breadcrumbs, parsley and seasoning in a bowl and mix well. Add the beaten egg and mix to bind the meatball mixture together.

2 Shape the mixture into 20 small even-size balls. Heat the olive oil in a frying pan, add the meatballs and cook over a high heat, stirring occasionally, until they are browned all over.

VARIATIONS
Minced (ground) beef or sausage meat (bulk sausage) can be used in place of the minced lamb in this dish.

3 Meanwhile, to make the sauce, mix together the chopped onion, tomatoes, passata, sugar, seeded and chopped chillies and oregano. Season well and pour the sauce into the clay pot.

4 Place the meatballs in the sauce, then cover and place in an unheated oven. Set the oven to 200°C/400°F/Gas 6 and cook for 1 hour, stirring after 30 minutes. Serve with Parmesan cheese and rocket.

FRAGRANT LAMB CURRY
with CARDAMOM-SPICED RICE

Wonderfully aromatic, this Indian-style lamb biriani, with the meat and rice cooked together, is a delicious meal in itself.

SERVES 4

1 large onion, quartered
2 garlic cloves
1 small green chilli, halved and seeded
5cm/2in piece fresh root ginger
15ml/1 tbsp ghee
15ml/1 tbsp vegetable oil
675 g/1½lb boned shoulder or leg of lamb,
    cut into chunks
15ml/1 tbsp ground coriander
10ml/2 tsp ground cumin
1 cinnamon stick, broken into 3 pieces
150ml/¼ pint/⅔ cup thick natural
    (plain) yogurt
150ml/¼ pint/⅔ cup water
75g/3oz/⅓ cup ready-to-eat dried apricots,
    cut into chunks
salt and ground black pepper

For the rice
250g/9oz/1¼ cups basmati rice
6 cardamom pods, split open
25g/1oz/2 tbsp butter, cut into small pieces
45ml/3 tbsp toasted cashew nuts or flaked
    (sliced) almonds

For the garnish
1 onion, sliced and fried until golden
a few sprigs of fresh coriander (cilantro)

1 Soak a large clay pot or chicken brick in cold water for 20 minutes, then drain. Place the onion, garlic, chilli and ginger in a food processor or blender and process with 15ml/1 tbsp water, to a smooth paste.

COOK'S TIP
Serve a cooling yogurt raita and a fresh fruit chutney or relish as an accompaniment.

2 Heat the ghee and vegetable oil in a heavy frying pan. Fry the lamb chunks in batches over a high heat until golden brown. Remove from the pan using a slotted spoon and set aside.

3 Add the onion paste to the remaining oil left in the frying pan, stir in the ground coriander and cumin, add the cinnamon stick pieces and fry for 1–2 minutes, stirring constantly with a wooden spoon.

4 Return the meat to the frying pan, then gradually add the yogurt, a spoonful at a time, stirring well between each addition with a wooden spoon. Season the meat well with plenty of salt and pepper and stir in the water.

5 Transfer the contents of the frying pan to the prepared clay pot, cover with the lid and place in an unheated oven. Set the oven to 180°C/350°F/Gas 4 and cook for 45 minutes.

6 Meanwhile prepare the basmati rice. Place it in a bowl, cover with cold water and leave to soak for 20 minutes. Drain the rice and place it in a large pan of boiling salted water, bring back to the boil and cook for 10 minutes. Drain and stir in the split cardamom pods.

7 Remove the clay pot from the oven and stir in the chopped ready-to-eat apricots. Pile the cooked rice on top of the lamb and dot with the butter. Drizzle over 60ml/4 tbsp water, then sprinkle the cashew nuts or flaked almonds on top. Cover the pot, reduce the oven temperature to 150°C/300°F/Gas 2 and cook the meat and rice for 30 minutes.

8 Remove the lid from the pot and fluff up the rice with a fork. Spoon into warmed individual bowls, then sprinkle over the fried onion slices and garnish with the sprigs of fresh coriander.

POT-ROAST LOIN of PORK with APPLE

Roasted pork loin with crisp crackling and a lightly spiced apple and raisin stuffing makes a wonderful Sunday-lunch main course.

SERVES 6–8

1.8kg/4lb boned loin of pork
300ml/½ pint/1¼ cups dry (hard) cider
150ml/¼ pint/⅔ cup sour cream
7.5ml/1½ tsp salt

For the stuffing
25g/1oz/2 tbsp butter
1 small onion, chopped
50g/2oz/1 cup fresh white breadcrumbs
2 apples, cored, peeled and chopped
50g/2oz/scant ½ cup raisins
finely grated rind of 1 orange
pinch of ground cloves
salt and ground black pepper

1 Preheat the oven to 220°C/425°F/ Gas 7. To make the stuffing, melt the butter in a frying pan and gently fry the onion for 10 minutes until soft. Stir in the remaining stuffing ingredients.

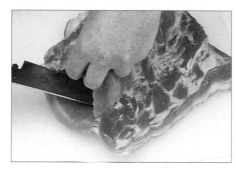

2 Put the pork, rind side down, on a board. Make a horizontal cut between the meat and outer layer of fat, cutting to within 2.5cm/1in of the edges to make a pocket.

3 Push the prepared stuffing into the pocket. Roll up the pork lengthwise and tie firmly with string. Score the rind at 2cm/¾in intervals with a sharp knife.

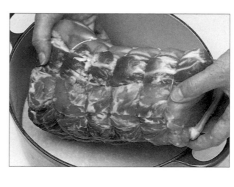

4 Pour the cider and sour cream into a large casserole. Stir to combine, then add the pork, rind-side down. Transfer to the oven and cook, uncovered, for 30 minutes.

5 Turn the joint over, so that the rind is on top. Baste with the juices, then sprinkle the rind with salt. Cook for a further 1 hour, basting after 30 minutes. Reduce the oven temperature to 180°C/ 350°F/Gas 4. Cook for 1½ hours, then remove the casserole from the oven and leave the joint to stand for 20 minutes before carving.

COOK'S TIP
Do not baste during the final 1½ hours of roasting, so the crackling becomes crisp.

BRAZILIAN PORK and RICE CASSEROLE

We tend to associate Brazil with beef recipes, but there are also some excellent pork recipes, including this hearty dish of marinated pork, vegetables and rice.

SERVES 4–6

500g/1¼lb lean pork, such as fillet
   (tenderloin), cut into strips
60ml/4 tbsp vegetable oil
1 onion, chopped
1 garlic clove, crushed
1 green (bell) pepper, cut into pieces
about 300ml/½ pint/1¼ cups chicken or
   vegetable stock
225g/8oz/generous 1 cup white long
   grain rice
150ml/¼ pint/⅔ cup single (light) cream
150g/5oz/1½ cups freshly grated
   Parmesan cheese
salt and ground black pepper

For the marinade
120ml/4fl oz/½ cup dry white wine
30ml/2 tbsp lemon juice
1 onion, chopped
4 juniper berries, lightly crushed
3 cloves
1 fresh red chilli, seeded and finely sliced

1 Mix the marinade ingredients in a shallow dish, add the pork strips and leave to marinate for 3–4 hours, stirring occasionally. Transfer the pork to a plate using a slotted spoon and pat dry. Strain the marinade and set aside.

2 Heat the oil in a heavy pan, add the pork strips and fry for a few minutes until evenly brown. Transfer to a plate using a slotted spoon.

3 Add the chopped onion and the garlic to the pan and fry for 3–4 minutes. Stir in the pieces of pepper and cook for 3–4 minutes more, then return the pork strips to the pan. Pour in the reserved marinade and the stock. Bring to the boil and season with salt and pepper, then lower the heat, cover the pan and simmer gently for 10 minutes, or until the meat is nearly tender.

VARIATION
Strips of chicken breast meat can be used in this recipe instead of the lean pork fillet.

4 Preheat the oven to 160°C/325°F/ Gas 3. Cook the rice in plenty of lightly salted boiling water for 8 minutes or until three-quarters cooked. Drain well. Spread half the rice over the base of a buttered, earthenware dish. Using a slotted spoon, make a neat layer of meat and vegetables on top, then spread over the remaining rice.

5 Stir the cream and 30ml/2 tbsp of the grated Parmesan into the liquid in which the pork was cooked. Tip into a jug (pitcher) and then carefully pour the cream mixture over the rice and sprinkle with the remaining Parmesan. Cover with foil and bake for 20 minutes, then remove the foil and cook for 5 minutes more, until the top is lightly brown.

PORK COOKED in CIDER with PARSLEY DUMPLINGS

Pork and fruit are a perfect combination. If you don't want to make dumplings, serve creamy mashed potatoes with the stew.

SERVES 6

115g/4oz/½ cup pitted prunes,
    roughly chopped
115g/4oz/½ cup ready-to-eat dried
    apricots, roughly chopped
300ml/½ pint/1¼ cups dry (hard) cider
30ml/2 tbsp plain (all-purpose) flour
675g/1½lb lean boneless pork, cut
    into cubes
30ml/2 tbsp vegetable oil
350g/12oz onions, roughly chopped
2 garlic cloves, crushed
6 celery sticks, roughly chopped
475ml/16fl oz/2 cups stock
12 juniper berries, lightly crushed
30ml/2 tbsp chopped fresh thyme
425g/15oz can black-eyed beans
    (peas), drained
salt and ground black pepper

For the dumplings
115g/4oz/1 cup self-raising (self-rising) flour
50g/2oz/scant ½ cup vegetable suet
45ml/3 tbsp chopped fresh parsley
90ml/6 tbsp water

1 Preheat the oven to 180°C/350°F/ Gas 4. Place the roughly chopped prunes and apricots in a small bowl. Pour over the cider and leave to soak for at least 20 minutes.

VARIATION
This recipe can also be made with lean lamb – leg steaks or diced shoulder would be ideal cuts to choose. Omit the juniper berries, try cannellini beans in place of the black-eyed beans and use red onions rather than brown ones.

2 Season the flour, then toss the pork in the flour to coat. Reserve any leftover flour. Heat the oil in a large flameproof casserole. Brown the meat in batches, adding a little more oil if necessary. Remove the meat with a slotted spoon and drain on kitchen paper.

3 Add the onions, garlic and celery to the casserole and cook for 5 minutes. Add any reserved flour and cook for a further 1 minute.

4 Blend in the stock until smooth. Add the cider and fruit, juniper berries, thyme and plenty of seasoning. Bring to the boil, add the pork, cover tightly and then cook in the oven for 50 minutes.

5 Just before the end of the cooking time prepare the dumplings. Sift the flour into a large bowl, add a pinch of salt, then stir in the suet and chopped fresh parsley. Add the water gradually and mix all the ingredients together to form a smooth, slightly sticky dough.

6 Remove the casserole from the oven, then stir in the black-eyed beans and adjust the seasoning. Divide the dumpling mixture into six, form into rough rounds and place on top of the stew. Return the casserole to the oven, then cover and cook for a further 20–25 minutes, or until the dumplings are cooked and the pork is tender.

COOK'S TIP
Black-eyed beans or peas, as they are called in America, are also sometimes referred to as cowpeas. They are a medium-size cream-coloured bean with a distinctive black spot or "eye" on the inner curve. They have a smooth, creamy texture and a subtle flavour. Black-eyed beans are a popular addition to soups and casseroles and are widely used in southern American cuisines.

PORK TENDERLOIN with SPINACH and PUY LENTILS

Lean pork tenderloin, wrapped in spinach and cooked in a clay pot on a bed of tiny French green lentils, flavoured with coconut.

SERVES 4

500–675g/1¼–1½lb pork tenderloin
15ml/1 tbsp sunflower oil
15g/½oz/1 tbsp butter
8–12 large spinach leaves
1 onion, chopped
1 garlic clove, finely chopped
2.5cm/1in piece fresh root ginger, finely grated
1 red chilli, finely chopped (optional)
250g/9oz/generous 1 cup Puy lentils
750ml/1¼ pints/3 cups chicken or vegetable stock
200ml/7fl oz/scant 1 cup coconut cream
salt and ground black pepper

1 Soak a small clay pot in cold water for about 15 minutes, then drain. Cut the pork tenderloin widthwise into two equal pieces. Season the pork well with salt and ground black pepper.

2 Heat the sunflower oil and butter in a heavy frying pan, add the pork tenderloin and cook over a high heat until browned on all sides. Remove the meat from the pan using a fish slice (spatula) and set aside.

3 Meanwhile, add the spinach leaves to a large pan of boiling water and cook for 1 minute, or until just wilted. Drain immediately in a colander and refresh under cold running water. Drain well.

4 Lay the spinach leaves on the work surface, overlapping them slightly to form a rectangle. Place the pork on top and wrap the leaves around the pork to enclose it completely.

5 Add the onion to the oil in the frying pan and cook for about 5 minutes, stirring occasionally, until softened. Add the chopped garlic, grated ginger and finely chopped chilli, if using, and fry for a further 1 minute.

6 Add the lentils to the onion mixture in the frying pan and then stir in the chicken or vegetable stock. Bring to the boil, then boil rapidly for 10 minutes. Remove the pan from the heat and stir in the coconut cream until well blended. Transfer the onion and lentil mixture to the clay pot and arrange the pork tenderloins on top.

7 Cover the clay pot and place it in an unheated oven. Set the oven to 190°C/375°F/Gas 5 and cook for 45 minutes, or until the lentils and pork are cooked.

8 To serve, remove the spinach-wrapped pork tenderloins from the clay pot using a slotted spoon or tongs and cut the pork into thick slices. Stir the lentils and spoon them, with some of the cooking juices, on to warmed, individual plates and top each portion with a few of the pork slices.

VARIATIONS
• Wrap the pork in slices of prosciutto, instead of the spinach leaves, and tie in place with string or secure with wooden cocktail sticks (toothpicks).
• Use 4 large chicken or duck breast portions in place of the pork tenderloin. Check the chicken or duck after about 30 minutes cooking time. Cut the breast portions into thick, diagonal slices to serve. The chicken would also be good wrapped with prosciutto.

POTATO and SAUSAGE CASSEROLE

You will find numerous variations of this traditional supper dish throughout Ireland, but the basic ingredients are the same wherever you go — potatoes, sausages and bacon.

2 Heat the oil in a frying pan, then add the bacon and fry for 2 minutes, stirring. Add the onions and fry for 5–6 minutes until golden. Add the garlic and fry for 1 minute, then remove the mixture from the pan and set aside.

3 Fry the sausages in the same pan for 5–6 minutes until golden brown.

SERVES 4

15ml/1 tbsp vegetable oil
4 bacon rashers (strips), cut into
    2.5cm/1in pieces
2 large onions, chopped
2 garlic cloves, crushed
8 large pork sausages
4 large baking potatoes, peeled and
    thinly sliced
1.5ml/¼ tsp fresh sage
300ml/½ pint/1¼ cups vegetable stock
salt and ground black pepper
crusty bread, to serve

1 Preheat the oven to 180°C/350°F/ Gas 4. Lightly grease a large, shallow earthenware baking dish and set aside.

4 Arrange the potatoes in the base of the prepared dish. Spoon the bacon and onion mixture on top. Season with the salt and pepper and sprinkle with the fresh sage. Pour on the stock and top with the sausages. Cover and bake for about 1 hour, or until the potatoes and sausages are tender. Serve hot with crusty bread.

TOAD-in-the-HOLE

This is one of those dishes that is classic comfort food – perfect for lifting the spirits on cold days. Use only the best sausages for this grown-up version, which includes chives.

SERVES 4–6

175g/6oz/1½ cups plain (all-purpose) flour
30ml/2 tbsp chopped fresh chives (optional)
2 eggs
300ml/½ pint/1¼ cups milk
50g/2oz/⅓ cup white vegetable fat
   or lard
450g/1lb Cumberland sausages or good-
   quality pork sausages
salt and ground black pepper

VARIATION
For a young children's supper, make small individual toad-in-the-holes: omit the chopped fresh chives from the batter and cook small cocktail sausages in patty tins (muffin pans) until golden. Add the batter and cook for 10–15 minutes, or until puffed and golden brown.

1 Preheat the oven to 220°C/425°F/ Gas 7. Sift the flour into a bowl with a pinch of salt and pepper. Make a well in the centre of the flour. Whisk the chives, if using, with the eggs and milk, then pour this into the well in the flour. Gradually whisk the flour into the liquid to make a smooth batter. Cover and leave to stand for at least 30 minutes.

2 Put the vegetable fat or lard into a small roasting pan and place in the oven for 3–5 minutes until very hot. Add the sausages and cook for 15 minutes. Turn the sausages twice during cooking.

3 Pour the batter over the sausages and cook for about 20 minutes, or until the batter is risen and golden. Serve immediately.

OVEN-ROASTED CHICKEN with MEDITERRANEAN VEGETABLES

This is a delicious – and trouble-free – alternative to a traditional roast chicken. The recipe also works very well with guinea fowl.

SERVES 4

1.8–2.25kg/4–5lb roasting chicken
150ml/¼ pint/⅔ cup extra virgin olive oil
½ lemon
a few sprigs of fresh thyme
450g/1lb small new potatoes
1 aubergine (eggplant), cut into
   2.5cm/1in cubes
1 red or yellow (bell) pepper, seeded
   and quartered
1 fennel bulb, trimmed and quartered
8 large garlic cloves, unpeeled
coarse salt and ground black pepper

1 Preheat the oven to 200°C/400°F/
Gas 6. Rub the chicken all over with
olive oil and season with pepper. Place
the lemon half inside the bird, with a
sprig or two of thyme. Put the chicken
breast side down in a large roasting pan.
Roast for about 30 minutes.

2 Remove the chicken from the oven
and season with salt. Turn the chicken
right side up, and baste with the juices
from the pan.

3 Arrange the potatoes around the
chicken and roll them in the cooking
juices until they are thoroughly coated.
Return the roasting pan to the oven, to
continue roasting.

4 After 30 minutes, add the aubergine,
red pepper, fennel and garlic cloves to
the pan. Drizzle the vegetables with the
remaining oil, and season to taste with
salt and pepper.

5 Add the remaining sprigs of thyme
to the roasting pan, tucking the sprigs
in among the vegetables. Return the
chicken and vegetables to the oven and
cook for 30–50 minutes more, basting
and turning the vegetables occasionally
during cooking.

6 To find out if the chicken is cooked,
push the tip of a small sharp knife
between the thigh and breast – if the
juices run clear, rather than pink, it is
done. The vegetables should be tender
and beginning to brown. Serve the
chicken and vegetables from the pan.

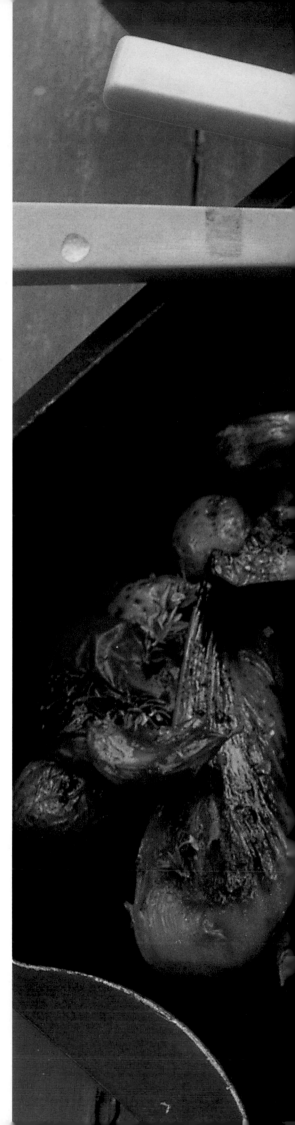

CHICKEN with FORTY CLOVES of GARLIC

This dish does not have to be mathematically exact, so do not worry if you have 35 or even 50 cloves of garlic – the important thing is that there should be lots. The smell that emanates from the oven as the chicken and garlic cook is indescribably delicious.

SERVES 4–5

5–6 whole heads of garlic
15g/½oz/1 tbsp butter
45ml/3 tbsp olive oil
1.8–2kg/4–4½lb chicken
150g/5oz/1¼ cups plain (all-purpose) flour,
    plus 5ml/1 tsp
75ml/5 tbsp white port, Pineau
    de Charentes or other white,
    fortified wine
2–3 fresh tarragon or rosemary sprigs
30ml/2 tbsp crème fraîche (optional)
a few drops of lemon juice (optional)
salt and ground black pepper

1 Separate three of the heads of garlic into cloves and peel them. Remove the first layer of papery skin from the remaining heads of garlic and cut off the tops to expose the cloves, if you like, or leave them whole. Preheat the oven to 180°C/350°F/Gas 4.

2 Heat the butter and 15ml/1 tbsp of the olive oil in a flameproof casserole that is just large enough to take the chicken and garlic. Add the chicken and cook over a medium heat, turning it frequently, for 10–15 minutes, until it is browned all over.

3 Sprinkle in 5ml/1 tsp flour and cook for 1 minute. Add the port or wine. Tuck in the whole heads of garlic and the peeled cloves with the sprigs of tarragon or rosemary. Pour over the remaining oil and season to taste with salt and pepper.

4 Mix the main batch of flour with sufficient water to make a firm dough. Roll it out into a long sausage and press it around the rim of the casserole, then press on the lid, folding the dough up and over it to create a tight seal. Cook in the oven for 1½ hours.

5 To serve, lift off the lid to break the seal and remove the chicken and whole garlic to a serving platter and keep warm. Remove and discard the herb sprigs, then place the casserole on the stove top and whisk the remaining ingredients to combine the garlic cloves with the juices. Add the crème fraîche, if using, and a little lemon juice to taste, if using. Process the sauce in a food processor or blender until smooth. Reheat the garlic sauce in a clean pan if necessary and serve it with the chicken.

CHICKEN BAKED with SHALLOTS, GARLIC and FENNEL

This is a very simple and delicious way to cook chicken. If you have time, leave the chicken to marinate for a few hours for the best flavour.

2 Preheat the oven to 190°C/375°F/ Gas 5. Add the wedges of fennel to the chicken, then season with salt and stir well to mix. Transfer the chicken to the oven and cook for 50–60 minutes, stirring once or twice, until the chicken is thoroughly cooked. The chicken juices should run clear, not pink, when the thick thigh meat is pierced with a skewer or a small sharp knife.

3 Transfer the chicken and vegetables to a serving dish and keep them warm. Skim off some of the fat and bring the cooking juices to the boil, then pour in the cream. Stir, scraping up all the juices. Whisk in the redcurrant jelly followed by the mustard. Check the seasoning, adding a little sugar, if necessary.

4 Finely chop the remaining garlic clove with the feathery fennel tops and mix them with the parsley. Pour the sauce over the chicken and then sprinkle the chopped garlic and herb mixture over the top. Serve immediately with rice or baked potatoes.

COOK'S TIPS

• If possible, use the fresh, new season's garlic for this dish, as it is plump, moist and full of flavour. Purple-skinned garlic is considered by many cooks to have the best flavour.
• The cut surfaces of fennel will quickly discolour, so do not prepare it too far in advance of using it. If you must prepare it beforehand, then put the wedges into a bowl of cold water acidulated with a little lemon juice.

SERVES 4

1.6 1.8kg/3½–4lb chicken, cut into
   8 pieces, or 8 chicken joints
250g/9oz shallots, peeled
1 head of garlic, separated into cloves
   and peeled
60ml/4 tbsp extra virgin olive oil
45ml/3 tbsp tarragon vinegar
45ml/3 tbsp white wine or
   vermouth (optional)
5ml/1 tsp fennel seeds, crushed
2 bulbs fennel, cut into wedges, feathery
   tops reserved
150ml/¼ pint/⅔ cup double (heavy) cream
5ml/1 tsp redcurrant jelly
15ml/1 tbsp tarragon mustard
a little sugar (optional)
30ml/2 tbsp chopped fresh flat leaf parsley
salt and ground black pepper

1 Place the chicken pieces, shallots and all but one of the garlic cloves in a large, shallow flameproof dish. Add the olive oil, tarragon vinegar, white wine or vermouth, if using, and the crushed fennel seeds. Season to taste with plenty of ground black pepper, then set aside and leave to marinate in a cool place for 2–3 hours.

STOVED CHICKEN

"Stovies" were originally potatoes slowly cooked on the stove with onions and dripping or butter until falling to pieces. This version includes a delicious layer of bacon and chicken.

2 Heat the butter and oil in a large, heavy frying pan, add the chopped bacon and chicken pieces and cook, turning occasionally, until brown on all sides. Using a slotted spoon, transfer the chicken and bacon to the earthenware dish. Reserve the fat in the pan.

3 Sprinkle the remaining chopped thyme over the chicken, season with salt and pepper, then cover with the remaining onion slices, followed by a neat, overlapping layer of the remaining potato slices. Season the top layer of potatoes with more salt and ground black pepper.

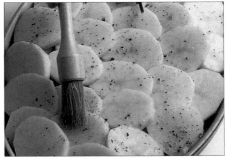

4 Pour the chicken stock into the casserole, add the bay leaf and brush the potatoes with the reserved fat from the frying pan. Cover tightly with foil and bake for about 2 hours, or until the chicken is cooked and tender.

SERVES 4

1kg/2¼lb baking potatoes, cut into
    5mm/¼in slices
butter, for greasing
2 large onions, thinly sliced
15ml/1 tbsp chopped fresh thyme
25g/1oz/2 tbsp butter
15ml/1 tbsp vegetable oil
2 large bacon rashers (strips), chopped
4 large chicken portions, halved
600ml/1 pint/2½ cups chicken stock
1 bay leaf
salt and ground black pepper

COOK'S TIP
Instead of chicken portions, choose eight chicken thighs or chicken drumsticks.

 Preheat the oven to 150°C/300°F/ Gas 2. Arrange a thick layer of half the potato slices in a large lightly greased, earthenware baking dish, then cover with half the onions. Sprinkle with half of the thyme, and season with salt and pepper to taste.

5 Preheat the grill (broiler) to medium-hot, then remove the foil from the earthenware dish and place the dish under the grill. Cook until the slices of potato are beginning to turn golden brown and crisp. Remove the bay leaf and serve immediately.

POT-ROAST CHICKEN with LEMON and GARLIC

This is a rustic dish that is easy to prepare. Lardons are thick strips of bacon fat; if you can't get them, use fatty bacon instead. Serve with thick bread to mop up the juices.

SERVES 4

30ml/2 tbsp olive oil
25g/1oz/2 tbsp butter
175g/6oz/1 cup smoked lardons, or
   roughly chopped streaky (fatty) bacon
8 garlic cloves, peeled
4 onions, quartered
10ml/2 tsp plain (all-purpose) flour
600ml/1 pint/2½ cups chicken stock
2 lemons, thickly sliced
45ml/3 tbsp chopped fresh thyme
1 chicken, about 1.3–1.6kg/3–3½lb
2 × 400g/14oz cans flageolet, cannellini
   or haricot (navy) beans, drained
   and rinsed
salt and ground black pepper

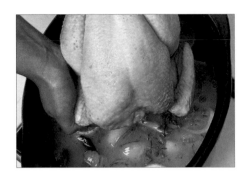

3 Bring the sauce to the boil, stirring constantly until thickened, then place the chicken on top. Season well. Transfer the casserole to the oven. Cook for 1 hour, basting the chicken once or twice during cooking to ensure it stays moist.

4 Baste the chicken again. Stir the beans into the casserole and return it to the oven for a further 30 minutes, or until the chicken is cooked through and tender. Carve the chicken into thick slices and serve with the beans.

1 Preheat the oven to 190°C/375°F/ Gas 5. Heat the oil and butter in a flameproof casserole that is large enough to hold the chicken with a little room around the sides. Add the lardons and cook until golden. Remove with a slotted spoon and drain on kitchen paper.

2 Add the garlic and onions and brown over a high heat. Stir in the flour, then the stock. Return the lardons to the pan with the lemon, thyme and seasoning.

POUSSINS and NEW POTATO POT-ROAST

Pot roasts are traditionally associated with the colder months, but this delicious version is a simple summer dish that makes the most of new season potatoes.

SERVES 4

2 poussins, about 500g/1¼lb each
25g/1oz/2 tbsp butter
15ml/1 tbsp clear honey
500g/1¼lb small new potatoes
1 red onion, halved lengthwise and cut into thin wedges
4–5 small rosemary sprigs
2 bay leaves
1 lemon, cut into wedges
450ml/¾ pint/scant 2 cups hot chicken stock
salt and ground black pepper

1 Soak a clay chicken brick in cold water for 20 minutes, then drain. Cut the poussins in half, along the breast bone.

2 Melt the butter, mix it together with the honey and brush over the poussins. Season with salt and pepper.

3 Place the small new potatoes and onion wedges in the base of the chicken brick. Tuck the rosemary sprigs, bay leaves and lemon wedges in among the vegetables. Pour over the hot chicken stock (see Cook's Tip).

4 Place the halved poussins on top of the vegetables. Cover the chicken brick and place it in an unheated oven. Set the oven to 200°C/400°F/Gas 6 and cook for 55–60 minutes, or until the poussin juices run clear and the vegetables are tender. Uncover the chicken brick for the last 10 minutes of cooking to add more colour to the poussins, if necessary.

COOK'S TIPS
• Make sure the stock is hot, but not boiling when it is added to the chicken brick otherwise the chicken brick may crack.
• A poussin is a baby chicken – usually around 4–6 weeks old. Poussins can be cooked by grilling (broiling), roasting or pot-roasting, but are especially tender and moist cooked in a chicken brick.

CORN-FED CHICKEN with WINTER VEGETABLES

Chicken cooked in a clay pot remains beautifully moist and tender. Flavoured with lemon, parsley and tarragon, serve this as an alternative to a traditional Sunday roast.

SERVES 4

3 large carrots, cut into batons
1 celery heart, thickly sliced
2 red onions, quartered
a few sprigs of fresh thyme
1.6kg/3½lb corn-fed chicken
40g/1½oz/3 tbsp butter, softened
15ml/1 tbsp chopped fresh parsley
15ml/1 tbsp chopped fresh tarragon
1 small lemon, halved
300ml/½ pint/1¼ cups dry white wine or
    chicken stock
salt and ground black pepper

COOK'S TIP
Cook some potatoes in the oven at the same time to accompany the pot roast – baked potatoes or roast potatoes both go well with this main course. Or, if you prefer, serve the pot-roast with creamy mashed potatoes.

1 Soak a chicken brick or large clay pot in cold water for 20 minutes, then drain. Place the carrots, celery, red onions and thyme in the pot.

2 Wash the chicken and dry thoroughly. Mix together the butter, parsley and tarragon. Ease up the breast skin of the chicken and spread the butter under it, taking care not to puncture the skin. Place the lemon halves inside the chicken.

3 Rub the chicken with seasoning and nestle on top of the vegetables. Add the wine or chicken stock and cover. Place the chicken brick or pot in an unheated oven. Set the oven temperature to 200°C/400°F/Gas 6 and cook for about 1¾ hours, or until the chicken is cooked.

4 Remove the lid from the brick or pot and cook for a further 10 minutes, or until the chicken is golden brown.

CHICKEN GUMBO with OKRA, HAM, TOMATOES and PRAWNS

This classic Creole dish is really a very hearty soup, but is usually served over rice as a delicious and filling main course, like a stew.

SERVES 4

30ml/2 tbsp olive oil
1 onion, chopped
225g/8oz skinless, boneless chicken
 breast portions, cut into
 small chunks
25g/1oz/¼ cup plain (all-purpose) flour
5ml/1 tsp paprika
30ml/2 tbsp tomato purée (paste)
600ml/1 pint/2½ cups well-flavoured
 chicken stock
400g/14oz can chopped tomatoes
 with herbs
a few drops of Tabasco
175g/6oz okra
1 red, orange or yellow (bell) pepper,
 seeded and chopped
2 celery sticks, sliced
225g/8oz/1⅓ cups diced lean
 cooked ham
225g/8oz large prawns (shrimp), peeled,
 deveined and heads removed, but with
 tails intact
salt and ground black pepper
boiled rice, to serve

1 Soak a large clay pot or chicken brick in cold water for 20 minutes, then drain. Heat the oil in a large frying pan, add the chopped onion and cook over a medium heat for about 5 minutes, stirring occasionally, until softened and lightly golden.

2 Add the chicken chunks to the pan and sauté for 1–2 minutes, to seal. Stir in the flour, paprika and tomato purée and cook, stirring constantly, for 1–2 minutes.

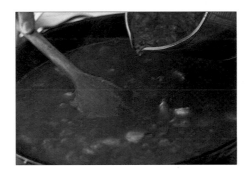

3 Gradually add the stock, stirring constantly, then bring the sauce to the boil, stirring. Add the chopped tomatoes, then remove the pan from the heat. Add a few drops of Tabasco and season with salt and pepper.

4 Cut the okra pods in half if they are large, then add them to the clay pot or chicken brick with the chopped red, orange or yellow pepper and the sliced celery. Add the chicken and tomato mixture and stir well to mix.

5 Cover the clay pot or chicken brick and place it in an unheated oven. Set the oven to 200°C/400°F/Gas 6 and cook for 30 minutes.

6 Remove the clay pot or chicken brick from the oven, then add the diced ham and the prawns and stir well to combine. Cover the pot or brick and return it to the oven for about 10 minutes, or until the ham is heated through and the prawns are just cooked. To serve, spoon some freshly boiled rice into four warmed, individual serving plates or bowls and ladle over the gumbo.

VARIATIONS
Replace the cooked ham with crab meat or cooked and shelled mussels or, for a special occasion, replace the peeled prawns with crayfish and replace the ham with cooked and shelled oysters.

COOK'S TIPS
• Okra is a favourite ingredient in the southern states of the USA and in African and Caribbean cooking. When buying, look for firm, bright green pods that are less than 10cm/4in long. Larger pods may be slightly tough and fibrous. When cooked, okra produces a rather viscous substance that thickens the liquid in which it is cooked – an essential part of many traditional okra recipes.
• If you don't have a bottle of Tabasco sauce to hand, add about 2.5ml/½ tsp chilli powder, or a finely chopped fresh or dried chilli. Remove the seeds from the chilli if you would prefer the gumbo to be only medium-hot.

CHICKEN PIRI-PIRI

This is a classic Portuguese dish, based on a hot sauce made from Angolan chillies. It is popular wherever there are Portuguese communities, and is often served in South Africa.

SERVES 4

4 chicken breast portions
30–45ml/2–3 tbsp olive oil
1 large onion, finely sliced
2 carrots, cut into thin strips
1 large parsnip or 2 small parsnips,
    cut into thin strips
1 red (bell) pepper, seeded and sliced
1 yellow (bell) pepper, seeded
    and sliced
1 litre/1¾ pints/4 cups chicken or
    vegetable stock
3 tomatoes, peeled, seeded and chopped
generous dash of piri-piri sauce
15ml/1 tbsp tomato purée (paste)
½ cinnamon stick
1 fresh thyme sprig, plus extra fresh thyme
    to garnish
1 bay leaf
275g/10oz/1½ cups white long grain rice
15ml/1 tbsp lime or lemon juice
salt and ground black pepper

1 Preheat the oven to 180°C/350°F/ Gas 4. Rub the chicken skin with a little salt and ground black pepper. Heat 30ml/2 tbsp of the olive oil in a large frying pan, add the chicken portions and cook, turning occasionally until browned on all sides. Transfer to a plate using a fish slice (spatula).

2 Add some more oil to the pan if necessary, add the sliced onion and fry for 2–3 minutes until slightly softened. Add the carrot and parsnip strips and the pepper slices and stir-fry for a few minutes more. Cover the pan and cook for 4–5 minutes until all the vegetables are quite soft.

3 Pour in the chicken or vegetable stock, then add the tomatoes, piri-piri sauce, tomato purée and cinnamon stick. Stir in the thyme and bay leaf. Season to taste and bring to the boil. Using a ladle, spoon off 300ml/½ pint/1¼ cups of the liquid and set aside in a small pan.

4 Put the rice in the base of a large earthenware dish. Using a slotted spoon, scoop the vegetables out of the frying pan and spread them over the rice. Arrange the chicken pieces on top. Pour over the spicy chicken stock from the frying pan, cover tightly and cook in the oven for about 45 minutes, until both the rice and chicken are completely tender.

5 Meanwhile, heat the reserved chicken stock, adding a few more drops of piri-piri sauce and the lime or lemon juice.

6 To serve, spoon the piri-piri chicken and rice on to warmed serving plates. Serve the remaining sauce separately or poured over the chicken.

CHICKEN BIRIANI

Easy to make and very tasty, this is the ideal one-pot dish for a family supper.

SERVES 4

10 green cardamom pods
275g/10oz/1½ cups basmati rice, soaked
    and drained
2.5ml/½ tsp salt
2–3 cloves
5cm/2in cinnamon stick
45ml/3 tbsp vegetable oil
3 onions, sliced
4 chicken breast portions, each about
    175g/6oz, cubed
1.5ml/¼ tsp ground cloves
5ml/1 tsp ground cumin
5ml/1 tsp ground coriander
2.5ml/½ tsp ground black pepper
3 garlic cloves, chopped
5ml/1 tsp finely chopped fresh root ginger
juice of 1 lemon
4 tomatoes, sliced
30ml/2 tbsp chopped fresh
    coriander (cilantro)
150ml/¼ pint/⅔ cup natural (plain) yogurt
4–5 saffron threads, soaked in 10ml/2 tsp
    hot milk
150ml/¼ pint/⅔ cup water
toasted flaked (sliced) almonds and fresh
    coriander (cilantro) sprigs, to garnish
natural (plain) yogurt, to serve

1 Preheat the oven to 190°C/375°F/
Gas 5. Remove the seeds from half the
cardamom pods and grind them finely, using
a mortar and pestle. Set the seeds aside.

2 Bring a flameproof casserole of water
to the boil and add the soaked and
drained basmati rice, then stir in the salt,
the remaining whole cardamom pods,
whole cloves and cinnamon stick. Boil
the rice for 2 minutes, then drain,
leaving the whole spices in the rice.

3 Heat the oil in the flameproof
casserole and fry the onions for about
8 minutes, until softened and browned.
Add the cubed chicken and the ground
spices, including the ground cardamom
seeds. Mix well, then add the chopped
garlic, ginger and lemon juice. Stir-fry the
mixture together for 5 minutes.

4 Arrange the sliced tomatoes on top.
Sprinkle on the coriander, spoon the
yogurt on top and cover with the rice.

5 Drizzle the saffron milk over the rice
and add the water. Cover and bake for
1 hour. Garnish with almonds and
coriander and serve with extra yogurt.

CASSOULET

Based on the traditional French dish, this recipe is full of delicious flavours and makes a welcoming and warming meal.

SERVES 6

3–4 boneless duck breast portions, about
    450g/1lb total weight
225g/8oz thick-cut streaky (fatty) pork
    or unsmoked streaky (fatty) bacon
    rashers (strips)
450g/1lb Toulouse or garlic sausages
45ml/3 tbsp vegetable oil
450g/1lb onions, chopped
2 garlic cloves, crushed
2 × 425g/15oz cans cannellini beans, rinsed
    and drained
225g/8oz carrots, roughly chopped
400g/14oz can chopped tomatoes
15ml/1 tbsp tomato purée (paste)
bouquet garni
30ml/2 tbsp chopped fresh thyme or
    15ml/1 tbsp dried
475ml/16fl oz/2 cups well-flavoured
    chicken stock
115g/4oz/2 cups fresh white or wholemeal
    (whole-wheat) breadcrumbs
salt and ground black pepper
fresh thyme sprigs, to garnish
warm crusty bread, to serve

1 Preheat the oven to 160°C/325°F/
Gas 3. Cut the duck portions and pork
or bacon rashers into large pieces. Twist
the sausages to shorten them and then
cut them into short lengths.

COOK'S TIP
Cannellini beans are large white beans
with a nutty flavour. They are especially
popular in Italy, particularly in Tuscany,
where they are included in a variety of
pasta and soup dishes. Cannellini beans
are sometimes referred to as white
kidney beans or fazola beans.

2 Heat the oil in a large flameproof
casserole. Cook the meat in batches,
until well browned. Remove from the
pan with a slotted spoon and drain on
kitchen paper.

3 Add the onions and garlic to the pan
and cook for 3–4 minutes, or until
beginning to soften, stirring frequently.

4 Stir in the beans, carrots, tomatoes,
tomato purée, bouquet garni, thyme and
seasoning. Return the meat to the
casserole and mix until well combined.

VARIATION
Canned butter (lima) beans or borlotti
beans can be used in this recipe instead
of the cannellini beans.

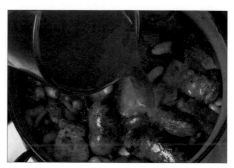

5 Add enough of the stock just to cover
the meat and beans. (The cassoulet
shouldn't be swimming in juices; if the
mixture becomes too dry during the
cooking time, add a little more stock or
water.) Bring to the boil. Cover the
casserole tightly and cook in the oven
for 1 hour.

6 Remove the cassoulet from the oven
and add a little more stock or water, if
necessary. Remove the bouquet garni.

7 Sprinkle the breadcrumbs in an even
layer over the top of the cassoulet and
return to the oven, uncovered, for a
further 40 minutes, or until the meat is
tender and the top crisp and lightly
brown. Garnish with fresh thyme sprigs
and serve hot with plenty of warm
crusty bread to mop up the juices.

BRAISED SAUSAGES with ONIONS, CELERIAC and APPLE

This richly flavoured casserole is comfort food at its best – serve with mashed potatoes and a glass or two of full-bodied red wine on a cold winter night.

SERVES 4

45ml/3 tbsp sunflower oil
450g/1lb duck or venison sausages
2 onions, sliced
15ml/1 tbsp plain (all-purpose) flour
400ml/14fl oz/1⅔ cups dry (hard) cider
350g/12oz celeriac, cut into
   large chunks
15ml/1 tbsp Worcestershire sauce
15ml/1 tbsp chopped fresh sage
2 small tart cooking apples, cored
   and sliced
salt and ground black pepper

1 Preheat the oven to 180°C/350°F/ Gas 4. Heat the oil in a frying pan, add the sausages and fry until evenly browned, about 5 minutes. Transfer to an earthenware casserole dish.

2 Drain off any excess oil from the pan to leave 15ml/1 tbsp. Add the onions and sauté for a few minutes until golden.

3 Stir in the flour, then gradually add the cider and bring to the boil, stirring. Add the celeriac and cook for 2 minutes. Stir in the Worcestershire sauce and sage. Season well with salt and black pepper.

4 Pour the cider and celeriac mixture over the sausages, then cover and cook in the oven for 30 minutes. Add the apples and cook for 10–15 minutes, or until the apples are just tender.

VARIATION
You can use good-quality pork and herb sausages instead, if you like.

MARINATED PIGEON in RED WINE

The time taken to marinate and cook this casserole is well rewarded by the fabulous rich flavour of the finished dish. Stir-fried green cabbage and celeriac purée are delicious accompaniments to this casserole.

SERVES 4

4 pigeons (US squabs), about 225g/
    8oz each
30ml/2 tbsp olive oil
1 onion, coarsely chopped
225g/8oz/3¼ cups chestnut
    mushrooms, sliced
15ml/1 tbsp plain (all-purpose) flour
300ml/½ pint/1¼ cups game stock
30ml/2 tbsp chopped fresh parsley
salt and ground black pepper
flat leaf parsley, to garnish

For the marinade
15ml/1 tbsp light olive oil
1 onion, chopped
1 carrot, peeled and chopped
1 celery stick, chopped
3 garlic cloves, sliced
6 allspice berries, bruised
2 bay leaves
8 black peppercorns, bruised
150ml/¼ pint/⅔ cup red wine vinegar
150ml/¼ pint/⅔ cup red wine
45ml/3 tbsp redcurrant jelly

1 Mix together all the ingredients for the marinade in a large bowl. Add the pigeons and turn them in the marinade, then cover the bowl and chill for about 12 hours, turning the pigeons frequently.

VARIATIONS
If you are unable to buy pigeon, this recipe works equally well with chicken or rabbit. Buy portions and make deep slashes in the flesh so that the marinade soaks into, and flavours right to, the centre of the pieces of meat.

2 Preheat the oven to 150°C/300°F/ Gas 2. Heat the oil in a large, flameproof casserole and cook the onion and mushrooms for about 5 minutes, or until the onion has softened.

3 Meanwhile, drain the pigeons and strain the marinade into a jug (pitcher), then set both aside separately.

4 Sprinkle the flour over the pigeons and add them to the casserole, breast-sides down. Pour in the marinade and stock, and add the chopped parsley and seasoning. Cover and cook for 2½ hours.

5 Check the seasoning, then serve the pigeons on warmed plates and ladle the sauce over them. Garnish with parsley.

GUINEA FOWL with BEANS and CURLY KALE

Cooking lean poultry such as guinea fowl, chicken or turkey in a clay pot or chicken brick gives a delicious, moist result. Here the guinea fowl is cooked atop a colourful bed of herb-flavoured beans and vegetables.

2 Remove the shallots, garlic and celery with a slotted spoon and place in the chicken brick. Stir in the tomatoes and beans. Tuck in the thyme and bay leaves.

3 Put the guinea fowl in the frying pan and brown on all sides, then pour in the wine and stock and bring to the boil. Lift the bird out of the pan, place it on top of the vegetables in the chicken brick and then pour the liquid over the top. Cover and place in an unheated oven and set to 200°C/400°F/Gas 6. Cook for 1 hour.

4 Add the curly kale to the chicken brick, nestling it among the beans. Cover and cook for 10–15 minutes, or until the guinea fowl is tender. Season the bean mixture and serve.

COOK'S TIP
Guinea fowl and quail were both originally classified as game birds but nowadays farmed varieties are sold, making them available in the stores all year round.

VARIATION
Use chard, spring greens (collards) or Savoy cabbage in place of curly kale.

SERVES 4

1.3kg/3lb guinea fowl
45ml/3 tbsp olive oil
4 shallots, chopped
1 garlic clove, crushed
3 celery sticks, sliced
400g/14oz can chopped tomatoes
2 × 400g/14oz cans mixed
    beans, drained
5 fresh thyme sprigs
2 bay leaves
150ml/¼ pint/⅔ cup dry white wine
300ml/½ pint/1¼ cups well-flavoured
    chicken stock
175g/6oz curly kale
salt and ground black pepper

1 Soak a clay chicken brick in cold water for 20 minutes, then drain. Rub the guinea fowl with 15ml/1 tbsp of the olive oil and season. Place the remaining oil in a frying pan, add the shallots, garlic and celery and sauté for 4–5 minutes.

BRAISED PHEASANT with WILD MUSHROOMS, CHESTNUTS and BACON

Pheasant at the end of their season are not suitable for roasting, so consider this tasty casserole enriched with wild mushrooms and chestnuts. Allow two birds for four people.

SERVES 4

2 mature pheasants
50g/2oz/¼ cup butter
75ml/5 tbsp brandy
12 baby (pearl) onions, peeled
1 celery stick, chopped
50g/2oz unsmoked rindless bacon,
    cut into strips
45ml/3 tbsp plain (all-purpose) flour
550ml/18fl oz/2¼ cups chicken
    stock, boiling
175g/6oz peeled, cooked chestnuts
350g/12oz/4 cups fresh ceps, trimmed and
    sliced, or 15g/½oz/¼ cup dried porcini
    mushrooms, soaked in warm water for
    20 minutes
15ml/1 tbsp lemon juice
salt and ground black pepper
watercress sprigs, to garnish

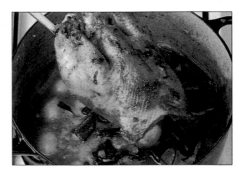

2 Wipe out the casserole and melt the remaining butter. Add the onions, celery and bacon and brown lightly. Stir in the flour. Remove from the heat.

3 Stir in the stock gradually so that it is completely absorbed by the flour. Add the chestnuts, mushrooms, the pheasants and their juices. Bring back to a gentle simmer, then cover and cook in the oven for 1½ hours.

4 Transfer the cooked pheasants and vegetables to a warmed serving plate. Bring the sauce back to the boil, add the lemon juice and season to taste. Pour the sauce into a jug (pitcher) or gravy boat and garnish the birds with watercress.

COOK'S TIP
Cooking and peeling fresh chestnuts can be hard work, so look out for ready-peeled canned or vacuum-packed varieties.

1 Preheat the oven to 160°C/325°F/ Gas 3. Season the pheasants with salt and pepper. Melt half of the butter in a large flameproof casserole and brown the pheasants over a medium heat. Transfer the pheasants to a shallow dish and pour off the cooking fat. Return the casserole to the heat and brown the sediment. Add the brandy, stir well to loosen the sediment using a flat wooden spoon, then pour all the cooking juices over the pheasant.

COOK'S TIP
When buying pheasant choose birds that look fresh. They should be plump and firm, with supple skin. Game birds have a strong odour but they should never smell unpleasant or "off".

STOVE-TOP FISH AND SHELLFISH

For a healthy, speedy meal with superb flavour, fish and shellfish are the perfect choice. Cooking on top of the stove means you can check the dish frequently, and serve it the moment it is ready. Italian Fish Stew would make a fine dish for a family meal, Seafood Risotto is a good choice for an impromptu supper with friends, while a more formal dinner would provide the perfect opportunity for trying Octopus and Red Wine Stew, Fish with Fregola or a colourful Seafood Paella.

ITALIAN FISH STEW

Italians are renowned for enjoying good food and this stew is a veritable feast of fish and shellfish in a delicious tomato broth – ideal for a family lunch.

SERVES 4

30ml/2 tbsp olive oil
1 onion, thinly sliced
a few saffron threads
5ml/1 tsp dried thyme
large pinch of cayenne pepper
2 garlic cloves, finely chopped
2 × 400g/14oz cans tomatoes, drained
   and chopped
175ml/6fl oz/¾ cup dry white wine
2 litres/3½ pints/8 cups hot fish stock
350g/12oz white, skinless fish fillets, such
   as haddock or cod, cut into pieces
450g/1lb monkfish, cut into pieces
450g/1lb mussels, scrubbed
225g/8oz small squid, cleaned and cut
   into rings
30ml/2 tbsp chopped fresh basil
   or parsley
salt and ground black pepper
thickly sliced bread, to serve

1 Heat the olive oil in a large, heavy pan. Add the onion, saffron threads, thyme, cayenne pepper and salt, to taste. Stir well and cook over a low heat for 10 minutes, until the onion is soft. Add the garlic and cook for 1 minute more.

2 Stir in the chopped tomatoes, dry white wine and hot fish stock. Bring to the boil and boil for 1 minute, then reduce the heat and simmer gently for 15 minutes.

COOK'S TIP
Cayenne pepper has quite a hot, spicy flavour and was originally made from a type of chilli from the Cayenne region of French Guiana. It should be used sparingly.

3 Add the fish pieces to the tomato mixture in the pan and stir gently. Simmer the stew over a low heat for a further 3 minutes.

4 Add the mussels and squid rings and simmer for about 2 minutes, until the mussels open. Discard any that remain closed. Stir in the basil or parsley and season to taste. Ladle into warmed soup bowls and serve with bread.

OCTOPUS and RED WINE STEW

Fresh octopus can be quite tricky to prepare so unless you're happy to clean and prepare it for this traditional Greek dish, buy one that's ready for cooking.

SERVES 4

900g/2lb prepared octopus
450g/1lb onions, sliced
2 bay leaves
450g/1lb ripe tomatoes
60ml/4 tbsp olive oil
4 garlic cloves, crushed
5ml/1 tsp sugar
15ml/1 tbsp chopped fresh oregano
   or rosemary
30ml/2 tbsp chopped fresh parsley
150ml/¼ pint/⅔ cup red wine
30ml/2 tbsp red wine vinegar
chopped fresh herbs, to garnish
warm bread and pine nuts, to serve

COOK'S TIP
The octopus, along with cuttlefish and squid, is a member of the mollusc family – their main shared characteristic is that they have no shell. Octopus can be very tough, so it needs long, slow cooking to tenderize it.

1 Put the octopus in a large pan of gently simmering water with one-quarter of the onions and the bay leaves. Cover the pan and cook gently for 1 hour.

2 While the octopus is cooking, plunge the tomatoes into boiling water for 30 seconds, then refresh in cold water. Peel away the skins and chop roughly.

3 Drain the octopus and, using a small sharp knife, cut it into bitesize pieces. Discard the head.

4 Heat the oil in the pan and fry the octopus, the remaining onions and the garlic for 3 minutes. Add the tomatoes, sugar, herbs, wine and vinegar and cook, stirring, for 5 minutes.

5 Cover the pan and cook over the lowest possible heat for about 1½ hours until the red wine and tomato sauce is thickened and the octopus is tender. To serve, garnish with fresh herbs and serve with plenty of warm bread, and pine nuts to scatter on top.

MOROCCAN FISH TAGINE

This spicy, aromatic dish proves just how exciting an ingredient fish can be. Serve it with couscous, which you can steam in the traditional way in a colander on top of the tagine.

SERVES 8

1.3kg/3lb firm fish fillets, skinned and cut
   into 5cm/2in chunks
60ml/4 tbsp olive oil
1 large aubergine (eggplant), cut into
   1cm/½in cubes
2 courgettes (zucchini), cut into
   1cm/½in cubes
4 onions, chopped
400g/14oz can chopped tomatoes
400ml/14fl oz/1⅔ cups passata (bottled
   strained tomatoes)
200ml/7fl oz/scant 1 cup fish stock
1 preserved lemon, chopped
90g/3½oz/scant 1 cup olives
60ml/4 tbsp chopped fresh coriander
   (cilantro), plus extra coriander leaves
   to garnish
salt and ground black pepper

For the harissa
3 large fresh red chillies, seeded
   and chopped
3 garlic cloves, peeled
15ml/1 tbsp ground coriander
30ml/2 tbsp ground cumin
5ml/1 tsp ground cinnamon
grated rind of 1 lemon
30ml/2 tbsp sunflower oil

3 Heat half the olive oil in a shallow heavy pan. Add the aubergine cubes and fry for about 10 minutes, or until they are golden brown. Add the courgettes and fry for a further 2 minutes. Remove the vegetables from the pan using a slotted spoon and set aside.

4 Add the remaining olive oil to the pan, add the onions and cook over a low heat for about 10 minutes until golden brown. Stir in the remaining harissa and cook for 5 minutes, stirring occasionally.

5 Add the vegetables and combine with the onions, then stir in the chopped tomatoes, the passata and fish stock. Bring to the boil, then lower the heat and simmer for about 20 minutes.

6 Stir the fish chunks and preserved lemon into the pan. Add the olives and stir gently. Cover and simmer over a low heat for about 15–20 minutes. Season to taste. Stir in the chopped coriander. Serve with couscous, if you like, and garnish with coriander leaves.

1 Make the harissa. Whizz everything in a food processor to a smooth paste.

2 Put the fish in a wide bowl and add 30ml/2 tbsp of the harissa. Toss to coat, cover and chill for at least 1 hour.

COOK'S TIP
To make the fish go further, add 225g/8oz/ 1¼ cups cooked chickpeas to the tagine.

FISH PLAKI

Greece has so much coastline, it's no wonder that fish is so popular there. Generally, it is treated simply, but in this recipe the fish is cooked with onions and tomatoes.

SERVES 6

300ml/½ pint/1¼ cups olive oil
2 onions, thinly sliced
3 large, well-flavoured tomatoes,
    roughly chopped
3 garlic cloves, thinly sliced
5ml/1 tsp sugar
5ml/1 tsp chopped fresh dill
5ml/1 tsp chopped fresh mint
5ml/1 tsp chopped fresh celery leaves
15ml/1 tbsp chopped fresh flat
    leaf parsley
300ml/½ pint/1¼ cups water
6 hake or cod steaks
juice of 1 lemon
salt and ground black pepper
extra fresh dill, mint or parsley sprigs,
    to garnish

1 Heat the oil in large heavy sauté pan or flameproof casserole. Add the onions and cook, stirring, until pale golden, then add the tomatoes, garlic, sugar, dill, mint, celery leaves and parsley with the water. Season with salt and pepper, then simmer, uncovered, for 25 minutes, until the liquid has reduced by one-third.

2 Add the fish steaks and cook gently for 10–12 minutes until the fish is just cooked. Remove the pan or casserole from the heat and add the lemon juice. Cover and leave to stand for 20 minutes before serving. Arrange the cod in a dish and pour the sauce over. Garnish with herbs and serve warm or cold.

FISH with SPINACH and LIME

Fresh herbs and hot spices are combined to make the charmoula marinade that is used to flavour this delicious Moroccan-style dish. Crusty bread makes a good accompaniment.

SERVES 4

675g/1½lb white fish, such as haddock,
   cod, sea bass or monkfish
sunflower oil, for frying
500g/1¼lb potatoes, sliced
1 onion, chopped
1–2 garlic cloves, crushed
5 tomatoes, peeled and chopped
375g/13oz fresh spinach, chopped
lime wedges, to garnish

For the charmoula
6 spring onions (scallions), chopped
10ml/2 tsp fresh thyme
60ml/4 tbsp chopped flat leaf parsley
30ml/2 tbsp chopped fresh
   coriander (cilantro)
10ml/2 tsp paprika
generous pinch of cayenne pepper
60ml/4 tbsp olive oil
grated rind of 1 lime and 60ml/4 tbsp
   lime juice
salt

1 Cut the white fish into large even-size pieces, discarding any skin and bones. Place the fish in a large shallow dish.

2 Blend together the ingredients for the charmoula. Season with salt. Pour over the fish, stir to mix and leave in a cool place, covered with clear film (plastic wrap), to marinate for 2–4 hours.

5 Place the marinated fish pieces on top of the chopped spinach in the pan and pour over all of the marinade. Cover the pan tightly and cook for 15–18 minutes. After about 8 minutes of the cooking time, carefully stir the contents of the pan with a wooden spoon, so that the pieces of fish at the top are distributed throughout the dish.

6 Cover the pan again and continue cooking, but check occasionally — the dish is cooked once the fish is just tender and opaque and the spinach has wilted. Serve the dish hot, with wedges of lime and plenty of warm crusty bread, if you like.

3 Heat about 5mm/¼in oil in a large heavy pan, add the potato slices and cook, turning them occasionally, until they are cooked right through and golden brown. Drain the fried potatoes on kitchen paper.

4 Pour off all but 15ml/1 tbsp of the oil from the pan and add the onion, garlic and tomatoes. Cook over a gentle heat for 5–6 minutes, stirring occasionally, until the onion is soft. Place the potatoes on top and then add the spinach.

FISH with FREGOLA

This Sardinian speciality is a cross between a soup and a stew. Serve it with crusty Italian country bread to mop up the juices.

SERVES 4–6

75ml/5 tbsp olive oil
4 garlic cloves, finely chopped
½ small fresh red chilli, seeded and
    finely chopped
1 large handful fresh flat leaf parsley,
    roughly chopped
1 red snapper, about 450g/1lb, cleaned,
    with head and tail removed
1 grey mullet or porgy, about 500g/1¼lb,
    cleaned, with head and tail removed
350–450g/12oz–1lb thick cod fillet
400g/14oz can chopped plum tomatoes
175g/6oz/1½ cups dried fregola
250ml/8fl oz/1 cup water
salt and ground black pepper

1 Heat 30ml/2 tbsp of the olive oil in a large flameproof casserole. Add the chopped garlic and chilli, with about half the chopped fresh parsley. Fry over a medium heat, stirring occasionally, for about 5 minutes.

2 Cut all of the fish into large chunks – including the skin and the bones in the case of the snapper and mullet – and add the pieces to the casserole. Sprinkle with a further 30ml/2 tbsp of the olive oil and fry for a few minutes more.

3 Add the tomatoes, then fill the empty can with water and add to the pan. Bring to the boil. Season to taste, lower the heat and cook for 10 minutes.

4 Add the fregola and simmer for about 5 minutes, then add the water and the remaining oil. Simmer for 15 minutes until the fregola is just tender.

5 If the sauce becomes too thick, add more water, then taste for seasoning. Serve hot, in warmed bowls, sprinkled with the remaining parsley.

VARIATION

Any white fish fillet can be used instead of cod in this dish. Monkfish, haddock, hake or plaice could all be used.

COOK'S TIPS

• Fregola is a tiny pasta shape from Sardinia. If you can't get it, use a tiny soup pasta (*pastina*), such as *corallini* or *semi de melone*.
• You can make the basic fish sauce several hours in advance or even the day before, bringing it to the boil and adding the fregola just before serving.

SEAFOOD PAELLA

There are as many versions of paella as there are regions of Spain. Those from near the coast contain a lot of seafood, while inland versions add chicken or pork. Here the only meat is the chorizo – essential for an authentic flavour.

SERVES 4

45ml/3 tbsp olive oil
1 large onion, chopped
2 fat garlic cloves, chopped
150g/5oz chorizo, sliced
300g/11oz small squid, cleaned
1 red (bell) pepper, seeded and sliced
4 tomatoes, peeled, seeded and diced,
  or 200g/7oz can tomatoes
about 500ml/17fl oz/generous 2 cups
  chicken stock
105ml/7 tbsp dry white wine
200g/7oz/1 cup short grain Spanish rice
  or risotto rice
a large pinch of saffron threads
150g/5oz/1¼ cups fresh or frozen peas
12 large cooked prawns (shrimp), in the
  shell, or 8 langoustines
450g/1lb mussels, scrubbed
450g/1lb clams, scrubbed
salt and ground black pepper

1 Heat the olive oil in a large sauté pan or a paella pan, add the onion and garlic and fry until the onion is translucent. Add the chorizo and fry until golden.

2 If the squid are very small, you can leave them whole; otherwise cut the bodies into rings and the tentacles into pieces. Add the squid to the pan and sauté over a high heat for 2 minutes, stirring occasionally.

3 Stir in the pepper slices and the seeded and diced tomatoes and simmer gently for 5 minutes, until the pepper slices are tender. Pour in the stock and wine, stir well and bring to the boil.

4 Stir in the rice and saffron and season to taste with salt and pepper. Spread the contents of the pan in an even layer over the base. Bring the liquid back to the boil, then lower the heat and simmer gently for 10 minutes.

5 Add the peas, prawns or langoustines, mussels and clams, stirring them gently into the rice. Cook gently for another 15–20 minutes, until the rice is tender and all the mussels and clams have opened. If any remain closed, discard them. If the paella seems dry, add a little more stock. Gently stir everything together and serve piping hot.

SEAFOOD RISOTTO

Creamy, saffron-flavoured rice makes the perfect foil for shellfish. Ready-prepared, frozen seafood mixtures, which include prawns, squid and mussels, are ideal for making this quick and easy dish – remember to thaw them before cooking.

SERVES 4

1 litre/1¾ pints/4 cups hot fish or
   shellfish stock
50g/2oz/¼ cup unsalted (sweet) butter
2 shallots, chopped
2 garlic cloves, chopped
350g/12oz/1¾ cups risotto rice
150ml/¼ pint/⅔ cup dry white wine
2.5ml/½ tsp powdered saffron, or a
   pinch of saffron threads
400g/14oz mixed prepared seafood,
   thawed if frozen
30ml/2 tbsp freshly grated
   Parmesan cheese
30ml/2 tbsp chopped fresh flat leaf parsley,
   to garnish
salt and ground black pepper

1 Pour the fish or shellfish stock into a large, heavy pan. Bring it to the boil, then pour it into a large, heatproof jug (pitcher) or bowl and keep warm.

2 Melt the butter in the rinsed-out pan pan, add the shallots and garlic and cook over a low heat for 3–5 minutes, stirring occasionally, until the shallots are soft but not coloured. Add the rice, stir well to coat the grains completely with butter, then pour in the dry white wine. Cook over a medium heat, stirring occasionally, until the wine has been absorbed by the rice.

COOK'S TIP
It is essential to use proper risotto rice, such as arborio or carnaroli for this dish, it has a wonderfully creamy texture when cooked but still retains a "bite".

3 Add a ladleful of hot stock and the saffron, and cook, stirring continuously, until the liquid has been absorbed. Add the seafood and stir well. Continue to add hot stock a ladleful at a time, waiting until each quantity has been absorbed before adding more. Stir the mixture for about 20 minutes in all until the rice is swollen and creamy, but still with a little bite in the middle.

VARIATION
Use peeled prawns (shrimp), or cubes of fish such as cod or salmon in place of the mixed prepared seafood.

4 Vigorously mix in the freshly grated Parmesan cheese and season to taste, then sprinkle over the chopped parsley and serve immediately.

OVEN-COOKED FISH AND SHELLFISH

Moist and succulent, fish tastes great when cooked in the oven, especially when baked in clay. Specially designed clay pots will hold a whole fish with ease, so you can treat yourself to Baked Sea Bass with Lemon Grass and Red Onions, or Monkfish with Rocket Pesto, Peppers and Onions. Also on the menu are delicious one-pot dishes such as Jansson's Temptation, a delectable potato and anchovy bake, and a very special Shellfish Tagine.

BAKED SEA BREAM with TOMATOES

John Dory, halibut or sea bass can all be cooked this way. If you prefer to use filleted fish, choose a chunky fillet, such as cod, and roast it skin-side up. Roasting the tomatoes brings out their sweetness, which contrasts beautifully with the flavour of the fish.

SERVES 4–6

8 ripe tomatoes
10ml/2 tsp sugar
200ml/7fl oz/scant 1 cup olive oil
450g/1lb new potatoes
1 lemon, sliced
1 bay leaf
1 fresh thyme sprig
8 fresh basil leaves
1 sea bream, about 900g–1kg/2–2¼lb,
    cleaned and scaled
150ml/¼ pint/⅔ cup dry white wine
30ml/2 tbsp fresh white breadcrumbs
2 garlic cloves, crushed
15ml/1 tbsp finely chopped fresh parsley
salt and ground black pepper
fresh flat parsley or basil leaves, chopped,
    to garnish

1 Preheat the oven to 240°C/475°F/ Gas 9. Cut the tomatoes in half lengthwise and arrange them in a single layer in a baking dish, cut-side up. Sprinkle with sugar, salt and pepper and drizzle over a little of the olive oil. Roast for 30–40 minutes, until lightly browned. Remove the tomatoes from the dish and set aside.

2 Meanwhile, cut the potatoes into 1cm/½in slices. Place in a large pan of salted water and par-boil for 5 minutes. Drain and set aside.

3 Grease the baking dish with a little more of the oil. Arrange the potatoes in a single layer with the lemon slices over; sprinkle on the herbs. Season and drizzle with half the remaining oil. Lay the fish on top and season. Pour over the wine and the rest of the oil. Arrange the tomatoes around the fish.

4 Mix together the breadcrumbs, garlic and parsley; sprinkle over the fish. Bake for 30 minutes. Garnish with chopped parsley or basil.

FILLETS of BRILL in RED WINE SAUCE

Forget the old maxim that red wine and fish do not go well together. The robust sauce adds colour and richness to this excellent dish, which is more than elegant enough for a dinner party. Halibut and John Dory are also good cooked this way.

SERVES 4

4 fillets of brill, about 175–200g/6–7oz
    each, skinned
150g/5oz/10 tbsp chilled butter, diced, plus
    extra for greasing
115g/4oz shallots, thinly sliced
200ml/7fl oz/scant 1 cup robust red wine
200ml/7fl oz/scant 1 cup fish stock
salt and ground black and white pepper
fresh flat leaf parsley leaves or chervil,
    to garnish

1 Preheat the oven to 180°C/350°F/ Gas 4. Season the fish fillets on both sides with salt and ground black pepper. Generously butter a shallow flameproof dish, which is large enough to take all the brill fillets in a single layer. Spread the shallots in an even layer in the dish and lay the fish fillets on top. Season well with salt and ground black pepper.

2 Pour in the red wine and fish stock, cover the dish with a lid or foil and then bring the liquid to just below boiling point. Transfer the dish to the oven and bake for 6–8 minutes, or until the brill is just cooked.

3 Using a fish slice (metal spatula), lift the fish and shallots on to a serving dish, cover with foil and keep hot.

4 Transfer the dish to the stove and bring the cooking liquid to the boil over a high heat. Cook it until it has reduced by half. Lower the heat and whisk in the chilled butter, one piece at a time, to make a smooth, shiny sauce. Season with salt and ground white pepper, set the sauce aside and keep hot.

5 Divide the shallots among four warmed plates and lay the brill fillets on top. Pour the sauce over and around the fish and garnish with the fresh flat leaf parsley or chervil.

MONKFISH with ROCKET PESTO, PEPPERS and ONIONS

Colourful Mediterranean vegetables complement richly flavoured monkfish layered with pesto sauce in this impressive-looking clay pot dish.

SERVES 4

900g/2lb monkfish tail
50g/2oz rocket (arugula)
30ml/2 tbsp pine nuts
1 garlic clove, chopped
25g/1oz/⅓ cup freshly grated
    Parmesan cheese
90ml/6 tbsp olive oil
45ml/3 tbsp lemon juice
2 red (bell) peppers, halved
2 yellow (bell) peppers, halved
1 red onion, cut into wedges
2 courgettes (zucchini), cut into
    2.5cm/1in slices
4 fresh rosemary sprigs
salt and ground black pepper

1 Remove any skin or membrane from the monkfish. Using a large, sharp knife cut along one side of the central bone, as close to the bone as possible and then remove the fish fillet. Repeat on the other side. Set aside.

2 Soak a fish clay pot in cold water for 20 minutes, then drain and set aside.

VARIATIONS
• Salmon tail fillets, or thick fillets of cod or haddock could be used in place of the monkfish. Remove the skin from the fish and run your hand along the other side to check for any hidden bones and, if necessary, remove these with tweezers.
• Rocket makes an interestingly peppery pesto, but other leafy herbs can be used to make this sauce. basil is the classic choice, but flat leaf parsley is also good.

3 Place the rocket, pine nuts, chopped garlic, freshly grated Parmesan cheese, 45ml/3 tbsp of the olive oil and 15ml/1 tbsp of the lemon juice in a food processor or blender and process to form a smooth paste.

4 Lay one fish fillet out flat, cut-side up and spread with the pesto. Place the remaining fillet on top, cut-side down, on top of the layer of pesto. Tie the fish with string at regular intervals to seal together. Sprinkle with plenty of salt and pepper to season and set aside.

5 Cut each pepper half into three lengthwise. Remove the core and seeds.

6 Place the pieces of pepper in the clay pot with the onion wedges and slices of courgette. In a small bowl, mix together 15ml/1 tbsp of the olive oil and the remaining lemon juice and sprinkle over the vegetables. Mix well and season with salt and plenty of black pepper.

7 Tuck the fresh rosemary sprigs in among the vegetables. Cover the clay pot and place in an unheated oven. Set the temperature to 220°C/425°F/Gas 7 and cook the vegetables for 20 minutes.

8 Remove the clay pot from the oven, place the monkfish parcel in the centre of the vegetables and brush it with 15ml/1 tbsp of the olive oil. Sprinkle the remaining oil over the vegetables. Cover the pot again, then return the pot to the oven and cook for 20–25 minutes more, or until the monkfish is cooked through and turns opaque.

9 To serve, cut the fish into thick slices, removing the string, if you prefer, and serve with the cooked vegetables.

BAKED MONKFISH with POTATOES and GARLIC

This simple supper dish can be made with other fish. Sauce tartare or a thick vinaigrette flavoured with chopped gherkins and hard-boiled egg are delicious accompaniments.

SERVES 4

50g/2oz/¼ cup butter
2 onions, thickly sliced
1kg/2¼lb waxy potatoes, peeled and cut
    into small chunks
4 garlic cloves
a few fresh thyme sprigs
2–3 fresh bay leaves
450ml/¾ pint/scant 2 cups vegetable
    or fish stock, plus 45ml/3 tbsp
900g/2lb monkfish tail in one piece,
    membrane removed
30–45ml/2–3 tbsp white wine
50g/2oz/1 cup fresh white breadcrumbs
15g/½oz fresh flat leaf parsley,
    finely chopped
15ml/1 tbsp olive oil
salt and ground black pepper

1 Preheat the oven to 190°C/375°F/ Gas 5. Melt half the butter in a shallow flameproof dish and cook the onions for 5 minutes until soft. Stir in the potatoes.

2 Slice two of the garlic cloves and add them to the dish with the thyme and bay leaves, and season with salt and pepper.

3 Pour the main batch of stock over the potatoes and bake, uncovered, stirring once or twice, for about 50 minutes, or until the potatoes are just tender.

4 Nestle the monkfish tail into the potatoes and season well with salt and ground black pepper. Mix the 45ml/ 3 tbsp stock with the wine and use to baste the monkfish two or three times during cooking. Bake the monkfish and potatoes for 10–15 minutes.

5 Finely chop the remaining garlic. Melt the remaining butter and toss it with the fresh breadcrumbs, chopped garlic, most of the chopped parsley and seasoning. Spread the crumb mixture over the monkfish, pressing it down gently with the back of a spoon.

6 Drizzle the olive oil over the crumb-covered fish, then return the dish to the oven and bake for a final 10–15 minutes, or until the breadcrumbs are crisp and golden brown and all the liquid has been absorbed. Sprinkle the remaining chopped parsley on to the potatoes and fish and serve immediately.

JANSSON'S TEMPTATION

A traditional Swedish favourite, this rich gratin is utterly moreish. As food writer Jane Grigson pointed out, the name probably does not refer to a specific Jansson but means "everyone's temptation" as Jansson is a common Swedish surname.

SERVES 4–6

50g/2oz/¼ cup butter
900g/2lb potatoes
2 large, sweet onions, sliced
2 × 50g/2oz cans anchovies in olive
 oil, drained
450ml/¾ pint/scant 2 cups whipping cream
 or half and half double (heavy) and
 single (light) cream
a little milk (optional)
salt and ground black pepper

1 Preheat the oven to 200°C/400°F/ Gas 6. Use 15g/½oz/1 tbsp of the butter to grease a shallow 1.5 litre/2½ pint/ 6¼ cup earthenware baking dish.

2 Using a small sharp knife, carefully cut the potatoes into thin slices, then cut the slices into fine matchstick strips.

3 Toss the potato strips with salt and ground black pepper and sprinkle half of them in the base of the prepared ovenproof dish.

COOK'S TIPS
• It is important to cover the gratin with foil for the first half of the cooking time so that the potatoes don't brown or dry out too much.
• If using whole, salted anchovies or Swedish salted sprats (US small whitebait or smelts) they will need to be boned. If they are very salty, soak in a little milk for about 30 minutes before using.
• Serve with small glasses of chilled schnapps and cold beer for an authentic Swedish flavour.

4 Lay half of the onions on top of the potatoes, season with black pepper and dot with butter. Lay the anchovies on top of the onions, then add the rest of the sliced onions and top with the remaining potatoes.

5 Mix the cream with 30ml/2 tbsp cold water and pour this mixture over the potatoes and onions in the dish. Add a little milk, if necessary, to bring the liquid to just below the top of the final layer of potato matchstick strips.

6 Dot the potatoes with the remaining butter, then cover the dish with foil and bake for 1 hour.

7 Reduce the oven temperature to 180°C/350°F/Gas 4 and remove the foil from the top of the dish. Bake for a further 40–50 minutes, or until the potatoes are tender when tested with a knife and brown in colour.

GOAN FISH CASSEROLE

The cooking of Goa is a mixture of Portuguese and Indian; the addition of tamarind gives a slightly sour note to the spicy coconut sauce.

SERVES 4

7.5ml/1½ tsp ground turmeric
5ml/1 tsp salt
450g/1lb monkfish fillet, cut into
    eight pieces
15ml/1 tbsp lemon juice
5ml/1 tsp cumin seeds
5ml/1 tsp coriander seeds
5ml/1 tsp black peppercorns
1 garlic clove, chopped
5cm/2in piece fresh root ginger,
    finely chopped
25g/1oz tamarind paste
150ml/¼ pint/⅔ cup hot water
30ml/2 tbsp vegetable oil
2 onions, halved and sliced lengthways
400ml/14fl oz/1⅔ cups coconut milk
4 mild green chillies, seeded and cut into
    thin strips
16 large raw prawns (shrimp), peeled
30ml/2 tbsp chopped fresh coriander
    (cilantro) leaves, to garnish

1 Mix together the ground turmeric and salt in a small bowl. Place the monkfish in a shallow dish and sprinkle over the lemon juice, then rub the turmeric and salt mixture over the fish fillets to coat them completely. Cover and chill until ready to cook.

COOK'S TIP
Tamarind, which is also known as Indian date, is a popular spice throughout India, South-east Asia and the Caribbean. It has little smell, but the distinctive sour, yet fruity taste makes up for this. It is often used in curries and spicy dishes and is available from Indian and South-east Asian stores and some large supermarkets.

2 Put the cumin seeds, coriander seeds and black peppercorns in a blender or small food processor and blend to a powder. Add the garlic and ginger and process for a few seconds more.

3 Preheat the oven to 200°C/400°F/ Gas 6. Mix the tamarind paste with the hot water and set aside.

4 Heat the oil in a frying pan, add the onions and cook for 5–6 minutes, until softened and golden. Transfer the onions to a shallow earthenware dish.

VARIATION
You may use any firm white fish fillets such as cod, halibut or hake instead of the monkfish in this casserole.

5 Add the fish fillets to the oil remaining in the frying pan, and fry briefly over a high heat, turning them to seal on all sides. Remove the fish from the pan and place on top of the onions.

6 Add the ground spice mixture to the frying pan and cook over a medium heat, stirring constantly, for 1–2 minutes. Stir in the tamarind liquid, coconut milk and chilli strips and bring to the boil. Pour the sauce into the earthenware dish to coat the fish completely.

7 Cover the earthenware dish and cook the fish casserole in the oven for about 10 minutes. Add the prawns, pushing them into the liquid, then cover the dish again and return it to the oven for 5 minutes, or until the prawns turn pink. Do not overcook them or they will toughen. Check the seasoning, sprinkle with coriander leaves and serve.

BAKED SARDINES with CAPER and TOMATO STUFFING

Sardines are often a popular choice for cooking on the barbecue but you can enjoy these delicious Mediterranean-style baked sardines all year round.

SERVES 4

16 fresh sardines, cleaned
8–12 cherry tomatoes, on the vine, sliced
45ml/3 tbsp capers, chopped
½ small red onion, very finely chopped
60ml/4 tbsp olive oil
grated rind and juice 1 lemon
45ml/3 tbsp chopped fresh parsley
15ml/1 tbsp chopped fresh basil
basil sprigs and lemon wedges,
   to garnish
crusty bread, to serve

COOK'S TIP
Removing the bones before cooking, as in step 1 of this recipe, makes the sardines easier to eat.

1 Remove the backbone from the sardines by placing slit side down on a chopping board. Using your fingers, push firmly along the length of the backbone to loosen it from the flesh. Turn the sardine over and pull out the bone; cut the ends with a sharp knife to release it. Repeat with the remaining sardines.

2 Place the tomato slices inside each sardine; they may stick out slightly, depending on the size of the fish. Mix the capers and red onion together and place on top of the tomatoes.

3 Preheat the oven to 200°C/400°F/ Gas 6. Lay the sardines in a single layer in a large earthenware dish.

4 Mix together the olive oil, lemon rind and juice, parsley and basil and drizzle over the sardines. Bake the sardines for about 10 minutes, or until the fish flesh flakes easily. Garnish with basil and lemon wedges and serve with plenty of crusty bread to mop up the sauce.

SALMON BAKED with POTATOES and THYME

This is clay-pot cooking at its most sophisticated – a mouthwatering combination of potatoes and onions braised in thyme-flavoured stock and topped with perfectly tender pepper-crusted salmon fillets.

SERVES 4

675g/1½lb waxy potatoes, thinly sliced
1 onion, thinly sliced
10ml/2 tsp fresh thyme leaves
450ml/¾ pint/scant 2 cups vegetable or
　fish stock
40g/1½oz/3 tbsp butter,
　finely diced
4 skinless salmon fillets, about
　150g/5oz each
30ml/2 tbsp olive oil
15ml/1 tbsp black peppercorns,
　roughly crushed
salt and ground black pepper
fresh thyme, to garnish
mangetouts (snow peas) or sugar snap
　peas, to serve

1 Soak a fish clay pot in cold water for 20 minutes, then drain.

2 Layer the potato and onion slices in the clay pot, seasoning each layer and sprinkling with thyme. Pour over the stock, dot with butter, cover and place in an unheated oven.

3 Set the oven to 190°C/375°F/Gas 5. Bake the potatoes for 40 minutes then remove the lid and bake for a further 20 minutes, or until they are almost cooked.

4 Meanwhile brush the salmon fillets with olive oil and coat with crushed black peppercorns, pressing them in, if necessary, with the back of a spoon. Place the salmon on top of the potatoes, cover and cook for 15 minutes, or until the salmon is opaque, removing the lid for the last 5 minutes. Serve garnished with fresh thyme sprigs and with mangetouts or sugar snap peas to accompany.

SEAFOOD PIE with RÖSTI TOPPING

In this variation of a classic fish pie, a mixture of white fish and shellfish are combined with a creamy herb-flavoured sauce and finished with a grated potato topping.

SERVES 4

750g/1lb 10oz potatoes, unpeeled
    and scrubbed
50g/2oz/¼ cup butter, melted
350g/12oz cod or haddock fillets, skinned
    and cut into bitesize pieces
115g/4oz cooked, peeled prawns (shrimp)
115g/4oz cooked, shelled mussels
8–12 shelled queen scallops
50g/2oz/¼ cup butter
1 onion, finely chopped
50g/2oz/½ cup plain (all-purpose) flour
200ml/7fl oz/scant 1 cup dry white wine
300ml/½ pint/1¼ cups fish or
    vegetable stock
105ml/7 tbsp double (heavy) cream
30ml/2 tbsp chopped fresh dill, plus extra
    sprigs to garnish
15ml/1 tbsp chopped fresh parsley
60ml/4 tbsp freshly grated
    Parmesan cheese
salt and ground black pepper

1 Place the potatoes in a large pan. Cover with cold water and bring to the boil. Cook for 10–15 minutes, or until they are only just tender.

VARIATIONS
• For a speedy version of these individual pies, buy ready-prepared potato rösti and sprinkle it evenly over the fish and sauce as in step 6.
• To make an alternative topping, cook the potatoes until soft, drain and mash with a little milk and butter. Spoon the mashed potato over the fish and sauce and top with cheese as in step 6.
• Add 30ml/2 tbsp chopped capers to the sauce at the end of step 5.

2 Drain the potatoes well, and set aside until they are cool enough to handle. Peel and coarsely grate the par-boiled potatoes into a large mixing bowl. Stir in the melted butter and season well with salt and pepper.

3 Preheat the oven to 220°C/425°F/ Gas 7. Divide the pieces of cod or haddock and the prawns, mussels and scallops among four individual 19cm/ 7½in rectangular earthenware dishes.

4 Melt the butter in a large pan, add the onion and cook for 6–8 minutes, stirring occasionally with a wooden spoon, or until softened and light golden. Sprinkle in the flour and stir thoroughly with a wooden spoon until well blended.

5 Remove the pan from the heat and gradually pour in the wine and stock, stirring constantly until smooth. Bring to the boil, stirring constantly, then stir in the cream, dill and parsley and season to taste. Pour the sauce over the fish.

6 Sprinkle the grated potato evenly over the fish and sauce in the dishes and top with the grated Parmesan cheese. Bake for 25 minutes, or until the topping is crisp and golden and the fish is cooked. Serve hot, garnished with dill.

COOK'S TIP
Choose waxy potatoes for this dish and cook until barely tender. Floury potatoes are too soft and will break up, so if you only have floury potatoes, opt for the mashed potato option (see Variations).

BAKED SEA BASS with LEMON GRASS and RED ONIONS

Moist, tender sea bass is flavoured with a combination of traditional Thai ingredients in this simple but mouthwatering clay pot dish.

SERVES 2–3

1 sea bass, about 675g/1½lb, cleaned
   and scaled
30ml/2 tbsp olive oil
2 lemon grass stalks, finely sliced
1 red onion, finely shredded
1 chilli, seeded and finely chopped
5cm/2in piece fresh root ginger,
   finely shredded
45ml/3 tbsp chopped fresh
   coriander (cilantro)
rind and juice of 2 limes
30ml/2 tbsp light soy sauce
salt and ground black pepper

COOK'S TIP
This recipe will taste delicious using a variety of fish, such as red or grey mullet, red snapper, salmon or tilapia. Depending on the weight of the fish you may need to use two smaller fish rather than one whole one.

1 Soak a fish clay pot in cold water for 20 minutes, then drain. Make four to five diagonal slashes on both sides of the fish. Repeat the slashes on one side in the opposite direction to give an attractive cross-hatched effect. Rub the sea bass inside and out with salt, pepper and 15ml/1 tbsp of the olive oil.

2 Mix together the Thai ingredients – the lemon grass, red onion, chilli, ginger, coriander and lime rind.

3 Place a little of the lemon grass and red onion mixture in the base of the clay pot, then lay the fish on top. Sprinkle the remaining mixture over the fish, then sprinkle over the lime juice, soy sauce and the remaining olive oil. Cover and place in an unheated oven.

4 Set the oven to 220°C/425°F/Gas 7 and cook the fish for 30–40 minutes, or until the flesh flakes easily when tested with a knife. Serve immediately.

SWORDFISH STEAKS with MANGO and AVOCADO SALSA

Meaty swordfish steaks, marinated in a tangy mix of lime juice, coriander and chilli, served with a vibrant fruity salsa.

SERVES 4

4 swordfish steaks, about 150g/5oz each
lime wedges and shredded spring onions
 (scallions), to garnish

For the marinade
rind and juice of 2 limes
2 garlic cloves, crushed
1 red chilli, seeded and finely chopped
30ml/2 tbsp olive oil
30ml/2 tbsp chopped fresh
 coriander (cilantro)
salt and ground black pepper

For the salsa
1 mango
4 spring onions (scallions), thinly sliced
1 red chilli, seeded and finely chopped
30ml/2 tbsp chopped fresh dill or
 coriander (cilantro)
30ml/2 tbsp lime juice
30ml/2 tbsp olive oil
1 ripe avocado

1 Place the swordfish steaks in a shallow non-metallic dish. Mix together the marinade ingredients and pour over the swordfish. Cover and leave to marinate in the refrigerator for 2 hours, or longer if time allows.

2 Soak a fish clay pot in cold water for 20 minutes, then drain. To prepare the salsa, peel the mango and slice the flesh off the stone (pit). Cut the flesh into rough dice. Add the spring onions, chilli, dill or coriander, lime juice and olive oil. Toss the ingredients together, cover and set aside to allow the flavours to blend.

3 Place the swordfish steaks in the clay pot and pour over the marinade. Cover and place in an unheated oven. Set the oven to 220°C/425°F/Gas 7 and bake for 15–20 minutes, or until the fish is cooked. The time will vary depending on the thickness of the steaks.

4 To complete the salsa, using a sharp knife, cut the avocado in half, remove the stone (pit), then roughly dice the flesh. Stir it into the prepared salsa ingredients and mix well. Serve the swordfish steaks with a mound of salsa, garnished with lime wedges and shredded spring onions.

SHELLFISH TAGINE

The distinctive mixture of spices and chillies used in this tagine is known as charmoula –
a classic Moroccan marinade for fish, meat and vegetable dishes.

SERVES 4

60ml/4 tbsp olive oil
4 garlic cloves, sliced
1–2 green chillies, seeded and chopped
a large handful of flat leaf parsley,
    roughly chopped
5ml/1 tsp coriander seeds
2.5ml/½ tsp ground allspice
6 cardamom pods, split open
2.5ml/½ tsp ground turmeric
15ml/1 tbsp lemon juice
350g/12oz scorpion fish, red mullet or red
    snapper fillets, cut into large chunks
225g/8oz squid, cleaned and cut into rings
1 onion, chopped
4 tomatoes, seeded and chopped
300ml/½ pint/1¼ cups warm fish or
    vegetable stock
225g/8oz large, raw prawns (shrimp)
15ml/1 tbsp chopped fresh
    coriander (cilantro)
salt and ground black pepper
lemon wedges, to garnish
couscous or rice and crusty bread,
    to serve

1 Place the olive oil, garlic, chillies, parsley, coriander seeds, allspice and cardamom pods in a mortar and pound to a smooth paste using a pestle. Stir in the ground turmeric, salt, pepper and lemon juice.

VARIATIONS
Scorpion fish is the traditional choice for this dish and red mullet or snapper makes a good, authentic alternative, but there's no reason why you shouldn't substitute other fish – try red bream, porgy or even halved cod or hake steaks.

2 Place the chunks of fish in a large glass or china bowl with the squid rings, add the spice paste and toss together. Cover and leave the fish to marinate in the refrigerator for about 2 hours, or longer, if time allows.

3 Place the chopped onion, seeded and chopped tomatoes and fish or vegetable stock in a tagine (see Cook's Tip) and cover. Place the tagine in an unheated oven and set the oven to 200°C/400°F/ Gas 6. Cook the vegetables for 20 minutes.

4 Remove the fish from the marinade, then drain well. Set aside the squid and any excess marinade, then place the fish in the tagine with the vegetables. Cover and cook in the oven for 5 minutes.

5 Add the prawns, squid rings and the remaining marinade to the tagine and stir to combine. Cover the tagine and return it to the oven for 5–10 minutes, or until all the fish, prawns and squid are cooked right through.

6 Taste the sauce and season to taste with salt and pepper if necessary, then stir in the chopped coriander. Serve immediately, garnished with lemon wedges. Serve the tagine with couscous or rice and crusty bread to soak up the juices.

COOK'S TIPS
• A tagine is a traditional Moroccan stew and it is also the name given to the shallow earthenware cooking dish with a tall, conical, earthenware lid in which the stew is traditionally cooked. A shallow, earthenware baking dish or a soaked, shallow clay pot can be used in place of a tagine.
• To ensure that the fish fillets have no tiny bones left in the flesh after filleting, lay the fillets on a board, skin-side down, and run your hand gently over the surface of the flesh. Pull out any bones that you find using a pair of tweezers.

STOVE-TOP VEGETARIAN DISHES

The great thing about these vegetarian dishes is that many of them are made with ingredients you will almost certainly have in your kitchen, so they are the recipes you'll make time and time again for all the family. Pan Haggerty, for instance, owes its excellent flavour to three simple ingredients: potatoes, Cheddar cheese and chives. Vegetable Korma is very adaptable, and Fettucine with Butter and Parmesan is as easy as its name suggests.

FRITTATA with LEEK, RED PEPPER and SPINACH

Apart from the fact that Italian frittata does not usually contain potato and is generally slightly softer in texture, it is not hugely different from Spanish tortilla. This combination of sweet leek, red pepper and spinach is delicious with the egg.

3 Add the spinach and cover the pan. Allow the spinach to wilt in the steam for 3–4 minutes, then stir to mix it into the vegetables, adding the pine nuts.

4 Beat the eggs with salt, pepper, the remaining cumin, basil and parsley. Add to the pan and cook over a gentle heat until the base of the omelette sets and turns golden brown. Pull the edges of the omelette away from the sides of the pan as it cooks and tilt the pan so that the uncooked egg runs underneath.

5 Preheat the grill (broiler). Flash the frittata under the hot grill to set the egg on top, but do not let it become too brown. Cut the frittata into wedges and serve warm, garnished with watercress and sprinkled with Parmesan, if using.

VARIATION
A delicious way to serve frittata is to pack it into a slightly hollowed-out loaf and then drizzle it with olive oil. Wrap tightly in clear film (plastic wrap) and stand for 1–2 hours before cutting into slices.

SERVES 3–4

30ml/2 tbsp olive oil
1 large red (bell) pepper, seeded and diced
2.5–5ml/½–1 tsp ground cumin
3 leeks (about 450g/1lb), thinly sliced
150g/5oz baby spinach leaves
45ml/3 tbsp pine nuts, toasted
5 large (US extra large) eggs
15ml/1 tbsp chopped fresh basil
15ml/1 tbsp chopped fresh flat leaf parsley
salt and ground black pepper
watercress, to garnish
50g/2oz/⅔ cup freshly grated Parmesan
    cheese, to serve (optional)

1 Heat a heavy, non-stick frying pan and add the olive oil. Add the diced red pepper and cook over a medium heat, stirring occasionally, for 6–8 minutes, until the pepper is soft and beginning to brown. Add 2.5ml/½ tsp of the ground cumin, mix well and cook for another 1–2 minutes.

2 Stir in the thinly sliced leeks, then partly cover the pan and cook gently for about 5 minutes, or until the leeks have softened and collapsed. Season the cooked vegetables with plenty of salt and ground black pepper.

PAN HAGGERTY

Use a firm-fleshed potato, such as Romano or Maris Piper, which will hold its shape when cooked. For a change, try adding chopped ham or salami between the layers.

SERVES 2

1 large onion
450g/1lb potatoes
30ml/2 tbsp olive oil
25g/1oz/2 tbsp butter
2 garlic cloves, crushed
115g/4oz/1 cup grated mature (sharp)
    Cheddar cheese
45ml/3 tbsp chopped fresh chives, plus
    extra to garnish
salt and ground black pepper

1 Halve and thinly slice the onion. Peel and thinly slice the potatoes.

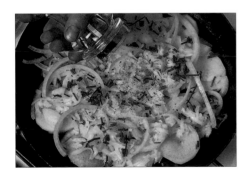

2 Heat the oil and butter in a large heavy or non-stick frying pan. Remove from the heat and cover the base with a layer of potatoes, followed by layers of onion slices, garlic, cheese, chives and plenty of seasoning.

VARIATIONS
• Other hard cheeses such as Red Leicester or Monterey Jack work well in this recipe.
• For a slightly sweeter flavour and extra colour, use 1 sliced red onion in place of the brown-skinned variety.

3 Continue layering, ending with grated cheese. Cover with a lid or foil and cook the pan haggerty over a gentle heat on the stove top for about 30 minutes, or until the potatoes and onion are tender when tested with a knife.

4 Preheat the grill (broiler) to hot. Uncover the pan, cover the pan handle with foil to protect it, if necessary, and brown the top under the grill. Serve the pan haggerty straight from the pan, sprinkled with extra chives to garnish.

RATATOUILLE

A highly versatile vegetable stew from Provence. Ratatouille is delicious hot or cold, on its own or with eggs, pasta, fish or meat – particularly roast lamb.

SERVES 6

900g/2lb ripe, well-flavoured tomatoes
120ml/4fl oz/½ cup olive oil
2 onions, thinly sliced
2 red (bell) peppers, seeded and
    cut into chunks
1 yellow or orange (bell) pepper,
    seeded and cut into chunks
1 large aubergine (eggplant),
    cut into chunks
2 courgettes (zucchini), cut
    into thick slices
4 garlic cloves, crushed
2 bay leaves
15ml/1 tbsp chopped fresh thyme
salt and ground black pepper

1 To skin the tomatoes plunge them into a bowl of boiling water for about 30 seconds, remove them using a slotted spoon and then refresh in cold water. Peel away the skins and roughly chop the tomato flesh.

2 Heat a little of the oil in a large, heavy pan and fry the onions for 5 minutes. Add the peppers and fry for a further 2 minutes. Drain. Add the aubergine and more oil and fry gently for 5 minutes. Add the remaining oil and courgettes and fry for 3 minutes. Drain.

3 Add the garlic and tomatoes to the pan with the bay leaves and thyme and a little salt and pepper. Cook gently until the tomatoes have softened and are turning pulpy.

4 Return all the vegetables to the pan and cook gently, stirring frequently, for about 15 minutes, until they are fairly pulpy but have retained a little texture. Season with more salt and pepper to taste if required.

COOK'S TIPS
• There are no specific quantities for the vegetables when making ratatouille so you can, to a large extent, vary the quantities and types of vegetables depending on what you have in the refrigerator.
• If the tomatoes are a little tasteless, add 30–45ml/2–3 tbsp tomato purée (paste) and a pinch of sugar to the mixture along with the tomatoes.
• Aubergines no longer need to be salted to draw out the bitter juices, however, this salting process does help prevent the aubergines from soaking up too much oil during frying. So, if you have the time, it is worth sprinkling the aubergine chunks with salt and leaving them in a colander in the sink for about 30 minutes to drain. Rinse them well and pat dry with kitchen paper before frying.

VEGETABLE KORMA

The blending of spices is an ancient art in India. Here the aim is to produce a subtle, aromatic curry rather than an assault on the senses.

SERVES 4

50g/2oz/¼ cup butter
2 onions, sliced
2 garlic cloves, crushed
2.5cm/1in piece fresh root ginger, grated
5ml/1 tsp ground cumin
15ml/1 tbsp ground coriander
6 cardamom pods
5cm/2in piece of cinnamon stick
5ml/1 tsp ground turmeric
1 fresh red chilli, seeded and
   finely chopped
1 potato, peeled and cut into
   2.5cm/1in cubes
1 small aubergine (eggplant), chopped
115g/4oz/1½ cups mushrooms,
   thickly sliced
175ml/6fl oz/¾ cup water
115g/4oz/1 cup green beans, cut into
   2.5cm/1in lengths
60ml/4 tbsp natural (plain) yogurt
150ml/¼ pint/⅔ cup double (heavy) cream
5ml/1 tsp garam masala
salt and ground black pepper
fresh coriander (cilantro) sprigs, to garnish
boiled rice and poppadums, to serve

1 Melt the butter in a heavy pan. Add the onions and cook for 5 minutes until soft. Add the garlic and ginger and cook for 2 minutes, then stir in the cumin, coriander, cardamom pods, cinnamon stick, turmeric and finely chopped chilli. Cook, stirring constantly, for 30 seconds.

VARIATION

All kinds of vegetables and pulses can be used for this korma; try broccoli, carrots, cauliflower, peas, canned or fresh beans and canned chickpeas.

2 Add the potato cubes, aubergine and mushrooms and the water. Cover the pan, bring to the boil, then lower the heat and simmer for 15 minutes. Add the beans and cook, uncovered, for 5 minutes. With a slotted spoon, remove the vegetables to a warmed serving dish and keep hot.

3 Allow the cooking liquid to bubble up until it has reduced a little. Season with salt and pepper, then stir in the yogurt, cream and garam masala. Pour the sauce over the vegetables and garnish with fresh coriander. Serve with boiled rice and poppadums.

BASMATI RICE and NUT PILAFF

Vegetarians will love this simple pilaff. Add wild or cultivated mushrooms, if you like.

SERVES 4

15–30ml/1–2 tbsp sunflower oil
1 onion, chopped
1 garlic clove, crushed
1 large carrot, coarsely grated
225g/8oz/generous 1 cup basmati
   rice, soaked
5ml/1 tsp cumin seeds
10ml/2 tsp ground coriander
10ml/2 tsp black mustard seeds (optional)
4 green cardamom pods
450ml/¾ pint/scant 2 cups vegetable
   stock or water
1 bay leaf
75g/3oz/½ cup shelled walnuts and/or
   unsalted cashew nuts
salt and ground black pepper
fresh parsley or coriander (cilantro)
   sprigs, to garnish

1 Heat the oil in a large frying pan. Add the onion, garlic and carrot and cook for 3–4 minutes, stirring occasionally.

2 Drain the rice and add it to the pan with the cumin seeds, ground coriander, black mustard seeds, if using, and the green cardamom pods. Cook for about 1 minute, stirring to coat the grains in oil.

3 Pour in the vegetable stock or water, add the bay leaf and season well with salt and pepper. Bring to the boil, then lower the heat, cover and simmer very gently for 10–12 minutes.

4 Remove the frying pan from the heat without lifting the lid. Leave to stand in a warm place for about 5 minutes, then check the rice. If it is cooked, there will be small steam holes on the surface of the rice. Remove the bay leaf and the cardamom pods.

5 Stir the walnuts and/or cashew nuts into the rice mixture. Taste to check the seasoning and add more salt and pepper if necessary. Spoon into warmed individual bowls or on to a large platter, garnish with the sprigs of fresh parsley or coriander and serve immediately.

COOK'S TIPS
• Use whichever nuts you prefer in this pilaff – even unsalted peanuts taste good – although almonds, brazil nuts, cashew nuts or pistachio nuts add a slightly more exotic flavour.
• If you don't have basmati rice, then use any other long grain rice. Thai jasmine rice has a particularly good flavour.

VEGETABLE COUSCOUS with SAFFRON and HARISSA

This spicy, north African dish makes an excellent main meal, or serve as part of a vegetarian buffet.

SERVES 4

45ml/3 tbsp olive oil
I onion, chopped
2 garlic cloves, crushed
5ml/I tsp ground cumin
5ml/I tsp paprika
400g/14oz can chopped tomatoes
300ml/½ pint/1¼ cups vegetable stock
I cinnamon stick
generous pinch of saffron threads
4 baby aubergines (eggplant), quartered
8 baby courgettes (zucchini), trimmed
8 baby carrots
225g/8oz/1⅓ cups couscous
425g/15oz can chickpeas, drained
175g/6oz/¾ cup pitted prunes
45ml/3 tbsp chopped fresh parsley
45ml/3 tbsp chopped fresh coriander
10–15ml/2–3 tsp harissa
salt

I Heat the olive oil in a large pan. Add the onion and garlic and cook gently for 5 minutes until soft. Add the cumin and paprika and cook, stirring, for I minute.

2 Add the tomatoes, stock, cinnamon stick, saffron, aubergines, courgettes and carrots, and season with salt. Bring to the boil, cover, lower the heat and cook gently for 20 minutes until the vegetables are just tender.

3 Line a steamer or colander with a double thickness of muslin (cheesecloth). Soak the couscous according to the instructions on the packet.

COOK'S TIPS
• Couscous is made from durum wheat and has a similar appearance to semolina. It has a very mild flavour and takes on the flavour of any ingredients it is mixed with. Most couscous is sold pre-cooked and only needs to be re-hydrated in boiling water or according to packet instructions.
• Harissa is a spicy paste made from red chillies, coriander, caraway, garlic, salt and olive oil. Its bright red/orange colour is an indicator of its fiery flavour. It is sold in cans, jars and tubes.

4 Add the chickpeas and prunes to the vegetables, stir and cook for 5 minutes.

5 Spread the couscous in the prepared steamer. Place the steamer on top of the vegetables, cover and cook for 5 minutes until the couscous is hot.

6 Stir the herbs into the vegetables. Heap the couscous on to a serving dish. Using a slotted spoon, remove the vegetables from the frying pan and add to the couscous. Spoon over a little sauce and toss gently. Stir the harissa into the remaining sauce and serve separately.

SPAGHETTI with ROCKET PESTO

*This is the pesto for real rocket lovers. It is sharp and peppery, and delicious for a
summer pasta meal with a glass of chilled dry white wine.*

SERVES 4

4 garlic cloves
90ml/6 tbsp pine nuts
2 large handfuls of rocket (arugula), total
    weight about 150g/5oz, stalks removed
50g/2oz/⅔ cup freshly grated
    Parmesan cheese
50g/2oz/⅔ cup freshly grated
    Pecorino cheese
90ml/6 tbsp extra virgin olive oil
400g/14oz fresh or dried spaghetti
salt and ground black pepper
freshly grated Parmesan and Pecorino
    cheese, to serve

1 Put the garlic and pine nuts in a food
processor or blender and process until
finely chopped. Add the rocket, grated
Parmesan and Pecorino, and olive oil.

2 Add salt and pepper, to taste and
process for 5 seconds. Stop and scrape
down the side of the bowl, then process
for 5–10 seconds more until a smooth
paste is formed.

3 Cook the spaghetti in a large pan of
boiling salted water until just tender, or
according to the packet instructions.

4 Spoon the pesto into a large mixing
bowl. Just before the pasta is ready, add
one or two ladlefuls of the cooking
water to the pesto and stir well to mix.

5 Drain the pasta, tip it into the bowl
of pesto and toss well to mix. Serve
immediately, with the grated cheeses
handed separately.

VARIATION
To temper the flavour of the rocket and
make the pesto milder, add 115g/4oz/
½ cup ricotta or mascarpone cheese to
the pesto in step 4 and mix well before
adding the water.

PASTA SHELLS with TOMATOES and RICOTTA

Nothing could be more simple than hot pasta tossed with fresh ripe tomatoes, ricotta cheese and sweet basil. Serve it on hot summer days – it is surprisingly refreshing.

SERVES 4–6

350g/12oz/3 cups dried conchiglie
130g/4½oz/generous ½ cup ricotta cheese
6 ripe plum tomatoes, diced
2 garlic cloves, crushed
a handful of fresh basil leaves, shredded,
    plus extra basil leaves to garnish
60ml/4 tbsp extra virgin olive oil
salt and ground black pepper

1 Cook the pasta in boiling salted water according to the packet instructions.

VARIATIONS
• Use diced mozzarella instead of ricotta.
• An avocado is the ideal ingredient for adding extra colour and flavour to this pasta dish. Halve, stone (pit) and peel, then dice the flesh. Toss it with the hot pasta at the last minute.

2 Meanwhile, put the ricotta cheese in a large mixing bowl and mash with a fork until soft and creamy.

3 Add the diced tomatoes (see Cook's Tip), crushed garlic and shredded basil to the softened ricotta cheese, with salt and pepper to taste, and mix well. Add the olive oil and whisk thoroughly. Taste for seasoning.

4 Drain the cooked pasta, tip it into the ricotta and tomato mixture and toss well to mix. Garnish with basil leaves and serve immediately, sprinkled with black pepper.

COOK'S TIP
If you like, skin the tomatoes before you dice them by plunging them into boiling water for 30 seconds and then refresh in cold water before peeling.

BUCKWHEAT NOODLES with CABBAGE, POTATOES and CHEESE

This is a very unusual pasta dish from Valtellina in the Italian Alps. The pale brown buckwheat noodles called pizzoccheri are unique to this area.

SERVES 6

400g/14oz Savoy cabbage, cut into
    1cm/½in strips
2 potatoes, total weight about 200g/7oz,
    cut into 5mm/¼in slices
400g/14oz dried pizzoccheri
    (buckwheat noodles)
75g/3oz/6 tbsp butter
1 generous bunch fresh sage
    leaves, shredded
2 garlic cloves
200g/7oz Fontina cheese, rind removed
    and thinly sliced
30–45ml/2–3 tbsp freshly grated
    Parmesan cheese, plus extra to serve
salt and ground black pepper

COOK'S TIPS
• Look for packets of dried pizzoccheri
pasta in Italian delicatessens.
• Fontina is an Italian mountain cheese
with a sweet, nutty taste. If you cannot
get it, look for Taleggio, Gruyère or
Emmenthal – they are all similar cheeses.

1 Bring a very large pan of salted water
to the boil. Add the cabbage strips and
potato slices and boil for 5 minutes.

2 Add the pasta to the pan, stir well and
let the water return to the boil over a
high heat. Lower the heat and simmer
for about 15 minutes, or according to
the instructions on the packet, until the
pasta is just tender.

3 Drain the pasta and vegetables and
set aside. Melt the butter in the pan.
Add the sage and whole garlic cloves
and fry over a low to medium heat until
the garlic is golden and sizzling. Lift the
garlic out of the pan and discard it. Set
the sage and garlic butter aside.

4 Pour one-quarter of the pasta and
vegetable mixture into a warmed large
bowl and arrange about one-third of
the Fontina slices on top. Repeat these
layers until all the ingredients have been
used, then sprinkle with the grated
Parmesan. Pour the sage and garlic
butter over the top and serve
immediately, with extra grated Parmesan
handed separately.

VARIATION
You could use chard or spinach instead
of the cabbage. Spinach will need much
less cooking, so add it to the pan about
5 minutes before the end of the cooking
time in step 2.

FETTUCINE with BUTTER and PARMESAN

Very few ingredients are needed to make up this incredibly simple dish. It comes from northern Italy, where butter and cheeses are the most popular ingredients for serving with pasta. This dish is especially popular with children.

SERVES 4

400g/14oz fresh or dried fettucine
50g/2oz/¼ cup unsalted (sweet)
    butter, cubed
115g/4oz/1¼ cups freshly grated
    Parmesan cheese
salt and ground black pepper

VARIATIONS
• Other long pastas would be just as good
in this recipe; try spaghetti, linguine or
tagliatelle. Spinach or tomato flavoured
versions would also work well.
• Try freshly grated Pecorino cheese
instead of the Parmesan.

1 Cook the pasta in a large pan of
salted boiling water until just tender, or
according to the instructions on the
packet. Drain thoroughly, then tip the
pasta into a large warmed bowl.

2 Add the cubes of butter and the
grated Parmesan, one-third at a time,
tossing the pasta after each addition until
it is evenly coated. Season to taste and
serve immediately.

PASTA TWISTS with PESTO

Bottled pesto is a useful stand-by, but if you have a food processor or blender, it is very easy to make a delicious home-made version.

SERVES 4

50g/2oz fresh basil leaves, plus extra fresh
   basil leaves, to garnish
2–4 garlic cloves
60ml/4 tbsp pine nuts
120ml/4fl oz/½ cup extra virgin
   olive oil
115g/4oz/1¼ cups freshly grated Parmesan
   cheese, plus extra to serve
25g/1oz/¼ cup freshly grated
   Pecorino cheese
400g/14oz/3½ cups dried pasta
   twists (fusilli)
salt and ground black pepper

1 Put the basil, garlic and pine nuts in a food processor. Add 60ml/4 tbsp of the oil. Process until chopped, then stop the machine and scrape the bowl.

2 Turn the machine on again and slowly add the remaining olive oil in a thin, steady stream through the feeder tube. You may need to stop the machine and scrape down the sides of the bowl once or twice to make sure that everything is evenly mixed.

3 Scrape the mixture into a large bowl and beat in the cheeses with a wooden spoon. Taste and add salt and ground black pepper if necessary.

4 Cook the pasta in a large pan of salted boiling water for 10 minutes, or according to the instructions on the packet, until just tender. Drain the pasta well, then add it to the bowl of pesto and toss well. Serve immediately, garnished with the extra fresh basil leaves. Hand around the extra shaved Parmesan separately.

COOK'S TIP
Fresh pesto can be made up to 2–3 days in advance. To store it, transfer the pesto to a small bowl and pour a thin film of olive oil over the surface. Cover the bowl tightly with clear film (plastic wrap) and keep it in the refrigerator.

PASTA with CHEESE and CREAM

The Italian name for this dish – Mezzanotte – means middle of the night, which is when this rich and filling dish is eaten – after a night on the tiles. When you arrive home hungry from a party, it's just the thing to sober you up!

SERVES 4

400g/14oz/3½ cups dried rigatoni
3 egg yolks
105ml/7 tbsp grated Parmesan cheese
200g/7oz/scant 1 cup ricotta cheese
60ml/4 tbsp double (heavy) cream
nutmeg
40g/1½oz/3 tbsp butter
salt and ground black pepper

1 Cook the pasta according to the instructions on the packet.

2 Meanwhile, mix the egg yolks, grated Parmesan and ricotta together in a bowl. Add the cream and mix with a fork.

3 Grate in nutmeg to taste, then season with plenty of black pepper and a little salt. Drain the pasta thoroughly when cooked. Return the clean pan to the heat. Melt the butter, add the drained pasta and toss over a medium heat.

4 Turn off the heat under the pan and add the ricotta mixture. Stir well with a large spoon for 10–15 seconds, or until all the pasta is coated in sauce. Serve immediately, in warmed individual bowls with plenty of ground black pepper.

OVEN-COOKED VEGETARIAN DISHES

Coming home to a delectable slow-cooked dish
is always a delight. You open the door to delicious,
tantalizing smells, take a few moments to assemble
plates and cutlery, and tuck in. On occasions like
these, a vegetarian dish such as Truffade is the ideal
choice. If you have a clay pot, try Clay-pot Risotto
with Spinach and Saffron or Vegetable Paella.
The steamy atmosphere inside the pot creates the
perfect cooking environment.

OKRA and TOMATO TAGINE

A spicy vegetarian dish that is delicious served either with other vegetable dishes or as a side dish to accompany a meat tagine.

SERVES 4

350g/12oz small okra
5–6 tomatoes
2 small onions
2 garlic cloves, crushed
1 green chilli, seeded
5ml/1 tsp paprika
a small handful of fresh coriander
    (cilantro) leaves
30ml/2 tbsp vegetable oil
juice of 1 lemon
120ml/4fl oz/½ cup water

1 Preheat the oven to 190°C/350°F/ Gas 5. Trim the okra, then cut the pods into 1cm/½in lengths. Set aside.

2 Peel the tomatoes, remove the seeds, then chop roughly. Set aside. Chop one of the onions, place in a food processor with the garlic, spices and 60ml/4 tbsp water and blend to form a paste.

3 Thinly slice the second onion. Heat the oil in a flameproof casserole or pan and fry the onion for 5–6 minutes until it turns golden brown. Transfer to a plate with a slotted spoon.

4 Reduce the heat and pour the onion and coriander paste over the onions. Cook for 1–2 minutes, stirring frequently, then add the okra, tomatoes and lemon juice. Pour in the water and stir well to mix. Cover tightly and transfer to the oven. Bake for about 15 minutes until the okra is tender.

5 Transfer the tagine to a serving dish, sprinkle with the fried onion rings and serve immediately.

VARIATION
Canned, chopped tomatoes can be used instead of the fresh tomatoes in this recipe – simply add the contents of a 200g/7oz can with the okra in step 4.

TOMATO, FETA CHEESE and OLIVE TARTS

These upside-down tartlets are filled with vegetables and chunks of salty cheese. They
make the perfect first course, or may be served with salad leaves for a lunchtime snack.

SERVES 4

25g/1oz sun-dried aubergine
   (eggplant) slices
300ml/½ pint/1¼ cups boiling water
45ml/3 tbsp sunflower oil
1 onion, thinly sliced
150g/5oz/2 cups button (white)
   mushrooms, sliced
1 garlic clove, crushed
12–16 cherry tomatoes, halved
8 black or green olives, pitted
   and chopped
115g/4oz/1 cup feta cheese, crumbled
350g/12oz ready-made puff pastry
salt and ground black pepper

1 Preheat the oven to 200°C/400°F/
Gas 6. Place the aubergine slices in a
shallow dish. Pour over the boiling water
and leave to soak for 10 minutes. Rinse
in cold water, drain and dry on kitchen
paper. Cut the aubergine slices in half or
quarters, depending on their size.

2 Heat 30ml/2 tbsp of the sunflower oil
in a frying pan and fry the onion over a
medium heat for 4–5 minutes. Add the
mushrooms and cook for 3–4 minutes,
or until the onions are light golden.
Remove and set aside.

3 Heat the remaining oil in the frying
pan, add the aubergine slices and garlic
and lightly fry for 1–2 minutes. Lightly oil
four individual cazuelas. Mix the halved
tomatoes with the onions, mushrooms,
aubergines, olives and feta cheese and
divide among the cazuelas. Season well.

4 Roll out the pastry thinly into an
oblong, then cut out four rounds, each
slightly larger than the diameter of the
cazuelas. Place the pastry on top of the
vegetable and cheese mixture, tucking
the overlap down inside the dish.

5 Bake for 20 minutes, or until the
pastry is risen and golden. Cool slightly
then invert on to individual warmed
serving plates to serve.

COOK'S TIP
Choose cherry tomatoes on the vine for
the very best flavour.

TOFU and VEGETABLE THAI CURRY

Traditional Thai ingredients – chillies, galangal, lemon grass and kaffir lime leaves – give this curry a wonderfully fragrant aroma.

SERVES 4

175g/6oz tofu, drained
45ml/3 tbsp dark soy sauce
15ml/1 tbsp sesame oil
5ml/1 tsp chilli sauce
2.5cm/1in piece fresh root ginger,
    finely grated
225g/8oz cauliflower
225g/8oz broccoli
30ml/2 tbsp vegetable oil
1 onion, sliced
400ml/14fl oz/1⅔ cups coconut milk
150ml/¼ pint/⅔ cup water
1 red (bell) pepper, seeded
    and chopped
175g/6oz green beans, halved
115g/4oz/1½ cups shiitake or button
    (white) mushrooms, halved
shredded spring onions (scallions),
    to garnish
boiled jasmine rice or noodles,
    to serve

For the curry paste
2 chillies, seeded and chopped
1 lemon grass stalk, chopped
2.5cm/1in piece fresh galangal, chopped
2 kaffir lime leaves
10ml/2 tsp ground coriander
a few sprigs fresh coriander (cilantro),
    including the stalks

1 Cut the drained tofu into 2.5cm/1in cubes and place in an ovenproof dish. Mix together the soy sauce, sesame oil, chilli sauce and ginger and pour over the tofu. Toss gently to coat all the cubes evenly, then leave to marinate for at least 2 hours or overnight if possible, turning and basting the tofu occasionally.

2 To make the curry paste, place the chopped chillies, lemon grass, galangal, kaffir lime leaves, ground coriander and fresh coriander in a food processor and process for a few seconds until well blended. Add 45ml/3 tbsp water and process to a thick paste.

3 Preheat the oven to 190°C/375°F/Gas 5. Using a large sharp knife, cut the cauliflower and broccoli into small florets and cut any stalks into thin slices.

4 Heat the vegetable oil in a frying pan, add the sliced onion and gently fry for about 8 minutes, or until soft and lightly browned. Stir in the prepared curry paste and the coconut milk. Add the water and bring to the boil.

5 Stir in the red pepper, green beans, cauliflower and broccoli. Transfer to a Chinese sand pot or earthenware casserole. Cover and place in the oven.

6 Stir the tofu and marinade, then place the dish in the top of the oven and cook for 30 minutes, then stir them into the curry with the mushrooms. Reduce the oven temperature to 180°C/350°F/Gas 4 and cook for about 15 minutes, or until the vegetables are tender. Garnish with spring onions and serve with boiled jasmine rice or noodles.

COOK'S TIP
Tofu or beancurd is made from soya beans and is sold in blocks. It is a creamy white colour and has a solid gel-like texture. Tofu has a bland flavour and its absorbent nature means that it takes on the flavours of marinades or any other food that it is cooked with.

MEDITERRANEAN BAKED VEGETABLES

This colourful selection of vegetables is baked in a shallow clay pot, known as a tian *in Provence where it is also the name given to the food baked in it.*

SERVES 4–6

75ml/5 tbsp olive oil
2 onions, halved and sliced
1 garlic clove, crushed
15ml/1 tbsp finely chopped
    fresh sage
4 large, well-flavoured
    tomatoes, quartered
3 courgettes (zucchini),
    thickly sliced
2 small yellow (bell) peppers, quartered
    and seeded
2 small red (bell) peppers, quartered
    and seeded
60ml/4 tbsp fresh white or wholemeal
    (whole-wheat) breadcrumbs
60ml/4 tbsp freshly grated
    Parmesan cheese
8–10 pitted black olives
salt and ground black pepper
sage leaves, to garnish

1 Heat 30ml/2 tbsp of the olive oil in a frying pan, add the onions and cook, stirring occasionally, until softened. Add the garlic and continue cooking until the onions are really soft and golden. Stir in the sage and season well.

2 Transfer the onions to a large oval *tian* or earthenware baking dish. Spread them evenly, then arrange the tomatoes, courgettes and peppers on top.

3 Preheat the oven to 200°F/400°C/ Gas 6. Drizzle the remaining oil over the mixed vegetables and season well. Bake for 30 minutes.

4 Sprinkle the fresh breadcrumbs and Parmesan cheese over the vegetables and arrange the olives on top. Return to the oven for a further 10–15 minutes, or until the vegetables are tender. Serve garnished with the sage leaves.

FIELD MUSHROOMS with HAZELNUTS

Large mushrooms, full of texture and flavour, are topped with crunchy hazelnut pieces and fresh parsley and garlic-flavoured olive oil.

SERVES 4

2 garlic cloves
grated rind of 1 lemon
90ml/6 tbsp olive oil
8 large field (portabello) mushrooms
50g/2oz/½ cup hazelnuts, coarsely chopped
30ml/2 tbsp chopped fresh parsley
salt and ground black pepper

1 Crush the garlic cloves with a little salt using a mortar and pestle or on a chopping board. Place the crushed garlic in a small bowl and stir in the grated lemon rind and the olive oil. If time allows, leave the mixture to stand to enable the flavours to infuse (steep).

2 Preheat the oven to 200°C/400°F/ Gas 6. Arrange the mushrooms, stalk side up, in a single layer in an ovenproof earthenware dish. Drizzle over about 60ml/4 tbsp of the oil mixture and bake for 10 minutes.

3 Remove the mushrooms from the oven and baste them with the remaining oil mixture, then sprinkle the chopped hazelnuts evenly over the top. Bake for a further 10–15 minutes, or until the mushrooms are tender. Season with salt and pepper and sprinkle with chopped parsley. Serve immediately.

COOK'S TIP
Almost any unsalted nuts can be used in place of the hazelnuts in this recipe – try pine nuts, cashew nuts, almonds or walnuts. Nuts can go rancid quickly so, for the freshest flavour, either buy nuts in small quantities or buy them in shells and remove the shells just before use.

ROASTED SQUASH with RICE STUFFING

Gem squash has a sweet, subtle taste that contrasts well with the olives and sun-dried tomatoes in this recipe. The rice adds substance without changing any of the flavour.

SERVES 4 AS A FIRST COURSE

4 whole gem squashes
225g/8oz cooked white long grain rice
    (about 90g/3½oz/½ cup raw weight)
75g/3oz sun-dried tomatoes in oil, drained
    and chopped
50g/2oz/½ cup pitted black olives, chopped
60ml/4 tbsp soft goat's cheese
30ml/2 tbsp olive oil
15ml/1 tbsp chopped fresh basil leaves,
    plus basil sprigs, to serve
yogurt and mint dressing and green salad,
    to serve

1 Preheat the oven to 180°C/350°F/ Gas 4. Using a sharp knife, trim the base of each squash, slice off the top of each and scoop out and discard the seeds.

2 Mix the rice, tomatoes, olives, cheese, half the oil and the basil in a bowl.

3 Oil a shallow baking dish with the remaining oil, just large enough to hold the squash side by side. Divide the rice mixture among the squash and place them in the dish.

4 Cover with foil and bake for about 45 minutes until the squash are tender when pierced with a skewer. Garnish with basil sprigs and serve with a yogurt and mint dressing and a green salad.

VARIATION
Try ricotta cheese or cream cheese with garlic and herbs in place of the soft goat's cheese in this recipe.

MEDITERRANEAN VEGETABLES BAKED in GOLDEN BATTER

Crunchy golden batter surrounds these vegetables, making them delicious and filling. Serve with salad as a light lunch, or with grilled sausages for a more substantial meal.

SERVES 6

1 small aubergine (eggplant), trimmed, halved and thickly sliced
1 egg
115g/4oz/1 cup plain (all-purpose) flour
300ml/½ pint/1¼ cups milk
30ml/2 tbsp fresh thyme leaves, or 10ml/2 tsp dried
1 red onion
2 large courgettes (zucchini)
1 red (bell) pepper
1 yellow (bell) pepper
60–75ml/4–5 tbsp sunflower oil
30ml/2 tbsp freshly grated Parmesan cheese
salt and ground black pepper
fresh herbs, to garnish

1 Place the aubergine in a colander or sieve, sprinkle generously with salt and leave for 10 minutes. Drain, rinse well and pat dry on kitchen paper.

2 Meanwhile, beat the egg in a bowl, then gradually beat in the flour and a little milk to make a smooth thick paste. Gradually blend in the rest of the milk, add the thyme leaves and seasoning to taste and stir until smooth. Leave the batter in a cool place until required. Preheat the oven to 220°C/425°F/Gas 7.

COOK'S TIP
As with Yorkshire pudding, it is essential to get the fat in the dish really hot before adding the batter, which should sizzle slightly as it goes in. If the fat is not hot enough, the batter will not rise well. Use a dish that is not too deep.

3 Cut the onion into quarters, slice the courgettes and seed and quarter the peppers. Put the oil in a shallow baking tray or roasting pan and heat in the oven. Add the prepared vegetables, toss them in the oil to coat thoroughly and return the pan to the oven for 20 minutes.

4 Give the batter another whisk, then pour it over the vegetables and return to the oven for about 30 minutes. When the batter is puffed up and golden, reduce the heat to 190°C/375°F/Gas 5 for about 10 minutes, or until the edges are crisp. Sprinkle with Parmesan and herbs.

TRUFFADE

*Baked until meltingly soft, this warming cheese and potato supper is the perfect slow
bake to come home to. In France, where it originated, it would be made with a Tomme or
Cantal cheese – look for them in good cheese stores.*

SERVES 4–6

a little sunflower oil or melted butter
1 large onion, thinly sliced
675g/1½lb baking potatoes, very
   thinly sliced
150g/5oz/1¼ cups grated hard cheese,
   such as Tomme, Cantal or mature
   (sharp) Cheddar
freshly grated nutmeg
salt and ground black pepper
mixed salad leaves, to serve

VARIATION
In France, they make a non-vegetarian
version of this dish, which is cooked with
finely diced fatty bacon (lardons) and
the cheese is chopped, not grated. The
ingredients are mixed and cooked slowly
in a little lard in a heavy frying pan on top
of the stove.

1 Preheat the oven to 180°C/350°F/
Gas 4. Lightly grease the base of a
shallow baking dish or roasting pan with
the oil or melted butter.

2 Arrange a layer of sliced onion over
the base of the dish, then add a layer of
sliced potatoes and about half of the
grated cheese. Finish with the remaining
onions and a layer of sliced potatoes.

3 Brush the top layer of potatoes with
oil or melted butter and season with
nutmeg, salt and pepper.

4 Sprinkle the remaining grated cheese
over the top and bake for about 1 hour,
or until the vegetables are tender and
the top is golden brown. Leave the dish
to stand for about 5 minutes, then serve
cut in wedges with a salad.

POTATOES BAKED with TOMATOES

*This simple, hearty dish from the south of Italy is best made in the summer when
fresh, ripe tomatoes are in season and bursting with flavour.*

SERVES 6

90ml/6 tbsp olive oil
2 large red or yellow onions, thinly sliced
1kg/2¼lb baking potatoes, thinly sliced
450g/1lb well-flavoured tomatoes, sliced,
   with their juice
115g/4oz/1 cup freshly grated Parmesan or
   Cheddar cheese
a few fresh basil leaves
50ml/2fl oz/¼ cup water
salt and ground black pepper

1 Preheat the oven to 180°C/350°F/
Gas 4. Brush a large baking dish
generously with 30ml/2 tbsp of the oil.

2 Arrange a layer of some of the thinly
sliced onions in the base of the prepared
dish, followed by a layer of the potatoes
and tomatoes.

3 Drizzle a little of the olive oil over
the potatoes and tomatoes, and sprinkle
with some of the grated cheese. Season
generously with plenty of salt and
ground black pepper.

4 Continue to layer the vegetables in
the dish until they are used up, ending
with an overlapping layer of potatoes
and tomatoes.

5 Reserve a sprig of fresh basil for the
garnish, tear the remaining leaves into
small pieces, and add them here and
there among the vegetables. Sprinkle the
top with the remaining grated cheese
and drizzle with the rest of the oil. Pour
the water evenly over the vegetables and
cheese, then bake for about 1 hour, or
until the vegetables are tender.

6 Check towards the end of the cooking
time and, if the top begins to brown
too much, place a sheet of foil, baking
parchment or a flat baking tray on top
of the dish. Garnish with the remaining
basil, once it is cooked, and serve hot.

VARIATION
If you can't get hold of really flavoursome
tomatoes, a 400g/14oz can of chopped
plum tomatoes can be used instead.

BAKED SCALLOPED POTATOES with FETA CHEESE and OLIVES

Thinly sliced potatoes are cooked with Greek feta cheese and black and green olives and olive oil. This dish is a good one to serve with toasted pitta bread.

SERVES 4

4–6 large, unpeeled potatoes, total weight
    about 900g/2lb
150ml/¼ pint/⅔ cup extra virgin
    olive oil
leaves from a sprig of rosemary
275g/10oz/2½ cups feta cheese,
    coarsely crumbled
115g/4oz/1 cup pitted mixed black and
    green olives
300ml/½ pint/1¼ cups hot vegetable stock
salt and ground black pepper
toasted pitta bread, to serve

1 Preheat the oven to 200°C/400°F/ Gas 6. Bring a large pan of salted water to the boil and cook the potatoes for 15 minutes until only just tender.

4 Arrange half the potatoes in the dish in an even layer. Top with half of the rosemary, cheese and olives and season with salt and pepper. Arrange the rest of the potatoes in an even layer on top.

5 Add the remaining rosemary leaves, crumbled cheese and olives, and drizzle with the remaining olive oil. Pour the hot vegetable stock over the top and season the top layer with salt and plenty of ground black pepper.

6 Bake for 35 minutes, covering the dish loosely with foil after about 20 minutes to prevent the potatoes from getting too brown. Serve hot, straight from the dish with the toasted pitta bread.

VARIATION
Thinly sliced sun-dried tomatoes would make a delicious addition.

2 Drain the potatoes and set them aside until they are cool enough to handle. Carefully remove the peel from the potatoes using a small sharp knife and then cut them into thin slices.

3 Brush the base and sides of a 1.5 litre/ 2½ pint/6¼ cup rectangular ovenproof dish with some of the olive oil.

COOK'S TIP
Cooking the potatoes with their skins on not only helps to preserve their vitamin content, but will also ensure that the potatoes cook more evenly. If you prefer, peel them before they are cooked.

CLAY-POT RISOTTO with SPINACH and SAFFRON

Rice cooks to perfection in the moist environment of a clay pot. This risotto can be made without the constant checking required when cooked on top of the stove.

SERVES 4

a few saffron threads
30ml/2 tbsp boiling water
15ml/1 tbsp olive oil
50g/2oz/¼ cup butter
1 onion, finely chopped
350g/12oz/1¾ cups risotto rice
900ml/1½ pints/3¾ cups warm
   vegetable stock
150ml/¼ pint/⅔ cup dry white wine
225g/8oz baby spinach leaves
300ml/½ pint/1¼ cups hot vegetable stock
40g/1½oz/¼ cup shelled walnuts, chopped
75g/3oz Parmesan cheese, very
   finely shaved
salt and ground black pepper

1 Soak a large clay pot in cold water for 20 minutes, then drain. Meanwhile, place the saffron in a bowl, cover with the boiling water and leave to infuse (steep).

2 Heat the oil and half the butter in a large, heavy pan. Add the finely chopped onion and cook gently for 5 minutes, or until soft, stirring occasionally. Add the rice and stir over the heat for about 3 minutes until the grains are thoroughly coated in oil and butter.

COOK'S TIP
Risotto rice is short grain rice that is widely used in Italy to make a variety of different types of risotto. Arborio rice is the most widely available type, but you may also find carnaroli and vialone nano. When cooked, risotto rice has a creamy consistency but the grains retain a slight "bite" to their texture.

3 Pour the warm stock into the clay pot, add the saffron water, wine and the rice mixture and stir together. Cover and place in an unheated oven. Set the oven to 190°C/375°F/Gas 5 and cook for 50 minutes, stirring after 30 minutes.

4 Stir in the spinach, add the stock, then cover and cook for 10 minutes, or until the rice is tender. Stir in the walnuts, the remaining butter and half the Parmesan cheese. Season and serve sprinkled with the remaining Parmesan cheese.

VEGETABLE PAELLA

A colourful assortment of vegetables is cooked slowly with rice to make this tasty –
slightly spicy – vegetarian meal.

SERVES 4

1 large aubergine (eggplant)
45ml/3 tbsp extra virgin olive or
    sunflower oil
2 onions, quartered and sliced
2 garlic cloves, crushed
300g/11oz/1½ cups short grain Spanish or
    risotto rice
1.2–1.5 litres/2–2½ pints/5–6¼ cups
    vegetable stock
1 red (bell) pepper, halved, seeded
    and sliced
1 yellow (bell) pepper, halved, seeded
    and sliced
200g/7oz fine green beans, halved
115g/4oz/scant 2 cups chestnut
    mushrooms, quartered, or brown
    cap (cremini) or button (white)
    mushrooms, halved
1 dried chilli, crushed
115g/4oz/1 cup frozen peas
salt and ground black pepper
fresh coriander (cilantro) leaves,
    to garnish

1 Soak a clay pot or Chinese sand pot in cold water for 20 minutes, then drain. Cut the aubergine in half lengthwise, then cut it crosswise into thin slices.

COOK'S TIP
Although nowadays aubergines don't need to be salted to remove the bitter flavour they used to have, salting them does ensure that they absorb less oil when they are fried. So, if you have the time, layer the slices in a colander and sprinkle each layer with salt. Leave the slices to drain for about 30 minutes, then rinse thoroughly and pat dry before frying.

2 Heat 30ml/2 tbsp of the oil in a large frying pan, add the aubergine slices and quickly sauté until slightly golden. Transfer to the clay pot.

3 Add the remaining oil, add the onion and cook, stirring occasionally, for a few minutes until golden.

4 Add the garlic and rice and cook for 1–2 minutes, stirring, until the rice becomes transparent. Pour in 900ml/ 1½ pints/3¾ cups of the stock into the clay pot, then add the rice mixture.

5 Add the peppers, halved green beans, mushrooms, crushed chilli and seasoning. Stir to mix, then cover the pot and place in an unheated oven.

6 Set the oven to 200°C/400°F/Gas 6 and cook for 1 hour, or until the rice is almost tender. After 40 minutes, remove the pot from the oven and add a little more stock to moisten the paella. Stir well, re-cover and return to the oven.

7 Add the peas and a little more stock to the paella and cook for a further 10 minutes. Adjust the seasoning and sprinkle over the coriander. Lightly stir through and then serve.

VARIATIONS
• Almost any roughly chopped or sliced vegetables can be used in this dish. Broccoli, carrots, cauliflower, courgettes (zucchini) and okra are all suitable – or try using frozen sweetcorn in place of all or some of the peas.
• For a tomato-flavoured paella, use a 400g/14oz can chopped tomatoes in place of 350ml/12floz/1½ cups of the stock.

LENTIL FRITTATA

Throughout the Mediterranean a variety of thick, vegetable omelettes are cooked. This tasty supper dish combines green lentils, red onions, broccoli and cherry tomatoes.

SERVES 4–6

75g/3oz/scant ½ cup green lentils
225g/8oz small broccoli florets
2 red onions, halved and thickly sliced
30ml/2 tbsp olive oil
8 eggs
45ml/3 tbsp milk or water
45ml/3 tbsp chopped mixed herbs, such as
    oregano, parsley, tarragon and chives,
    plus extra sprigs to garnish
175g/6oz cherry tomatoes, halved
salt and ground black pepper

I Place the lentils in a pan, cover with cold water and bring to the boil, reduce the heat and simmer for 25 minutes until tender. Add the broccoli, return to the boil and cook for 1 minute.

VARIATIONS
Add about 50g/2oz/⅔ cup freshly grated Parmesan cheese or 115g/4oz/1 cup diced mozzarella cheese to the egg mixture.

2 Meanwhile place the onion slices and olive oil in a shallow earthenware dish or cazuela about 23–25cm/9–10in in diameter and place in an unheated oven. Set the oven to 200°C/400°F/Gas 6 and cook for 25 minutes.

3 In a bowl, whisk together the eggs, milk or water, a pinch of salt and plenty of black pepper. Stir in the herbs. Drain the lentils and broccoli and stir into the onions. Add the cherry tomatoes. Stir gently to combine.

4 Pour the egg mixture evenly over the vegetables. Reduce the oven to 190°C/375°F/Gas 5. Return the dish to the oven and cook for 10 minutes, then push the mixture into the centre of the dish using a spatula, allowing the raw mixture in the centre to flow to the edges.

5 Return the dish to the oven and cook the frittata for a further 15 minutes, or until it is just set. Garnish with sprigs of fresh herbs and serve warm, cut into thick wedges.

TAGLIATELLE BAKED with MUSHROOMS, GORGONZOLA and WALNUTS

This rich, creamy dish is perfect served as a lunch or supper dish with a mixed leaf salad.

2 Meanwhile, place the tagliatelle in a large pan of boiling salted water and cook according to packet instructions or until just tender.

3 Remove the mushrooms and leeks and set aside. Crumble the Gorgonzola cheese into the frying pan and stir over a gentle heat, until melted. Stir in the creams and the dry vermouth or white wine and season to taste.

4 Drain the pasta and divide it among four individual cazuelas or other shallow ovenproof earthenware dishes. Top with the mushrooms and leeks, spreading them over the pasta. Pour over the sauce, sprinkle the chopped walnuts and Parmesan cheese on top and bake for about 15 minutes, or until the cheese is golden brown and bubbling.

VARIATION

Any type of pasta shapes can be used in this bake in place of the tagliatelle. However, other long ribbon pastas, such as linguine and bucatini, and hollow tube pastas that scoop up the sauce, such as macaroni, penne or rigatoni, will work particularly well.

SERVES 4

25g/1oz/2 tbsp butter
15ml/1 tbsp vegetable oil
350g/12oz/4 cups chestnut mushrooms, quartered, or brown cap (crimini) mushrooms, halved
2 leeks, thinly sliced
400g/14oz mixed spinach and plain tagliatelle
175g/6oz Gorgonzola cheese
150ml/¼ pint/⅔ cup double (heavy) cream
200ml/7fl oz/scant 1 cup thick single (light) cream
90ml/6 tbsp dry vermouth or white wine
50g/2oz/½ cup walnuts, finely chopped
75g/3oz/1 cup grated Parmesan cheese
salt and ground black pepper

1 Preheat the oven to 200°C/400°F/ Gas 6. Melt the butter with the oil in a large sauté pan or deep frying pan, add the quartered chestnut mushrooms or halved brown cap mushrooms and the thinly sliced leeks and stir-fry the vegetables together for 4–5 minutes.

MIXED BEAN and AUBERGINE TAGINE with MINT YOGURT

In this traditional-style Moroccan dish, the mixed beans and aubergine provide both texture and flavour, which are enhanced by the herbs and chillies.

SERVES 4

115g/4oz/generous ½ cup dried red kidney beans, soaked overnight in cold water and drained
115g/4oz/generous ½ cup dried black-eyed beans (peas) or cannellini beans, soaked overnight in cold water and drained
600ml/1 pint/2½ cups water
2 bay leaves
2 celery sticks, each cut into 4 batons
75ml/5 tbsp olive oil
1 aubergine (eggplant), about 350g/12oz, cut into chunks
1 onion, thinly sliced
3 garlic cloves, crushed
1–2 fresh red chillies, seeded and finely chopped
30ml/2 tbsp tomato purée (paste)
5ml/1 tsp paprika
2 large tomatoes, roughly chopped
300ml/½ pint/1¼ cups vegetable stock
15ml/1 tbsp each chopped fresh mint, parsley and coriander (cilantro)
salt and ground black pepper
fresh herb sprigs, to garnish

For the mint yogurt
150ml/¼ pint/⅔ cup natural (plain) yogurt
30ml/2 tbsp chopped fresh mint
2 spring onions (scallions), chopped

1 Place the soaked and drained kidney beans in a large pan of unsalted boiling water. Bring back to the boil and boil rapidly for 10 minutes, then drain. Place the soaked and drained black-eyed or cannellini beans in a separate large pan of boiling unsalted water and boil rapidly for 10 minutes, then drain.

2 Place the 600ml/1 pint/2½ cups of water in a soaked bean pot or a large tagine, add the bay leaves, celery and beans. Cover and place in an unheated oven. Set the oven to 190°C/375°F/Gas 5. Cook for 1–1½ hours or until the beans are tender. Drain.

3 Heat 60ml/4 tbsp of the oil in a large frying pan or cast iron tagine base. Add the aubergine and cook, stirring for 4–5 minutes, until evenly browned. Remove and set aside.

4 Add the remaining oil to the tagine base or frying pan, then add the onion and cook, stirring, for 4–5 minutes, until softened. Add the garlic and chillies and cook for a further 5 minutes, stirring frequently, until the onion is golden.

VARIATIONS
• Use 10–15ml/2–3 tsp harissa paste or chilli sauce instead of fresh chillies.
• A mixture of courgettes (zucchini) and red and yellow (bell) peppers can be used instead of the aubergines. Cut them into small chunks and fry them in the oil as in step 3 above.

5 Reduce the oven temperature to 160°C/325°F/Gas 3. Add the tomato purée and paprika and cook, stirring, for 1–2 minutes. Add the tomatoes, browned aubergine, drained red kidney and black-eyed or cannellini beans and stock. Season with salt and pepper.

6 Cover the iron tagine base with the earthenware lid or, if using a frying pan, transfer the contents to a clay tagine. Place in the oven and cook for 1 hour.

7 Meanwhile, mix together the yogurt, mint and spring onions and place in a small serving dish. To serve, add the mint, parsley and coriander to the tagine and lightly mix through the vegetables. Season to taste. Garnish with fresh herb sprigs and serve with the mint yogurt.

COOK'S TIP
The cooking time for the dried beans will vary depending on the age of the beans. Older beans will take longer to cook until tender. The tagine will happily keep warm once it's ready, so if you are serving this to guests, it is a good idea to allow extra time for the beans to become tender.

MOROCCAN BRAISED CHICKPEAS

This sweet and spicy vegetarian dish is a real treat. Serve it hot as a main course with rice or couscous or serve cold as a salad, drizzled with olive oil and lemon juice.

SERVES 4

250g/9oz/1½ cups dried chickpeas, soaked
    overnight in cold water
30ml/2 tbsp olive oil
2 onions, cut into wedges
10ml/2 tsp ground cumin
1.5ml/¼ tsp ground turmeric
1.5ml/¼ tsp cayenne pepper
15ml/1 tbsp ground coriander
5ml/1 tsp ground cinnamon
300ml/½ pint/1¼ cups vegetable stock
2 carrots, sliced
115g/4oz/½ cup ready-to-eat dried
    apricots, halved
50g/2oz/scant ½ cup raisins
25g/1oz/¼ cup flaked (sliced) almonds
30ml/2 tbsp chopped fresh
    coriander (cilantro)
30ml/2 tbsp chopped fresh flat leaf parsley
salt and ground black pepper

3 Meanwhile, place the olive oil and onions in a frying pan and cook for about 6 minutes, or until softened. Add the cumin, turmeric, cayenne, coriander and cinnamon and cook for 2–3 minutes. Stir in the stock, carrots, apricots, raisins and almonds and bring to the boil.

4 Drain the chickpeas, add the spicy vegetable mixture and stir. Cover and return to the oven for 30 minutes.

5 Season with salt and pepper, lightly stir in half the fresh coriander and parsley and serve sprinkled with the remainder.

1 Soak a bean clay pot in cold water for 20 minutes, then drain. Place the chickpeas in a pan with plenty of cold water. Bring to the boil and boil rapidly for 10 minutes, then place the chickpeas in the bean pot, cover with lukewarm water and cover.

2 Place in an unheated oven and set the temperature to 200°C/400°F/Gas 6. Cook for 1 hour, then reduce the oven temperature to 160°C/325°/Gas 3. Cook for another hour, or until the chickpeas are tender.

COOK'S TIP
The cooking time for the chickpeas will vary depending on their age – if old, they could take a further 30 minutes.

JAMAICAN BLACK BEAN POT

Molasses imparts a rich treacly flavour to the spicy sauce, which incorporates a stunning mix of black beans, vibrant red and yellow peppers and orange butternut squash.

SERVES 4

225g/8oz/1¼ cups dried black beans
1 bay leaf
30ml/2 tbsp vegetable oil
1 large onion, chopped
1 garlic clove, chopped
5ml/1 tsp mustard powder
15ml/1 tbsp molasses or black treacle
30ml/2 tbsp soft dark brown sugar
5ml/1 tsp dried thyme
2.5ml/½ tsp dried chilli flakes
5ml/1 tsp vegetable bouillon powder
1 red (bell) pepper, seeded and diced
1 yellow (bell) pepper, seeded
   and diced
675g/1½lb butternut squash or pumpkin,
   seeded and cut into 1cm/½in dice
salt and ground black pepper
sprigs of thyme, to garnish
cornbread or plain boiled rice, to serve

1 Soak the beans overnight in plenty of water, then drain and rinse well. Place in a large pan, cover with fresh water and add the bay leaf. Bring to the boil, then boil rapidly for 10 minutes. Reduce the heat, cover the pan, and simmer for about 30 minutes until tender. Drain, reserving the cooking water. Preheat the oven to 180°C/350°F/Gas 4.

COOK'S TIPS
• To prepare squash or pumpkin, cut it in half using a large sharp knife, then cut off the skin. Remove the seeds using a spoon and cut the flesh into chunks. Choose firm specimens that are blemish-free.
• If you don't have bouillon powder, then dissolve half a stock (bouillon) cube in the bean cooking water.

2 Heat the vegetable oil in a flameproof casserole, add the onion and garlic and sauté for about 5 minutes until softened, stirring occasionally. Stir in the mustard powder, molasses or treacle, sugar, dried thyme, chilli flakes and seasoning. Cook for about 1 minute, stirring, then stir in the black beans.

3 Add enough water to the reserved liquid to make 400ml/14fl oz/1⅔ cups, mix in the bouillon powder and pour into the casserole. Bake for 25 minutes.

4 Add the peppers and the squash or pumpkin and mix well. Cover, then bake for 45 minutes. Garnish with thyme.

BULGUR WHEAT, ASPARAGUS and BROAD BEAN PILAFF

Nutty-textured bulgur wheat is usually simply soaked in boiling water until it is softened, but it can be cooked like rice to make a pilaff. Here it is combined with broad beans, herbs and lemon and orange rinds, which add a fresh, springtime flavour.

SERVES 4

250g/9oz/1½ cups bulgur wheat
750–900ml/1¼–1½ pints/3–3¾ cups warm
    vegetable stock
225g/8oz asparagus spears
225g/8oz/2 cups frozen broad (fava)
    beans, thawed
8 spring onions (scallions), chopped
15ml/1 tbsp grated lemon rind
15ml/1 tbsp grated orange rind
40g/1½oz/3 tbsp butter, cut into
    small pieces
60ml/4 tbsp chopped fresh flat leaf parsley
30ml/2 tbsp chopped fresh dill, plus extra
    sprigs to garnish
salt and ground black pepper

1 If using a clay pot, soak in cold water for 20 minutes, then drain. Place the bulgur wheat in the clay pot or in a shallow, ovenproof earthenware dish and pour over 600ml/1 pint/2½ cups of the stock. Season with salt and pepper.

VARIATIONS
• Try using fresh green beans and either fresh or frozen peas in place of the asparagus and broad beans and, instead of using dill, stir in plenty of chopped fresh mint along with the parsley.
• If you'd like to add a little extra colour to the pilaff, then stir in some finely shredded red (bell) pepper, or some peeled and seeded wedges of tomato.
• To make a richer pilaff, stir in some finely grated Parmesan cheese along with the butter in step 6.

2 Cut the asparagus spears into 2.5cm/1in lengths, discarding any hard, woody ends from the stems. Add the asparagus pieces to the clay pot or dish and gently stir these into the bulgur wheat.

3 Cover the clay pot or dish tightly and place in an unheated oven. Set the oven to 200°C/400°F/Gas 6 and then cook the bulgur wheat and asparagus for 20 minutes.

4 Meanwhile pop the broad beans out of their shells and then stir the beans into the bulgur pilaff after it has cooked for about 20 minutes, adding a little more stock at the same time. Re-cover the clay pot or dish and return the dish to the oven for about 10 minutes.

COOK'S TIP
If your clay pot or earthenware dish doesn't have its own lid, then cover the pot or dish with foil, crimping it around the edge to seal. Or, if the top of the dish is completely flat, then you can simply place a flat, heavy baking sheet on top.

5 Stir in the spring onions, grated lemon and orange rind. Add a little more stock, if necessary. Cover and return to the oven for 5 minutes.

6 Dot the pieces of butter over the top of the pilaff and leave to stand, covered, for 5 minutes.

7 Add the chopped parsley and dill to the pilaff and stir well with a fork, to fluff up the bulgur wheat and distribute the herbs evenly. Check the seasoning and add salt and plenty of black pepper. Serve the pilaff hot, garnished with sprigs of fresh dill.

DESSERTS

The clever cook who saves time and effort by mastering one-pot and clay-pot cooking deserves a sweet reward, and what better way to celebrate success than with Baked Maple and Pecan Croissant Pudding or Honey-baked Figs – cooked in a clay pot, of course – served with Hazelnut Ice Cream. Black Cherry Clafoutis is another treat or, for pots of pleasure, try sweet and tangy Citrus and Caramel Custards, which are baked in individual cazuelas, or elegant and impressive Plum Charlottes with Foamy Kirsch Sauce.

PLUM CHARLOTTES with FOAMY KIRSCH SAUCE

These individual puddings, cooked in mini earthenware dishes, conceal a fresh plum filling and are served on a pool of light, frothy Kirsch-flavoured sauce.

SERVES 4

115g/4oz/½ cup butter, melted
50g/2oz/4 tbsp demerara (raw) sugar
450g/1lb ripe plums, stoned (pitted) and
    thickly sliced
25g/1oz/2 tbsp caster (superfine) sugar
30ml/2 tbsp water
1.5ml/¼ tsp ground cinnamon
25g/1oz/¼ cup ground almonds
8–10 large slices of white bread

For the Kirsch sauce
3 egg yolks
40g/1½oz/3 tbsp caster
    (superfine) sugar
30ml/2 tbsp Kirsch

2 Place the stoned plum slices in a pan with the caster sugar, water and ground cinnamon and cook gently for 5 minutes, or until the plums have softened slightly. Leave them to cool, then stir in the ground almonds.

5 Divide the plum mixture among the lined dishes. Place the bread rounds on top and brush with the remaining butter. Place the ramekins on a baking sheet and bake for 25 minutes.

1 Preheat the oven to 190°C/375°F/ Gas 5. Line the base of four individual 10cm/4in-diameter deep, earthenware ramekin dishes with baking parchment. Brush evenly and thoroughly with a little of the melted butter, then sprinkle each dish with a little of the demerara sugar, rotating the dish in your hands to coat each dish evenly.

VARIATIONS
• Slices of peeled pear or eating apples can be used in this recipe instead of the stoned, sliced plums.
• If using apples or pears substitute the Kirsch in the foamy sauce with Calvados or another apple brandy.
• If you are short on time, drained canned fruit such as pineapple, apricots, pears or plums can be used – simply stir in the ground almonds as in step 2 and add to the prepared ramekins.

3 Cut the crusts off the bread and then use a plain pastry cutter to cut out four rounds to fit the bases of the ramekins. Dip the bread rounds into the melted butter and fit them into the dishes. Cut four more rounds to fit the tops of the dishes and set aside.

4 Cut the remaining bread into strips, dip into the melted butter and use to line the sides of the ramekins completely.

6 Just before the charlottes are ready place the egg yolks and caster sugar for the sauce in a bowl. Whisk together until pale. Place the bowl over a pan of simmering water and whisk in the Kirsch. Continue whisking until the mixture is very light and frothy.

7 Remove the charlottes from the oven and turn out on to warm serving plates. Pour a little sauce over and around the charlottes and serve immediately.

COOK'S TIP
For an extra indulgent dessert, serve the puddings with lightly whipped double (heavy) cream flavoured with extra Kirsch and sweetened to taste with a little sieved icing (confectioners') sugar.

BAKED MAPLE and PECAN CROISSANT PUDDING

This variation of the classic English bread and butter pudding uses croissants, which give a light fluffy texture. Pecans, brandy-laced sultanas and maple syrup-flavoured custard complete this mouthwatering dessert.

SERVES 4

75g/3oz/generous ½ cup sultanas
   (golden raisins)
45ml/3 tbsp brandy
50g/2oz/¼ cup butter, plus extra for greasing
4 large croissants
40g/1½oz/⅓ cup pecan nuts,
   roughly chopped
3 eggs, lightly beaten
300ml/½ pint/1¼ cups milk
150ml/¼ pint/⅔ cup single (light) cream
120ml/4fl oz/½ cup maple syrup
25g/1oz/2 tbsp demerara (raw) sugar
maple syrup and pouring (half-and-half)
   cream, to serve (optional)

1 Place the sultanas and brandy in a small pan and heat gently, until warm. Leave to stand for 1 hour. Soak a small clay pot in cold water for 15 minutes, then drain, leave for 2–3 minutes and lightly grease the base and sides.

2 Cut the croissants (see Cook's Tip) into thick slices, then spread with butter on one side.

3 Arrange the croissant slices, butter-side uppermost and slightly overlapping in the soaked clay pot. Sprinkle the brandy-soaked sultanas and the roughly chopped pecan nuts over the buttered croissant slices.

4 In a large bowl, beat the eggs and milk together, then gradually beat in the single cream and maple syrup.

5 Pour the egg custard through a sieve, over the croissants, fruit and nuts in the dish. Leave the uncooked pudding to stand for 30 minutes, so that some of the egg custard liquid is absorbed by the croissants.

6 Sprinkle the demerara sugar evenly over the top, then cover the dish and place in an unheated oven. Set the oven to 180°C/350°F/Gas 4 and bake for 40 minutes. Remove the lid and continue to cook for about 20 minutes, or until the custard is set and the top is golden.

7 Leave the pudding to cool for about 15 minutes before serving warm with extra maple syrup and a little pouring cream, if you like.

COOK'S TIPS
• This dessert is perfect for using up leftover croissants. Slightly stale one-day-old croissants are easier to slice and butter; they also soak up the custard more easily. Thickly sliced one-day-old bread or large slices of brioche could be used instead.
• Pecan nuts are an elongated nut in a glossy red oval-shaped shell, but are usually sold shelled. They are native to the USA and have a sweet, mild flavour. Pecans are most commonly used in pecan pie but are also popular in ice creams and cakes. Walnuts can be substituted for pecans in most recipes, and they would be perfect in this one if you don't have any pecan nuts.

COCONUT RICE PUDDING

A delicious adaptation of the classic creamy rice pudding, this dessert is flavoured with coconut milk and finished with a coconut crust.

SERVES 4

75g/3oz/scant ½ cup short grain
   pudding rice
40g/1½oz/3 tbsp caster
   (superfine) sugar
2.5ml/½ tsp vanilla essence (extract)
300ml/½ pint/1¼ cups milk
400ml/14fl oz/1⅔ cups coconut milk
105ml/7 tbsp single (light) cream
30ml/2 tbsp desiccated (dry unsweetened
   shredded) coconut or slivers of
   fresh coconut

VARIATION

If preferred, this pudding can be made
with extra milk instead of the single
cream. Use full cream (whole) milk, for
a rich, creamy flavour.

1 Soak a small clay pot in cold water for
15 minutes, then drain. Add the rice,
sugar, vanilla essence, milk, coconut milk
and cream.

2 Cover the clay pot and place in a cold
oven. Set the oven to 180°C/350°F/
Gas 4 and cook for 1 hour.

3 Remove the lid from the clay pot, stir
the pudding gently, then re-cover and
cook for a further 30–45 minutes, or
until the rice is tender.

4 Remove the lid, stir the pudding, then
sprinkle with desiccated or fresh coconut
and bake uncovered for 10–15 minutes.

CITRUS and CARAMEL CUSTARDS

*These Spanish-style custards, made rich with cream and egg yolks, are delicately scented
with tangy citrus flavours and aromatic cinnamon.*

SERVES 4

450ml/¾ pint/scant 2 cups milk
150ml/¼ pint/⅔ cup single
    (light) cream
1 cinnamon stick, broken in half
thinly pared rind of ½ lemon
thinly pared rind of ½ orange
4 egg yolks
5ml/1 tsp cornflour (cornstarch)
40g/1½oz/3 tbsp caster (superfine) sugar
grated rind of ½ lemon
grated rind of ½ orange
a little icing (confectioner's) sugar,
    for sprinkling

1 Place the milk and cream in a pan. Add the cinnamon stick and the strips of pared citrus rind. Bring to the boil, then simmer for 10 minutes.

2 Preheat the oven to 160°C/325°F/ Gas 3. Whisk the egg yolks, cornflour and caster sugar together. Remove the rinds and cinnamon from the hot milk and cream and discard. Whisk the hot milk and cream into the egg yolk mixture.

3 Stir the grated citrus rind into the custard mixture. Pour into four individual cazuelas, each about 13cm/5in in diameter. Place in a roasting pan and pour warm water into the pan to reach three-quarters of the way up the sides. Bake for 25–30 minutes, or until the custards are just set. Remove the dishes from the water; leave to cool, then chill.

4 Preheat the grill (broiler) to high. Sprinkle the custards liberally with icing sugar and place under the grill until the tops turn golden brown and caramelize.

COOK'S TIPS
• Prepare the grated rind first, then cut a few strips of rind from the ungrated side of the citrus fruits using a swivel-bladed vegetable peeler.
• You can use a special cook's gas-gun or salamander to caramelize the tops instead of grilling (broiling) them.

HONEY-BAKED FIGS with HAZELNUT ICE CREAM

This is a delectable dessert – fresh figs are baked in a lightly spiced lemon and honey syrup and served with a gorgeous, home-made roasted hazelnut ice cream.

SERVES 4

1 lemon grass stalk, finely chopped
1 cinnamon stick, roughly broken
60ml/4 tbsp clear honey
200ml/7fl oz/scant 1 cup water
8 large figs

For the hazelnut ice cream
450ml/¾ pint/scant 2 cups double (heavy) cream
50g/2oz/¼ cup caster (superfine) sugar
3 egg yolks
1.5ml/¼ tsp vanilla essence (extract)
75g/3oz/¾ cup hazelnuts

1 To make the ice cream, place the cream in a pan and heat slowly until almost boiling. Place the sugar and egg yolks in a bowl and beat until creamy.

2 Pour a little of the cream on to the egg yolk mixture and stir. Pour into the pan and mix with the rest of the cream. Cook over a low heat, stirring constantly, until the mixture thickens slightly and lightly coats the back of the spoon – do not allow it to boil. Pour into a bowl, then stir in the vanilla and leave to cool.

3 Preheat the oven to 180°C/350°F/Gas 4. Place the hazelnuts on a baking sheet and roast for 10–12 minutes, or until golden. Leave the nuts to cool, then place them in a food processor or blender and process until they are coarsely ground.

4 Transfer the ice cream mixture to a metal or plastic freezer container and freeze for 2 hours, or until the mixture feels firm around the edge. Remove the container from the freezer and whisk the ice cream to break down the ice crystals. Stir in the ground hazelnuts and freeze the mixture again until half-frozen. Whisk again, then freeze until firm.

COOK'S TIPS
• If you prefer, rather than whisking the semi-frozen ice cream, tip it into a food processor and process until smooth.
• There are several different types of figs available and they can all be used in this recipe. Choose from green-skinned figs that have an amber-coloured flesh, dark purple-skinned fruit with a deep red flesh or green/yellow-skinned figs with a pinky-coloured flesh.

5 Place the lemon grass, cinnamon stick, honey and water in a small pan and heat slowly until boiling. Simmer the mixture for 5 minutes, then leave the syrup to stand for 15 minutes.

6 Meanwhile, soak a small clay pot in cold water for 15 minutes. Cut the figs into quarters, leaving them intact at the bases. Place the figs in the clay pot and pour over the honey-flavoured syrup.

7 Cover the clay pot and place in an unheated oven. Set the oven to 200°C/400°F/Gas 6 and bake the figs for about 15 minutes, or until tender.

8 Take the ice cream from the freezer about 10 minutes before serving, to soften slightly. Transfer the figs to serving plates. Strain a little of the cooking liquid over the figs and then serve them with a scoop or two of hazelnut ice cream.

VARIATION
This recipe also works well with halved, stoned (pitted) nectarines or peaches – simply cook as from step 6 and serve with the home-made ice cream.

SPICED PEARS with NUT CRUMBLE

An all-time favourite, this crumble has a crunchy pecan nut and oat topping,
which complements the spicy pears hidden beneath.

SERVES 4–6

900g/2lb pears
30ml/2 tbsp lemon juice
40g/1½oz/3 tbsp caster (superfine) sugar
5ml/1 tsp mixed (apple pie) spice
2.5ml/½ tsp grated nutmeg
vanilla ice cream, to serve

For the crumble topping
75g/3oz/⅔ cup plain (all-purpose) flour
75g/3oz/6 tbsp butter
50g/2oz/¼ cup light muscovado
   (brown) sugar
50g/2oz/½ cup pecan nuts or
   walnuts, chopped
40g/1½oz/scant ½ cup rolled oats

COOK'S TIP
Look out for golden-skinned Forelle pears,
which are especially good for cooking, or
try Anjou, Williams or Conference pears.

1 Soak a small clay pot in cold water for
15 minutes, then drain. Peel the pears
if wished, then halve them and remove
the cores. Cut each pear into six wedges
and toss in the lemon juice.

2 Place the pears in the clay pot, add
the sugar, mixed spice and nutmeg and
mix together. Place in an unheated oven,
set the oven to 200°C/400°F/Gas 6 and
cook for 25 minutes.

3 Meanwhile, prepare the crumble
topping. Sift the flour into a bowl and
rub in the butter, then stir in the sugar,
nuts and rolled oats.

4 Uncover the clay pot and stir gently to
rearrange the fruit. Spoon the crumble
mixture over the pears, then return the
clay pot to the oven for 25–30 minutes,
or until the crumble is golden. Serve
warm, with vanilla ice cream.

NECTARINES BAKED with ALMONDS and PISTACHIO NUTS

Fresh nectarines stuffed with a ground almond and chopped pistachio nut filling, baked in a clay pot until meltingly tender, then served with a passion fruit sauce.

SERVES 4

50g/2oz/½ cup ground almonds
15ml/1 tbsp caster (superfine) sugar
1 egg yolk
50g/2oz/⅓ cup shelled pistachio
 nuts, chopped
4 nectarines
200ml/7fl oz/scant 1 cup orange juice
2 ripe passion fruits
45ml/3 tbsp Cointreau or other
 orange liqueur

1 Soak a small clay pot, if using, in cold water for 15 minutes. Mix the ground almonds, sugar and egg yolk to a paste, then stir in the pistachio nuts.

2 Cut the nectarines in half and carefully remove the stones (pits). Pile the ground almond and pistachio filling into the nectarine halves and then place them in a single layer in the base of the clay pot or cazuela.

3 Pour the orange juice around the nectarines, then cover the pot or dish and place in an unheated oven. Set the oven to 200°C/400°F/Gas 6 and cook for 15 minutes.

4 Remove the lid from the pot or dish and bake for a further 5–10 minutes, or until the nectarines are soft. Transfer the nectarines to individual, warmed serving plates and keep warm.

5 Cut the passion fruits in half, scoop out the seeds and stir into the cooking juices in the clay pot or dish with the liqueur. Spoon the sauce around the nectarines and serve.

STRAWBERRY OAT CRUNCH

This simple dessert looks good and tastes delicious. The strawberries form a tasty filling between the layers of oat crumble.

SERVES 4

150g/5oz/1¼ cups rolled oats
50g/2oz/½ cup wholemeal
    (whole-wheat) flour
75g/3oz/6 tbsp butter
30ml/2 tbsp pear and apple concentrate
500g/1¼lb strawberries
10ml/2 tsp arrowroot
natural (plain) yogurt, custard or cream,
    to serve

VARIATIONS
• Use dried apricots (chop half and cook the rest to a purée with a little apple juice) instead of the strawberries.
• Add a few chopped almonds or walnuts to the crumble mixture.

COOK'S TIP
You'll find pear and apple concentrate in good health food stores.

1 Preheat the oven to 180°C/350°F/ Gas 4. Mix the oats and flour in a bowl. Melt the butter with the apple and pear concentrate in a pan; stir into the bowl.

2 Purée half the strawberries in a food processor; chop the rest. Mix the arrowroot with a little of the strawberry purée in a small pan, then add the rest of the purée. Heat gently until thickened, then stir in the chopped strawberries.

3 Spread half the crumble mixture over the base of a shallow 18cm/7in round ovenproof earthenware dish to form a layer at least 1cm/½in thick. Top the crumble with the chopped and puréed strawberry mixture, then add the remaining crumble mixture, patting it down gently to form an even layer. Bake the oat crunch for about 30 minutes until golden brown. Serve warm or cold, with yogurt, custard or cream.

FRESH CURRANT BREAD and BUTTER PUDDING

Fresh mixed red- and blackcurrants add a tart touch to this scrumptious hot pudding in which layers of custard-soaked bread are cooked to a crisp golden crust.

SERVES 6

8 medium-thick slices day-old white bread,
    crusts removed
50g/2oz/¼ cup butter, softened
115g/4oz/1 cup redcurrants
115g/4oz/1 cup blackcurrants
4 eggs, beaten
75g/3oz/6 tbsp caster (superfine) sugar
475ml/16fl oz/2 cups creamy milk
5ml/1 tsp vanilla essence (extract)
freshly grated nutmeg
30ml/2 tbsp demerara (raw) sugar
single (light) cream, to serve

1 Preheat the oven to 160°C/325°F/ Gas 3. Butter a 1.2 litre/2 pint/5 cup ovenproof earthenware dish.

VARIATION
A mixture of blueberries and raspberries would work just as well as the currants.

2 Spread the slices of bread generously with the butter, then cut them in half diagonally. Layer the slices in the dish, buttered side up, sprinkling the currants between the layers.

3 Beat the eggs and caster sugar lightly together in a large mixing bowl, then gradually whisk in the creamy milk and vanilla essence along with a large pinch of freshly grated nutmeg.

4 Pour the milk mixture over the bread, pushing the slices down into the liquid. Sprinkle the demerara sugar and a little more nutmeg over the top. Place the dish in a roasting pan and fill with hot water to come halfway up the sides of the dish. Bake for 40 minutes, then increase the oven temperature to 180°C/350°F/Gas 4 and bake for about 20 minutes more, or until the top is golden. Serve warm, with single cream.

APRICOT PANETTONE PUDDING

Panettone and pecan nuts make a rich addition to this "no-butter" version of a traditional bread and butter pudding.

SERVES 6

sunflower oil, for greasing
350g/12oz panettone, sliced
    into triangles
25g/1oz/¼ cup pecan nuts
75g/3oz/⅓ cup ready-to-eat dried
    apricots, chopped
500ml/17fl oz/generous 2 cups full-cream
    (whole) milk
5ml/1 tsp vanilla essence (extract)
1 large (US extra large) egg, beaten
30ml/2 tbsp maple syrup
nutmeg
demerara (raw) sugar,
    for sprinkling

1 Lightly grease a 1 litre/1¾ pint/4 cup ovenproof earthenware dish. Arrange half of the panettone triangles in the dish, sprinkle over half the pecan nuts and all of the chopped, dried apricots, then add another layer of panettone on top.

COOK'S TIP
Panettone is a light fruit cake originally from northern Italy but now popular all over the world. It is traditionally eaten at festivals such as Christmas or Easter. Panettone is baked in cylindrical moulds, giving it a distinctive shape. You can now find panettone in different flavours – the coffee-flavoured type is particularly good.

2 Heat the milk and vanilla essence in a small pan until the milk just simmers. Put the egg and maple syrup in a large bowl, grate in about 2.5ml/½ tsp nutmeg, then whisk in the hot milk.

3 Preheat the oven to 200°C/400°F/ Gas 6. Pour the egg mixture over the panettone, lightly pressing down the bread so that it is submerged. Leave the pudding to stand for about 10 minutes, to allow the panettone slices to soak up a little of the liquid.

4 Sprinkle over the reserved pecan nuts and sprinkle a little demerara sugar and freshly grated nutmeg over the top. Bake for 40–45 minutes until the pudding is risen and golden brown. Serve hot.

PEAR, ALMOND and GROUND RICE PIE

Ground rice gives a distinctive, slightly grainy texture to puddings that goes particularly well with autumn fruit. Pears and almonds are a divine combination.

2 Place the butter and caster sugar in a mixing bowl and beat together using a wooden spoon or electric mixer until light and fluffy, then beat in the eggs, one at a time, and the almond essence. Fold in the flour and the ground rice.

3 Carefully spoon the creamed mixture over the quartered pears in the flan or pie dish and then level the surface with a palette knife or metal spatula.

4 Sprinkle the flaked almonds evenly over the top of the creamed mixture, then bake the flan for about 30 minutes, or until the topping springs back when touched lightly and is a golden brown colour. Serve warm or cold with custard or crème fraîche.

SERVES 6

4 ripe pears
25g/1oz/2 tbsp soft light brown sugar
115g/4oz/½ cup unsalted (sweet) butter, at room temperature
115g/4oz/generous ½ cup caster (superfine) sugar
2 eggs
a few drops of almond essence (extract)
75g/3oz/⅔ cup self-raising (self-rising) flour
50g/2oz/⅓ cup ground rice
25g/1oz/¼ cup flaked (sliced) almonds
pouring custard or crème fraîche, to serve

1 Preheat the oven to 180°C/350°F/ Gas 4. Grease a shallow 25cm/10in flan or pie dish, then peel and quarter the pears and arrange them in the dish. Sprinkle with the brown sugar.

SPICED BLACKBERRY and APPLE CRUMBLE

*Any fruit can be used in this popular dessert, but you can't beat the favourites of
blackberry and apple. Hazelnuts and cardamom seeds give the topping extra flavour.*

SERVES 4–6

butter, for greasing
450g/1lb tart cooking apples
115g/4oz/1 cup blackberries
grated rind and juice of 1 orange
50g/2oz/¼ cup soft light brown sugar
custard, to serve

For the topping
175g/6oz/1½ cups plain (all-purpose) flour
75g/3oz/6 tbsp butter
75g/3oz/⅓ cup caster (superfine) sugar
25g/1oz/¼ cup chopped hazelnuts
2.5ml/½ tsp crushed cardamom seeds

VARIATIONS

This pudding can be made with all kinds
of fruit. Try plums, apricots, peaches or
pears, alone or in combination with
apples. Rhubarb is especially good when
partnered with bananas.

1 Preheat the oven to 200°C/400°F/
Gas 6. Generously butter a 1.2 litre/
2 pint/5 cup baking dish. Peel and core
the apples, then slice them into the
prepared baking dish. Level the surface
with the back of a spoon, then sprinkle
the blackberries over. Sprinkle the
orange rind and light brown sugar evenly
over the top, then pour over the orange
juice. Set the fruit mixture aside while
you make the crumble topping.

2 Sift the flour into a large bowl and rub
in the butter until the mixture resembles
coarse breadcrumbs. Stir in the caster
sugar, hazelnuts and cardamom seeds,
then sprinkle the topping over the top
of the fruit.

3 Press the topping around the edges of
the dish to seal in the juices. Bake for
30–35 minutes, or until the crumble is
golden. Serve hot, with custard.

TARTE TATIN

This upside-down apple tart is remarkably easy to make – especially if you use ready-rolled pastry. The apples are cooked in butter and sugar to make a caramel topping.

SERVES 6–8

3 eating apples
juice of ½ lemon
50g/2oz/¼ cup butter, softened
75g/3oz/⅓ cup caster (superfine) sugar
250g/9oz ready-rolled puff pastry
cream, to serve

COOK'S TIPS
• Tarte Tatin is a popular traditional French dessert. It is basically an upside-down apple pie cooked in a pan. The tart is inverted before serving to reveal a rich caramel topping.
• To turn out the tarte Tatin, place the serving plate upside down on top of it, then, protecting your arms with oven gloves, hold both pan and plate firmly together and deftly turn them over. Lift off the pan.

I Preheat the oven to 220°C/425°F/ Gas 7. Cut the apples in quarters and then remove the cores. Toss the apple quarters in the lemon juice.

2 Spread the butter over the base of a 20cm/8in heavy, ovenproof omelette pan. Sprinkle the caster sugar over the base of the pan and arrange the apple wedges on top, rounded side down.

3 Cook over a medium heat for about 15 minutes, or until the sugar and butter have melted and the apples are golden. Cut the pastry into a 25cm/10in round and place on top of the apples; tuck the edges in with a knife. Place the pan in the oven and bake for 15–20 minutes or until the pastry is golden. Carefully invert the tart on to a serving plate, then cool slightly before serving with cream.

BLACK CHERRY CLAFOUTIS

Clafoutis is a batter pudding that originated in the Limousin area of central France. It is often made with cream in place of milk and traditionally uses slightly tart black cherries.

SERVES 6

butter, for greasing
450g/1lb/2 cups fresh black
  cherries, pitted
25g/1oz/¼ cup plain (all-purpose) flour
50g/2oz/½ cup icing (confectioner's) sugar,
  plus extra for dusting
4 eggs, beaten
250ml/8fl oz/1 cup full-cream
  (whole) milk
30ml/2 tbsp cherry liqueur, such as Kirsch
  or maraschino
vanilla ice cream, to serve

1 Preheat the oven to 180°C/350°F/ Gas 4. Grease a 1.2 litre/2 pint/5 cup baking dish and add the cherries.

2 Sift the flour and icing sugar into a large mixing bowl, then gradually whisk in the beaten eggs until the mixture is smooth. Whisk in the milk until well blended, then stir in the liqueur.

3 Pour the batter into the baking dish and then stir gently to ensure that the cherries are evenly distributed. Transfer to the oven and bake for about 40 minutes, or until just set and light golden brown. Insert a small knife into the centre of the pudding to test if it is cooked in the middle; the blade should come out clean.

4 Allow the pudding to cool for at least 15 minutes, then dust liberally with icing sugar just before serving, either warm or at room temperature. Vanilla ice cream makes a good accompaniment.

VARIATIONS
Try other fruit or nut liqueurs in this dessert. Almond-flavoured liqueur is delicious teamed with cherries, while hazelnut, raspberry or orange liqueurs will also work well. Other fruits that can be used in this pudding include blackberries, blueberries, plums, peaches, nectarines and apricots.

LEMON SURPRISE PUDDING

This is a much-loved dessert that many of us remember from childhood. The surprise is the unexpected sauce concealed beneath the delectable sponge.

SERVES 4

50g/2oz/¼ cup butter, plus extra
    for greasing
grated rind and juice of 2 lemons
115g/4oz/½ cup caster (superfine) sugar
2 eggs, separated
50g/2oz/½ cup self-raising (self-rising) flour
300ml/½ pint/1¼ cups milk

1 Preheat the oven to 190°C/375°F/ Gas 5. Use a little butter to grease a 1.2 litre/2 pint/5 cup baking dish.

COOK'S TIP
Lemons are often waxed before packing. If a recipe uses the rind of the lemons either buy unwaxed lemons or scrub the peel thoroughly to remove the wax.

2 Beat the lemon rind, remaining butter and caster sugar in a bowl until pale and fluffy. Add the egg yolks and flour and beat together well. Gradually whisk in the lemon juice and milk (don't be alarmed – the mixture will curdle horribly). In a grease-free bowl, whisk the egg whites until they form stiff peaks.

3 Fold the egg whites lightly into the lemon mixture using a metal spoon, then pour into the prepared baking dish.

4 Place the dish in a roasting pan and pour in hot water to come halfway up the side of the dish. Bake for 45 minutes until golden. Serve immediately.

INDEX